ROYAL INSTITUTE OF PHILOSOPHY LECTURES
VOLUME TWELVE · 1977–78

PHILOSOPHERS OF THE ENLIGHTENMENT

ROYAL INSTITUTE OF PHILOSOPHY LECTURES
GENERAL EDITOR: Godfrey Vesey

1. THE HUMAN AGENT Godfrey Vesey (ed.)
2. TALK OF GOD Godfrey Vesey (ed.)
3. KNOWLEDGE AND NECESSITY Godfrey Vesey (ed.)
4. THE PROPER STUDY OF MAN Godfrey Vesey (ed.)
5. REASON AND REALITY Godfrey Vesey (ed.)
6. PHILOSOPHY AND THE ARTS Godfrey Vesey (ed.)
7. UNDERSTANDING WITTGENSTEIN Godfrey Vesey (ed.)
8. NATURE AND CONDUCT Richard Peters (ed.)
9. IMPRESSIONS OF EMPIRICISM Godfrey Vesey (ed.)
10. COMMUNICATION AND UNDERSTANDING Godfrey Vesey (ed.)
11. HUMAN VALUES Godfrey Vesey (ed.)
12. PHILOSOPHERS OF THE ENLIGHTENMENT Stuart Brown (ed.)

ROYAL INSTITUTE OF PHILOSOPHY LECTURES

VOLUME TWELVE · 1977—78

PHILOSOPHERS
OF THE
ENLIGHTENMENT

Edited by

S. C. BROWN

Honorary Assistant Director
The Royal Institute of Philosophy

THE HARVESTER PRESS · SUSSEX

HUMANITIES PRESS INC. · NEW JERSEY

First published in Great Britain in 1979 by
THE HARVESTER PRESS LIMITED
Publisher: John Spiers
7 Ship Street, Brighton

and in the USA by
HUMANITIES PRESS INC.
Atlantic Highlands, New Jersey 07716

British Library Cataloguing in Publication Data
Royal Institute of Philosophy
  Lectures.
  Vol. 12: 1977–78: Philosophers of the Enlightenment
  1. Philosophy,—Periodicals
  I. Title II. Brown, S. C. III. Philosophers of
  the Enlightenment
  192'.08   B1

ISBN 0-85527-605-3

Humanities Press Inc.
ISBN 0-391-01638-5

Printed in Great Britain by
Latimer Trend & Company Ltd Plymouth

CONTENTS

Foreword by S. C. Brown   vii

1   The Empiricism of Locke and Newton   1

    G. A. J. ROGERS, *Senior Lecturer in Philosophy at the
    University of Keele*

2   Hume, Newton and 'the Hill called Difficulty'   31

    CHRISTINE BATTERSBY, *Lecturer in Philosophy at the
    University of Warwick*

3   The 'Principle' of Natural Order: *or* What the En-
    lightened Sceptics did not doubt   56

    S. C. BROWN, *Senior Lecturer in Philosophy at the Open
    University*

4   Adam Smith: Philosophy, Science, and Social Science   77

    D. D. RAPHAEL, *Professor of Philosophy at Imperial
    College, University of London*

5   Hume and the Scottish Enlightenment   94

    DUNCAN FORBES, *Fellow of Clare College and Lecturer
    in History at Cambridge University*

6   Condorcet: Politics and Reason   110

    IAN WHITE, *Assistant Lecturer in Philosophy at the
    University of Cambridge*

7   Hume as Moralist: a Social Historian's Perspective 140

    NICHOLAS PHILLIPSON, *Lecturer in History at the
    University of Edinburgh*

8   Diderot: Man and Society   162

    J. H. BRUMFITT, *Professor of French at the University of
    St. Andrews*

9   Jean-Jacques Rousseau, Philosopher of Nature   184

    RONALD GRIMSLEY, *Professor of French Language and
    Literature at the University of Bristol*

10 Butler's Theory of Moral Judgment   199

    R. A. SHINER, *Associate Professor of Philosophy at the
    University of Alberta, Edmonton*

11 Kant and the Sincere Fanatic   226

    BERNARD HARRISON, *Reader in Philosophy at the
    University of Sussex*

    Index   263

FOREWORD

The phrase 'philosophers of the Enlightenment' may be variously seen as vague, ambiguous or pleonastic. To historians, perhaps, it will seem vague, for fewer of the periodizing terms which historians have found it convenient to employ have a less certain application. Who belongs to the Enlightenment and who does not? Everyone would include Diderot, d'Alembert and Voltaire. Everyone will allow honorary and retrospective membership to Locke and Newton. Few would demur at the inclusion of Hume, Adam Smith, Condorcet or Kant. But this Royal Institute of Philosophy lecture series includes contributions on Rousseau and Butler. Can they be included among the philosophers of 'the Enlightenment' without stretching that phrase to the point of meaninglessness? I think they can. But first let me table the other complaints which may be pressed by those who now call themselves philosophers or by students of eighteenth-century literature. The title of 'philosopher' is as jealously guarded today as it ever was. It would surprise me if such a title as 'philosopher of the Enlightenment' did not strike many contemporary students of philosophy as ambiguous. Such a sense of ambiguity would be heightened by noticing the inclusion of Newton, Condorcet and Diderot among the figures discussed in this volume. Does 'philosopher' in the title mean something distinct from the special sciences or is it, and it commonly was in the eighteenth century, used to include the special sciences? If the latter – if the philosophical spirit is, in the words of the anonymous author of the entry on 'Philosopher' in the *Encyclopédie*,[1] 'characterized by observation and precision and relates everything to its true principles', then is the philosopher much different from the enlightened man? Is not the age of Enlightenment just the age of 'philosophy' in this broad sense? D'Alembert would certainly have agreed, to judge from his observation that 'our century' has called itself 'supremely the *century of philosophy*'.[2] For the Encyclopedists the phrase 'enlightened philosopher' is almost pleonastic.

TWO CONCEPTIONS OF 'PHILOSOPHY'

These three lines of criticism reflect the different discipline-perspectives which are represented in this collection of papers. Broadly these are history, philosophy and literature. Most of the lecturers are indeed professional philosophers but only two of them address themselves to the history of philosophy in a purely philosophical manner. Only two, that is to say, treat their chosen authors as though they were contemporaries. Mr. Bernard Harrison's paper on 'Kant and the Sincere Fanatic' begins with a problem (viz. the problem posed by the alleged possibility of sincere fanaticism) which arises for the moral philosophy of R. M. Hare. He suggests that Kant's moral rationalism is not exposed to the same difficulties as in Hare's. Dr. R. A. Shiner, in his 'Butler's Theory of Moral Judgement', also starts from problems in moral epistemology which arise for 'the Humean model' of moral judgement. Central to this model is a rivalry between Reason and Sentiment. Butler is represented, together with Aristotle, as offering an account of moral judgement which, because it is free of this dichotomy, deserves the attention of those who are confronted by the difficulties of the Humean model.

It is a peculiarity of philosophy that philosophers can redefine their subject and still look back with profit at the writings of others who thought of themselves as doing something rather different. There is now a well-established tradition of modernizing Hume, of transposing his psychological claims into the formal mode and converting his 'mental geography' into logical geography.[3] But not all philosophers believe nowadays that such a separation of psychological and philosophical considerations is desirable. Dr. Christine Battersby, in her lecture on 'Hume, Newton and "the Hill called Difficulty"', is concerned with Hume's mental mechanics. But her interest in Hume's psychological system is not antiquarian. Her point is, rather, that we must understand it if we are to understand Hume's epistemology. It is, as she puts it, 'an epistemology of ease'. The epistemological 'wheat' is not, on her account, to be separated from the psychological 'chaff'. Battersby is thus more sympathetic to Hume's avowed project in the *Treatise* of introducing 'the experimental Method of Reasoning into moral Subjects'. For that project does not separate psychology from moral philosophy. At the same time she by no means accepts the eighteenth-century conception of 'moral philosophy' which would include what is now called 'psychology' as one of its branches.

On an eighteenth-century conception of philosophy it is highly appropriate that Locke and Newton should be bracketed together, the first as a 'moral' and the second as a 'natural' philosopher. But, although they are bracketed together by Dr. G. A. J. Rogers, his lecture – as its title, 'The Empiricism of Locke and Newton', indicates – is concerned with them as 'philosophers' in a more modern sense. He compares their views on a range of philosophical topics, on innate ideas, perception, mind-body dualism, substance, hypotheses and the scientific enterprise. An eighteenth-century writer would, of course, have regarded Locke and Newton as 'philosophers' in the broader sense. D'Alembert, in his *Preliminary Discourse to the Encyclopedia*, writes of Newton that he 'gave philosophy a form which apparently it is to keep'. By its 'form' he meant the way in which science was done. It was not that d'Alembert wished to underplay Newton's 'innumerable discoveries'. 'But', he suggested, 'perhaps he has done more by teaching philosophy to be judicious . . .'[4] Locke brought the same qualities to metaphysics. 'It can be said that he created metaphysics, almost as Newton had created physics.' (*op. cit.* p. 83.) Locke's *Essay Concerning Human Understanding* is described as a work which 'reduced metaphysics to what it really ought to be: the experimental physics of the soul' (*op. cit.* p. 84). It is difficult to avoid comparison between this conception of Locke's enterprise and the self-conscious Newtonianism which Battersby traces in Hume.

The judiciousness with which D'Alembert credits both Newton and Locke is one of the intellectual virtues which was prized by those (including Voltaire and Condillac) whom I refer to in my own lecture as 'enlightened sceptics'. It involves for d'Alembert a due sense of the limits of human knowledge. 'Newton, who had studied Nature, did not flatter himself that he knew more than the ancients concerning the first cause which produces phenomena.' (*Preliminary Discourse*, p. 82.) Hume saw Newton in the same light and his writings frequently echo his thought that 'nature has kept us at a great distance from all her secrets'.[5] That scepticism, as I try to bring out, goes hand in hand with a rejection of more extreme sceptical positions such as that attributed to Berkeley. It reflects both the modesty and the confidence which Rogers discusses in connection with the rejection by Locke and Newton of 'hypotheses'.

For d'Alembert, a philosopher should have an encyclopaedic grasp of the order and connection of human knowledge. The object of an encyclopaedia, for him, is to produce a 'world map' of human knowledge. Such maps can be as different, he admits, as the different projections in use with actual maps. But, difficult though it is 'to encompass the infinitely varied branches of human knowledge in a truly unified system', d'Alembert thought 'it is readily apparent that . . . there is a chain that binds them together' (*Preliminary Discourse*, p. 5). D'Alembert's conception of philosophy depends upon this belief in the unity of knowledge. 'Philosophy', 'science' and 'enlightenment' are, for him, closely associated terms.

Adam Smith, in *The Wealth of Nations*, articulates a conception of the philosopher which does not differ greatly from d'Alembert's. The 'trade of philosophers', according to Smith, is 'to observe everything' and the philosopher, as Professor

D. D. Raphael explains in his lecture, is thus capable of making connections between 'distant and dissimilar objects'. Raphael notes too that Smith's economics have an underlying 'philosophical' character in a more familiar sense. For instance, his belief in the working of the 'invisible hand' that makes self-interested behaviour contribute to the general good 'show the permanent influence on Adam Smith of Stoic philosophy, with its belief in cosmic harmony', a cosmic harmony also displayed in Newton's 'natural philosophy'.

Not all 'philosophers' in the eighteenth-century sense are 'philosophers' in the modern sense. Smith counted James Watt as a philosopher, d'Alembert includes William Harvey and Christian Huyghens among a list of 'illustrious philosophers who . . . have contributed much to the advancement of the sciences . . . and lifted, so to speak, a corner of the veil that concealed truth from us' (*Preliminary Discourse*, p. 85). I believe, however, that all the philosophers of the Enlightenment discussed in this volume deserve the attention of modern philosophers, if not equally. Moreover, I hope readers of this volume will be persuaded that some of the philosophers discussed are unjustly neglected in contemporary philosophical discussion.

Condorcet has suffered such neglect more than most. But, as Mr. Ian White argues in 'Condorcet: Politics and Reason', his theory of voting is by no means of purely antiquarian interest. In seeking to relate Condorcet's work to contemporary issues in criminal jurisprudence and about social choice, White goes some way to deserving, as few modern philosophers have done, the title of 'philosopher' in the eighteenth-century sense. Nor is he alone in this. It is by no means an orthodoxy nowadays that philosophical questions are categorially different from practical questions on the one hand, or the questions of other specialist inquiries, on the other. An emphasis on the continuity of philosophical discussions with other kinds of discussion does not, of course, imply a straightforward restoration of an eighteenth-century conception of philosophy. It does, however, bring into question the assumption that the word 'philosopher' is straight-forwardly ambiguous as between modern and eighteenth-century uses.

'THE ENLIGHTENMENT'

In my remarks so far I have made frequent references to d'Alembert's *Preliminary Discourse*. I have done so because it seems to me that, if any work may be taken as *paradigmatically* the production of a 'philosopher of the Enlightenment', none would be a more appropriate choice than this preface to the *Encyclopedia*. It is an apologia for a work which the chief editors were not alone in seeing as an instrument for the spread of 'enlightenment'. That is not to say that d'Alembert should be elevated above Voltaire and Diderot. I do not disagree with Professor J. H. Brumfitt's suggestion in 'Diderot: Man and Society' that 'Diderot perhaps embodies the rich variety of the Enlightenment spirit more than any other man' or with his claim that Diderot's 'only real rival' for this status is Voltaire. The *Preliminary Discourse* is not the work of a free-thinker and indeed makes concessions to revealed religion of just the kind which, if Raphael is right, should lead us to doubt whether d'Alembert belongs to the Enlightenment at all.

The context of d'Alembert's concessions to revealed religion makes it clear, however, that they are marginal and that indeed they may be merely diplomatic. His main purpose in one case is to deny that it is within the province of revealed religion 'to enlighten us . . . on the system of the world' (*op. cit.* p. 73). Such matters are ones 'which the All-Powerful has expressly left to our own disputations'. The implication of this remark is that there are matters not 'left to our own disputations', i.e. matters which do belong within the province of religious dogma. Elsewhere d'Alembert gives some further indication of what these matters are: 'The nature of man . . . is an impenetrable mystery for man himself when he is enlightened by reason alone. . . . Thus, nothing is more necessary than a revealed Religion.' (p. 25 f.) But even here d'Alembert is concerned to limit rather than augment the pretensions of theologians. 'A few truths to be believed, a small number of precepts to be practised: such are the essentials to which revealed Religion is reduced.'

The *Preliminary Discourse* reveals the public persona of d'Alembert. In private he was by no means prepared to make such concessions. Voltaire frequently urged him to a more militant stance against *l'infâme* ('the infamous thing') but D'Alembert believed in a more gradualist approach. 'Mankind' he once wrote 'is today more enlightened only because people have been cautious or fortunate enough to enlighten it gradually. If the sun suddenly appeared in a cave, the in-habitants would be aware only of the pain it caused their eyes: the excess of light would only serve to blind them immediately.'[6] It was all very well for Voltaire in his situation to call for the infamous thing to be crushed. Someone living as close as d'Alembert to 'the wolf's jaws' could not afford to be so bold:[7]

> *Écrasez l'infâme!* That is soon said when one is living hundreds of miles away from the rogues and fanatics, when one has an income of 100,000 livres, when through one's reputation and fortune one has been able to make oneself independent of everything . . . But *un pauvre diable* cannot crush the snakes, lest, as they turn their heads, they bite him in the heel. He has to take care not to walk on their tails, because the snakes are only waiting for an excuse to bite him. The surest and least dangerous method of destroying snakes is to cut off their food, for direct attacks merely provide them with it . . . The only thing is to ignore them and by perfecting natural morality show them that it alone is reasonable, that it alone is necessary for men's happiness.

It is not revealed religion that is to show us how to live but 'natural morality'. The contradiction between the publicly professed view and the privately confessed view of d'Alembert is plain enough. Nor could he resist putting in some glimpse of his real view in the *Preliminary Discourse*. In a passage which drew the charge of impiety from an alert reviewer, d'Alembert gives a sketchy account of 'the origin of the concept of the unjust, and consequently of moral good and evil'. This concept is made understood 'among even the most savage people' by 'the cry of Nature' (p. 12).

It is difficult to avoid the impression that had d'Alembert's own intellectual interests lain in 'moral' rather than 'natural' philosophy he could not have kept up any pretence of believing that men needed revealed religion to enlighten them as to the 'precepts to be practiced'. It is perhaps significant that d'Alembert should have put so much stress on the mysteriousness of man rather than, as Hume did, the mysteriousness of bread. Hume, as Mr. Duncan Forbes points out in 'Hume and the Scottish Enlightenment', rejected the idea that religion – either revealed or natural – provided any foundation for morality. Natural law, Forbes suggests, was 'the matrix of the social theory of the Scottish Enlightenment'. Politics, for Hume, was to be grounded on the observed facts of human nature. Hume saw regularity as the distinguishing mark of modern governments compared with which the distinction between monarchies and republics was of secondary importance. His ability to see beyond a 'vulgar Whiggism' removed one barrier to a science of comparative politics.

Hume's opposition to prejudice, superstition and enthusiasm, his attraction to the Newtonian method of philosophizing, his rejection of religion as a foundation of morality – such characteristics mark him as an 'enlightened' man by the standards of d'Alembert. They were to become close friends during and after Hume's visit to France from 1763 to 1766. (D'Alembert indeed was to receive a legacy of £200 from Hume's Will.) But by that time each had written his most seminal work and their likemindedness must be seen as antecedent to their friendship rather than as a result of it.

For d'Alembert, 'enlightenment' is to be contrasted, above all, with ignorance and barbarism. It could only be spread gradually because men can only be made reasonable gradually. There was nothing inevitable about such a process. On the contrary, d'Alembert thought, it may only be a passing phase. 'Barbarism lasts for centuries; it seems that it is our natural element; reason and good taste are only passing.' (*Preliminary Discourse*, p. 103.) Hume was no more optimistic. In his essay 'Of Miracles' he claimed to have found an argument which would be 'an everlasting check to all kinds of superstitious delusion'. He qualified this with the remark that the argument, if just, will carry weight with 'the wise and learned'. He did not imagine that it could tackle the tendency to give accounts of miracles and prodigies at its root source. Because that tendency is not at its root touched by argument, the argument against miracles is no more than a 'check' to keep the bigot at bay. The hope that it will be an *everlasting* check is at the same time an expression of resignation to the continuation of bigotry and superstition 'as long as the world endures'.[8]

There are problems, as Brumfitt points out in his lecture, about including either Hume or Kant as 'philosophers of the Enlightenment'. In the case of Hume they appear, on the surface at least, to be insurmountable. The faculty which makes enlightenment possible, for d'Alembert certainly, is Reason. Yet what philosopher ever laid more stress on the impotence of Reason than Hume? On this matter Hume and d'Alembert appear to be diametrically opposed. On closer examination, however, the opposition is less straightforward. D'Alembert attacks Descartes and Leibniz not for giving *too much* weight to Reason but for not giving *enough*. The taste for systems indulged by Descartes, Malebranche and Leibniz is 'more suited to flatter the imagination than to enlighten reason' (*Preliminary Discourse*, p. 94). The 'age of reason', as understood by d'Alembert, was not inaugurated by those now commonly called 'rationalists' but by Locke and Newton. In championing Reason d'Alembert was championing *their* cause. He was, for example, *against* innate ideas and 'hypotheses', to mention two topics discussed by Rogers.

D'Alembert had some praise, more for Descartes than Leibniz, for the metaphysical writings of the 'rationalists'. He valued them for their scepticism about received systems and for their 'independence of thought'. They lacked one of the cardinal virtues of the enlightened philosopher, however – the quality exhibited, as we have seen, above all by Locke and Newton – 'judiciousness'.

Now if that is what is to be understood as being involved in championing Reason it is difficult to see the supposed opposition between Hume and d'Alembert. On the contrary, Hume shared d'Alembert's view that metaphysics practised without an exact analysis of the nature of the human mind was one of the 'airy sciences'. He shared his admiration for Newton. If he never showed much generosity towards Locke it seems plausible to suppose that this had more to do with rivalry than with intellectual distance. Like d'Alembert he favours 'the experimental method'. His remarks about the 'other scientific method' in Section I of *An Enquiry Concerning the Principles of Morals* almost seems to echo a passage in the *Preliminary Discourse*. (Both works were published in 1751.) Where Hume writes: 'Men are now cured of their passion for hypotheses and systems in natural philosophy . . .', d'Alembert wrote 'the taste for systems . . . is today almost banished from works of merit'.[9]

The acceptance of 'natural morality' as opposed to 'revealed morality' does seem to be sufficiently pervasive to be worth citing as *one* characteristic of 'enlightenment'. In the cases of Butler and Kant, of course, it turns out to be very different. Where we might quite appropriately speak, as Harrison does, of the 'moral rationalism' of Kant's ethical philosophy, Butler, like Hume, belongs to the empiricist tradition of seeking to base morality on the observed facts of human nature.

Rousseau's 'natural morality' is closer to that envisaged by d'Alembert, at least in being opposed to conventional morality. As Professor Grimsley points out in his 'Jean-Jacques Rousseau, Philosopher of Nature', man's true nature had been corrupted and distorted by the development of civilization. The nature of man is something which, for Rousseau, has to be reconstituted through an analysis of its gradual historical development. This, Grimsley suggests, could be done 'only imaginatively and hypothetically'. In the Preface to his *Discourse on the Origin of Inequality* Rousseau expresses the opinion that 'our greatest philosophers would not be too good to direct such experiments' as would 'discover the natural man'. But, although he raises no difficulties of principle about such a programme, his own methodology is quite different. He does not proceed to offer 'solid observations' on civilized man but what he calls a 'moral picture'. He writes, for example, that 'the less natural and pressing his wants, the more headstrong are his passions'. In practice Rousseau regards the study of man as calling for a quite different methodology from the study of nature. In this he is out of step with other major Enlightenment figures.

In other respects too there are reasons to doubt the in-clusion of Rousseau in the Enlightenment at all. There is much to confirm Shelley's verdict, in *The Defence of Poetry*, that Rousseau was 'essentially a poet' and not to be classed with the 'mere reasoners' (such as Locke and Hume) or 'the French writers [who] have defaced, the eternal truths charactered upon the imagination of men'. Rousseau's way of proceeding in *A Discourse on the Origin of Inequality* gives, in effect, a role to imaginative insight which there is no room for in d'Alembert's conception of 'enlightenment'.

There were other disagreements too, for example about the crucial question as to whether the rise of the arts and sciences had benefited mankind. For d'Alembert and the *philosophes* this was a matter of ideological commitment. If Rousseau may himself be classed as a '*philosophe*' it is only in a marginal way. Indeed one way of thinking about the Enlightenment, follow-ing Nicholas Phillipson's lecture on 'Hume as Moralist: A Social Historian's Perspective', in terms of specific groups of men in clubs and societies which have an ideological co-hesion. Such groups flourished in many cities in the eighteenth century. Phillipson notes that Edinburgh, after the Treaty of Union, became a city of para-parliamentary clubs of men devoted to the regeneration of the nation's manners. Hume, he suggests, may have been 'trimming his sails to meet the prevailing ideological winds' in turning to essay-writing after the manner of Addison. When Hume returned to the topics of his *Treatise*, according to Phillipson, he pruned back his treatment so that in the *Enquiries* his discussion of those topics is curtailed or subordinated where it seemed 'irrelevant to his moral teaching'.

It may be, of course, that if one tries to think of what such diverse groups had in common – the Select Society in Edinburgh, the salons of Paris or the Academy of Dijon, for example – it would be no easier to arrive at generalizations which would give interesting content to talk of 'the Enlightenment' than it is to arrive at them through the study of texts. But such an approach has the merit of directing attention to different questions – for example about the changing status of men of letters – which would seem to have an important bearing on any such generalization.

If there is any truth in this last remark then the right approach to a study of the Enlightenment must be an interdisciplinary one. To say this is not to decry the excellent monographs which already exist.[10] It is, however, some defence of multi-authored contributions to such an area of study even when they have, as a volume of lectures in the Royal Institute of Philosophy series is bound to have, an emphasis on one particular discipline.

S. C. Brown
Honorary Assistant Director
The Royal Institute of Philosophy

NOTES

[1] *Encyclopédie ou Dictionnaire raisonné des Sciences des Arts et des Metiers* (1751–65). The article 'Philosopher' is translated in *Encyclopedia: Selections*, trans. by N. Y. Hoyt and T. Cassirer, Library of Liberal Arts, Bobbs-Merrill, 1965.
[2] In his *Élémens de philosophie* (1759), *Oeuvres complètes de d'Alembert* (Paris, 1821–2), Vol. I, p. 122.
[3] See, for example, Antony Flew's commentary on the first *Enquiry, Hume's Philosophy of Belief* (London: Routledge).
[4] *Preliminary Discourse to the Encyclopedia of Diderot* (1751). Trans.

Richard N. Schwab, Library of Liberal Arts Edition, Indianapolis (Bobbs-Merrill) 1963, p. 81.

[5] *Enquiry* Sect. IV, Pt. II, Oxford University Press Edition of *Hume's Enquiries* (3rd edition, 1975), p. 32.

[6] Quoted in *Jean D'Alembert*, by Ronald Grimsley (Oxford University Press, 1963), p. 122. I am indebted to Professor Grimsley's book for introducing me to this dimension of D'Alembert's thought.

[7] Quoted by Grimsley, *op. cit.* p. 112.

[8] *An Enquiry Concerning Human Understanding, Hume's Enquiries*, p. 110.

[9] Respectively *Enquiries*, p. 174 f. and *Preliminary Discourse*, p. 94.

[10] Among these are Ernst Cassirer's *The Philosophy of the Englightenment* (1932) (Princeton University Press, 1951), Peter Gay's *The Enlightenment: An Interpretation* (1969), 2 volumes (London: Wildewood House, 1973) and Norman Hampson's shorter *The Enlightenment* (Penguin Books, 1968).

1

THE EMPIRICISM
OF LOCKE AND NEWTON

G. A. J. Rogers

A man may puzzle me by arguments against local motion
but I'le believe my eyes. (Isaac Newton)
[ULC. MS Add, 3970.9, f. 619.]

INTRODUCTION

The relationship between John Locke and Isaac Newton, his
co-founder of, in the apt phrase of one recent writer, 'the
Moderate Enlightenment'[1] of the eighteenth century, has
many dimensions. There is their friendship, which began
only after each had written his major work,[2] and which had
its stormy interlude.[3] There is the difficult question of their
mutual impact.[4] In what ways did each draw intellectually
on the other? That there was some debt of each to the other
is almost certain, but its exact extent is problematic. Questions
may be asked over a whole range of intellectual issues, but not
always answered. Thus their theology, which was in many
respects close, and which forms the bulk of their surviving
correspondence, may yet reveal mutual influence.[5] There is
the question of their political views, where both were firmly
Whig.[6] But it is upon their philosophy, and certain aspects of
their philosophy in particular, that this paper will concentrate.
My main theme is the nature of their empiricism, and my main

contention is that between them they produced a powerful and comprehensive philosophy.

'Empiricism', as a word, has much to be said against it. It is both vague and ambiguous. But I doubt if we can do without it when we are talking about either possible theories of, or possible methods to, knowledge – this disjunction itself reflecting the term's ambiguity. Introducing the term 'empiricism' also helps to underline the fact that there are many other facets of the philosophical positions of Locke and Newton which might be compared, other than those of epistemology. There is, pre-eminently, their metaphysics. Certain aspects of their metaphysics cannot be separated from their epistemology – some portion of their views about ontology, for example – but my major concern will be with their accounts of knowledge.

There are some basic facts about the two men which must be kept clearly in mind if misunderstandings about them are to be avoided.[7] First their dates. Locke was born in 1632 and died in 1704. Newton was born in 1642 and died in 1727. Locke's major epistemological work, the *Essay Concerning Human Understanding*, was published in 1690, but was to almost all intents and purposes finished by the end of 1686,[8] nearly a year before Locke read Newton's *Philosophiae Naturalis Principia Mathematica*, published in July 1687.[9] Locke and Newton met in 1689 or 1690 after Locke's return from Holland where he had been since 1683. Their friendship soon developed, and lasted until Locke's death. The first edition of Newton's *Principia* contains very little about either epistemology or scientific method. It is only in the second edition of 1713 that Newton expresses so clearly his philosophy of science.[10] His other major work, the *Opticks*, was published in 1704, only months before Locke's death.[11] Further, although Newton was less cautious about expressing his more conjectural views in the *Opticks* than he had been in the first edition of the *Principia*, his more speculative thoughts did not first appear until the *Opticks*' Latin edition of 1706.[12]

These facts suggest, what I have elsewhere argued, that

Locke was not indebted to Newton for his major intellectual positions, and certainly not for his epistemology. Although it is not the object of this paper to consider in detail the issue of mutual influence, we shall find that there are certain further bits of evidence to support the contention that Locke added to the philosophical depth of Newton's own, largely empiricist, epistemology.[13]

Locke wrote a major work of epistemology and Newton did not. Further, whilst Locke is remembered primarily as a philosopher, Newton equally obviously is remembered primarily as a mathematical physicist. As a result, whilst the text of the *Essay* is often taken as sufficient evidence for Locke's position on a matter of epistemology, Newton's position is not so clear. Are we to accept as Newton's beliefs what Newton says? Or should we be only impressed by his actual working practice as a scientist? The matter is of some importance as there is mounting evidence that there is often a disparity between Newton's claims as to method and his actual practice.[14]

In the sections which follow I shall employ a distinction to meet this difficulty in the understanding of Newton. The distinction I shall label as that between the logic of justification and the logic of discovery. Whether there is a *logic* of discovery is doubtful, though clearly some techniques are more likely to bring about discoveries (have in the past been more fruitful in bringing about discoveries) than others. But there is surely, in some minimal sense at least, a logic of justification. There is, that is, a variety of possible grounds for somebody believing that an explanation of natural phenomena (to take no more) is true or probably true, and the relationship between evidence and conclusion may be rationally assessed. Newton believed that only in certain situations, i.e. only when certain conditions were satisfied, did the case for the acceptance of some statement about the natural world demand our assent. For Newton these grounds were largely to be understood in terms of direct empirical evidence for the truth of the statement.

But this is far from claiming that Newton believed only those things for which he had such direct evidence. Often, like the rest of us, he was convinced of the truth of something for which, on his own account, he did not have sufficient evidence.[15] What does appear to be true, however, is that Newton did not believe that such ill-supported conjectures should be allowed to be propagated as pieces of natural philosophy. At least in principle Newton was an inductivist.

Clearly Locke and Newton shared similar ontologies. The influence of Descartes on each, either directly or indirectly, was substantial.[16] Like him, they were dualists, believing in mind and matter as two separate substances. Each subscribed to a causal theory of perception, and each was ambivalent about the objects of perception, switching from the language of ideas to that of some form of direct realism. Each claimed that the origin of ideas was experience, and denied the existence of any innate ideas. Both of them clearly believed the physical world to be one in which there occur genuine causal interactions between physical objects. Both of them thought the Scholastic account of substance and properties to be totally misconceived and, whilst both believed in some form of corpuscular theory of matter, each acknowledged that theories of matter were not, as yet, well grounded. Each recognized the obscurity of the notion of substance. They agreed that general propositions about the world were not logically certain. Such propositions should be based upon observation, and were liable to exception. It followed from this that both rejected any aspiration to an *a priori* physics. On the other side, each totally rejected the view that all that could be expected was some sort of hypothetical physics. Each accepted that the properties of matter could be divided into two sorts: the famous primary-secondary quality distinction. Each believed in God, believed that God's existence was evidenced by experience, though their proffered proofs differed.

Such a list points to a substantial body of intellectual agreement between the two men. But these agreed points should not cause us to ignore important differences. Some of these differences include the following: although their ontologies were much the same, they were not identical. Newton's list of primary and secondary qualities, for example, is different from that of Locke. This in part reflects Newton's much more sophisticated account of the origin and nature of force, a central achievement of his physics and his philosophy of nature. Put at its simplest, Newton seems to have come to believe that matter only possesses passive qualities, and that active properties were a direct intervention of God in the physical world. Locke was more cautious on these issues and there is no evidence that he gave the matter the attention which Newton did.[17]

But if Locke has left us little to suggest that he devoted much time to speculative thought about the ultimate forces of nature, Newton offers us no detailed argument for much of his epistemology. Here the two men were in important respects complementary. It is precisely in this sense that they were the twin founders of much of eighteenth-century thought.

There are other points of difference. Locke was not a great mathematician even though he saw the relevance and power of mathematics to handle many problems. Newton was always the mathematician, seeking ways to embrace phenomena within the quantified fold. But Locke's mathematical weaknesses, if they may be so called, must be seen in the light of an undoubted strength, his substantial contributions to our understanding of the nature of language. Here Newton shows no such comparable quality. A major contribution of Locke is his rejection of the possibility of our obtaining definitive knowledge of the real essences of natural kinds, which itself entailed the rejection of any sort of definitive scientific language, a *characteristica universalis*. Newton at an early stage, seems to have been attracted by the project of John Wilkins and others to produce such a language, a project which Locke's account of language must surely have challenged.

Although, as we have already hinted, both Locke and Newton were opposed to speculative theory in science, there were some differences between their two views. Despite Newton's well-known hostility to hypotheses in natural science, he was, in the end, much more prone to them – if that is the right expression – that Locke was. In part this reflects the areas of natural science with which each was most concerned. Seventeenth-century mathematical physics probably gained more from speculation than did either seventeenth-century medicine or chemistry, the two branches of science in which Locke was most deeply engaged.[18] Probably, also, it is a measure of their innate interest in the sciences. Newton's mind was for ever probing the secrets of nature, Locke's did so only intermittently.

THE EPISTEMOLOGIES OF LOCKE AND NEWTON

Locke's well-known rejection of innate ideas is the negative half of his positive thesis that all the ideas with which the mind is furnished are the product of experience, through the two routes of sensation and reflection.[19] Locke was well aware of important implications of his claim. One of these related to moral theory and another to the natural sciences.

First let us notice how Locke sees the dangers of the claim that there are innate practical principles (that is, moral principles) of which we are all really aware though we will not always admit it. One danger was that it was much easier for the dogmatist to lay claim to knowledge of the moral law. This is how Locke explained it:

> When men have found some general propositions that could not be doubted of, as soon as understood, it was, I know, a short and easy way to conclude them innate. This being once received, it eased the lazy from the pains of search, and stopp'd the enquiry of the doubtful, concerning all that was once stiled innate: and it was of no small advantage to those who affected to be masters and teachers, to make this the principle of principles, that principles must not be questioned: For having once established this tenet, That there are innate principles, it put their followers upon a necessity of receiving some doctrines as such; which was to take them off from the use of their own reason and

judgment, and put them upon believing and taking them upon trust, without farther examination: In which posture of blind credulity, they might be more easily governed by, and made useful to some sort of men, who had the skill and office to principle and guide them.[20]

Such a position was to be contrasted with what Locke believed to be the correct one, namely, that 'our knowledge depends upon the right use of those powers nature hath bestowed upon us.'[21] In other words, we may reach a knowledge of what is right and wrong by information which ultimately has its source in experience, rather than by an appeal to any innate practical principles. One implication is clear. To know what is right may be difficult, but it is not impossible, and such knowledge is grounded in experience.

Locke's rejection of innate practical principles was aimed widely. There were many contemporary thinkers who subscribed to some version or other of the view he rejected. His attack on innate speculative principles was probably aimed no less widely, but it certainly included the Cartesians. In the first Book of the *Essay* Locke makes a special point of denying that we have an innate idea of substance,[22] and in Book Two, in a sustained attack on Cartesian theory he says:

To ask, at what time a Man has first any ideas, is to ask, when he begins to perceive; having ideas, and perception being the same thing. I know it is an opinion, that the soul always thinks, and that it has the actual perception of ideas in it self constantly, as long as it exists; and that actual thinking is as inseparable from the soul, as actual extension is from the body; which if true, to enquire after the beginning of a man's ideas, is the same, as to enquire after the beginning of his soul. For by this account, soul and its ideas, as body and its extension, will begin to exist both at the same time.[23]

To believe that the soul always thinks 'is to be sure, without proofs, and to know without perceiving', itself, in Locke's eyes, a contradiction. 'Tis . . . a confused notion, taken up to

serve an hypothesis . . .'[24] which was to accuse the Cartesians
of building upon a fundamentally unsound method in philosophy, reinforced a little later by, 'He that will suffer himself,
to be informed by observation and experience, and not make
his own hypothesis the rule of nature, will find few signs of a
soul accustomed to much thinking in a new born child, and
much fewer of any reasoning at all.'[25]

Locke's rejection of innate ideas is supported by substantial
argument, but this is not the place to assess it. There is one
methodological point, however, to which it is worth making
brief reference. It is that the structure of the argument of
Book I of the *Essay* has in many respects the character of
showing that the assumption of innate ideas is an unsupported
and unnecessary hypothesis. Unsupported by any evidence,
and unnecessary because the facts can be better explained by
the inductively supported generalization that all our ideas are
derived from experience, evidence offered in considerable
detail in the 'historical, plain method'[26] of the second Book
of the *Essay*.

Newton's philosophical views about the origins and nature
of knowledge were never fully expressed in his published
works. But in his manuscripts there are some important
sources. The single most relevant text is a draft Rule V which
he at one time contemplated including in the *Regulae Philosophandie* at the beginning of Book III, *De Mundi Systemate*,
of the *Principia*.[27] The Rule, in translation, reads:

Whatever is not derived from things themselves, whether
by the external senses or by the perception of internal
thoughts, is to be taken for an hypothesis. Thus I perceive
that I am thinking which could not happen unless at the
same time I were to perceive that I exist. But I do not
perceive that any idea whatever shall be innate. And I
take for a phenomenon not only that which is made known
to us by the five external senses, but also that which we
contemplate in our minds when thinking: such as, I exist,
I believe, I understand, I remember, I think, I wish, I am

unwilling, I am thirsty, I am hungry, I rejoice, I suffer, etc. And those things which can neither be demonstrated from phenomena nor follow from it by the argument of induction, I hold as hypotheses.[28]

This position is clearly very close to that of Locke. So close, indeed, that one might suspect direct influence. The rejection of innate ideas, the distinction between ideas of sensation and reflection, and the attack on hypothetical explanation are all common themes. Was it Newton's considered opinion? The evidence suggests that it was. There are several other manuscript sources stating the same or similar positions. Further, the view expressed in the draft Rule is entirely consistent with all his published methodological and epistemological remarks, and, so far as I have discovered, all his unpublished ones as well. But Newton, unlike Locke, offers no sustained argument for his views. Perhaps he believed no detailed argument was called for after the publication of Locke's *Essay*. It also suggests that Newton did not pay a great deal of attention to matters of epistemology. Just as Locke by temperament was not strongly attracted to the mathematical sciences, so Newton was only weakly moved towards epistemology.

THE ACCOUNTS OF PERCEPTION

Locke believed that an account of perception was not to the purpose of the *Essay*. He tells us in the second paragraph of Chapter I:

I shall not at present meddle with the physical considerations of the mind; or trouble myself to examine, wherein its essence consists, or by what motions of our spirits, or alterations of our bodies, we come to have any sensation by our organs, or any *ideas* in our understandings; and whether those ideas do in their formation, any, or all of them, depend on matter or no.

The implication is that he does not wish to be committed to

any theory or hypothesis which might be thought part of
natural philosophy. 'These are speculations', he goes on,
'which, however curious and entertaining, I shall decline.'
This promise he was not altogether able to keep. For in Book II,
Chapter VIII, when he is considering how privative causes
may produce positive ideas, he puts forward what is clearly
his own view on the causes of perception:

> If it were the design of my present undertaking, to enquire
> into the natural causes and manner of perception, I should
> offer this as a reason why a privative cause might, in some
> cases at least, produce a positive idea, viz. That all sensation
> being produced in us, only by different degrees and modes
> of motion in our animal spirits, variously agitated by
> external objects, the abatement of any former motion,
> must as necessarily produce a new sensation, as the variation
> or increase of it; and so introduce a new idea, which depends
> only on a different motion of the animal spirits in that
> organ.[29]

Later, in accounting for our perception of bodies, in the
discussion of primary and secondary qualities, he says that
bodies produce ideas in us 'by impulse', 'the only way which
we can conceive bodies operate in'.[30] It is the 'operation of
insensible particles on our senses'[31] which causally produces
the ideas in our minds.

Notoriously, this account of perception is often held to lead
inevitably to a contradiction within Locke's philosophy. But
(as has also often been noticed) it does not appear to have
unduly worried Locke, who happily launched a strong attack
on Malebranche for a fault not dis-similar to that alleged
against himself.[32] But, be that as it may, Locke's account of
how it is that we may be justified in moving from ideas to
objects is worth noting for reasons which link him with Newton.

Locke's problem manifests itself in its most acute form when
he is attempting to justify his claim that we have knowledge
of the existence of particular things without the mind. He sees
of course that on his account 'the mind knows not things

immediately, but only by the intervention of the *ideas* it has of them'.[33] Granting 'some difficulty' Locke argues that there are two sorts of idea which we can be morally certain 'agree with things'. In fact only one of these arguments is at all relevant. It is that there are simple ideas which we know that the mind cannot make itself. They must, therefore be 'the product of things operating on the mind in a natural way'.[34] On this argument it is clear that Locke's justification is inferential, and he describes it as a necessary inference.

Locke's further justification for claims to knowledge of the existence of particular things without us does not purport to establish their existence as a necessary consequence of some given fact, but as a matter of such high probability that it deserves to be called knowledge: 'for I think nobody can, in earnest, be so sceptical, as to be uncertain of the existence of those things which he sees and feels'.[35] A substantial difficulty with his argument is that it clearly presupposes that which it is intended to prove, but I do not now wish to dwell on the limitations of Locke's arguments so much as their nature. It reveals, what is sometimes taken to be a particular Lockian fault, namely, moving at will from ideas to things as the objects of perception. Fault or not, it is certainly not confined to Locke, and reappears in the writings of Newton.

Newtonian accounts of perception may be found in many places in his published works and in his papers. His account is in general very similar to Locke's, as indeed it is to those of both Descartes and Robert Boyle. In the *Opticks* Newton states the facts of visual perception thus:

When a man views any object . . . the light which comes from the several points of the object is refracted by the transparent skins and humors of the eye (that is, by the outward coat . . . called the tunica cornea, and by the crystalline humor . . . which is beyond the pupil . . .) as to converge and meet again in so many points in the bottom of the eye, and there to paint the picture of the object upon the skin (called the tunica retina) with which the bottom

of the eye is covered . . . and these pictures, propagated by
motion along the fibers of the optic nerves in the brain, are
the cause of vision.[36]

The pictures are the cause of vision. But Newton believed
that that which actually sees is the soul. He explained it thus
in a letter:

> Let us now consider what may be the cause of the various
> situations of things to the eyes. If when we look but with
> one eye it be asked why objects appear thus and thus situated
> one to another, the answer would be because they are really
> so situated among themselves and make their collored
> pictures in the retina so situated one to another as they are;
> and those pictures transmit motional pictures into the
> sensorium in the same situation, and by the situation of
> those motional pictures one to another the soul judges of
> the situation of things without.[37]

There are numerous manuscript sources which link Newton's
account of perception with his dualism. Thus he wrote:
'The organs of sense are not for enabling the soul to perceive
the species of things in its sensorium, but only for conveying
them thither & God has no used (*sic*) of such organs, he
being everywhere present to the things themselves.'[38]

Newton is not at all embarrassed by the transition from
objects of perception as external entities, and objects as ideas
or pictures within the head. In the letter, quoted above,
Newton goes on to talk of double vision and remarks 'through
the two eyes are transmitted into the sensorium two motional
pictures by whose situation and distance from another the
soul judges she sees two things so situate and distant'.

Do these remarks reflect a lack of clarity and commitment
about the true objects of perception, in the same way as such
ambivalence is often read in, or into, Locke? The answer
appears to be affirmative. Newton does not wish either to
deny his dualism or to abandon a position which makes the
observation of the world non-inferential. This lack of penetra-

tion into the implications of his descriptions of what he takes the facts of perception to be are well illustrated by a remark in a draft for the 31st Query:

> . . . A man must argue from phenomena). We find in our-selves a power of moving our bodies by o^r thoughts (but the laws of this power we do not know) & see ye same power in other living creatures but how this is done & by what laws we do not know.[39]

Here we have a clear example where Newton asserts that we see what on Newton's own dualist principles, we cannot possibly ever have seen, namely a causal connection between the thoughts of others and the movement of their limbs.

There is, then, a problem in the interpretation of Newton, just as there is in the interpretation of Locke, as to exactly what the objects of perception, the phenomena, are. Newton, as much as Locke ever did, usually wishes to identify these objects with public things. The lists of phenomena which he gives at various places are not mental entities or descriptions of mental events, but such things as 'the earth is a round body in the form of a globe',[40] or 'the celebrated phenomena of colours'.[41] As Newton makes clear, in the draft Rule V already quoted, he is totally committed to the position that the senses inform us about phenomena. We gain knowledge of pheno-mena, say, by sight, directly, not inferentially. We *see* the colours of the prism, or the phases of Venus. They are not, for Newton, hypotheses assumed to save the appearances.

DUALISM AND THE ISSUE OF SUBSTANCE

Newton was puzzled by the occurrence of double vision, and discussions of it occur several times in his papers.[42] The roots of this puzzlement appear in an early notebook[43] in passages which probably owe more than a little to Henry More, and which are directed against Hobbes's materialism. Newton, in these immature reflections – though many were to become his considered opinions – links double vision, or rather the

B

lack of it in normal circumstances, with his dualism. His
argument is that if the soul were 'nothing but modified matter
& did memory consist in action' we could never recall things
at will. Our memories would depend only upon the motions
in the brain. Further, 'If sense consisted in reaction we should
perceive things double . . .'.[44]

Two things which emerge clearly from Newton's remarks
in this notebook are that he believed empirical evidence –
the phenomena – point unambiguously towards dualism, and
that it is only from the phenomena that we may learn more
about both soul and body. Under the heading 'Philosophy'
he entered:

> The nature of things is more securely & naturally deduced
> from their operacons one upon another & upon o[er] senses.
> And when by ye former experiments we have found ye
> nature of bodys, by ye latter wee may more clearaly find
> ye nature of o[r] senses. But so long as wee are ignorant of
> ye nature of both soule & body wee cannot clearly dis-
> tinguish how far an act of sensation proceeds from y[e] soule
> & how far from y[e] body Etc.[45]

In a series of questions and answers entered under 'Of ye
soule' Newton's dualism emerges unambiguously and power-
fully:

> Memory is a faculty of ye soule (in some measure) for
> else how can divers sounds, or words excite her to divers
> thoughts or 3.4.5 or more words beget ye same thought
> in her. Perhaps she remembers by ye helpe of characters
> in ye Braine, but yn how doth shee remember the significa-
> tion of those characters.
>   Quase 1. why Objects appear not inversed Resp. The
> mind or Soule cannot judge ye image in ye Braine to be
> inversed in less she perceived externall things wth w[ch] shee
> might compare y[t] Image.
>   2. Why doe [objects?] appear to bee without (i.e. out-
> side) our body? Resp: Because in the image of things

delineated in the braine by sight, ye bodys image is placed ye midst of ye images of other things is moved at o^e [our] command towars & from those other images &c.

3. But why are not these objects then judged to bee in the braine Resp. Because ye image of ye braine is not painted there, nor is ye Braine perceived [*sic*] by ye soule it not being in motion, & probably ye soule perceives noe body but by ye helpe of their motion. But were ye Braine perceived together with those images in it wee should thinke wee saw a body like the braine encompassing & comprehending our selves ye starrs & all other visible objects. &c.[46]

Newton clearly believed on both direct empirical grounds, and on the basis of inference, that we have both a body and a soul. We can be sure also, both on independent grounds and from the implications of his remarks, that he thought the soul to be an immaterial entity. Matter was governed by the laws of motion (still far from understood by Newton in the 1660's when he made his notebook entries). It was essentially passive. Mind, however, was active, capable of being a direct and sufficient causal agent, as exemplified in deliberate human actions, whether mental or physical: 'Were ye soule nothing but modified matter . . . we could never call things into o^r memory'.[47]

But what of the real nature of both soul and body? Here Newton, like Locke, and in sharp contrast to Descartes, is very cautious and uncertain. Of Newton's conception of the nature of the soul there is almost no evidence. There is much more, however, on the nature of body. Much more than can be satisfactorily discussed here. I shall therefore confine my remarks to some aspects of Newton's account which are particularly relevant to a comparison with Locke.

In a comparatively early composition, *De Gravitatione et aequipondio fluidorum* (about 1671) Newton puts forward a rich collection of ideas about matter, many of which were to remain with him until the end of his life. His account of body begins as follows:

Now that extension has been described, it remains to give an explanation of the nature of body. Of this, however, the explanation must be more uncertain, for it does not exist necessarily but by divine will, because it is hardly given to us to know the limits of the divine power, that is to say whether matter could be created in one way only, or whether there are several ways by which different beings similar to bodies could be produced. And although it scarcely seems credible that God could create beings similar to bodies which display all their actions and exhibit all their phenomena and yet are not in essential and metaphysical constitution bodies; as I have no clear and distinct perception of this matter I should not dare to affirm the contrary, and hence I am reluctant to say positively what the nature of bodies is, but I rather describe a certain kind of being similar in every way to bodies, and whose creation we cannot deny to be within the power of God, so that we can hardly say that it is not body.[48]

Although Descartes's influence can be detected in this passage, there is also clear hostility to Cartesian positions. In so far as Newton sees the creation of matter not as the product of some necessity in nature, but as the result of divine will, and in so far as Newton makes use of the criterion of clear and distinct perception [*claram ac distinctam perceptionem*] there is a debt to Descartes. On the other side, in the denial of knowledge of the essence of body, and in the style of that denial, Newton places himself in strong opposition both to the method of discovery and to the first truth of the physical world presented in Cartesian metaphysics. That claim was that 'the true nature of body consists solely in extension'.[49]

Newton's mature account of the properties of bodies is found in Rule III of the *Regulae Philosophandie*, but the Rule contains no remarks about substance. In a draft version of the *Scholium Generale*, however, added to the second edition of the *Principia*, Newton expressed entirely Lockian sentiments:

From phenomena we know the properties of things, and

from the properties we infer that the things themselves exist and we call them substances: but we do not have any idea of substances. We see but the shapes and colours of bodies, we hear but sounds, we touch but external surfaces, we smell odours and taste flavours; but we know the substances or essences themselves by no sense, by no reflex action, and therefore we have no more idea of them than a blind man has of colours. And when it is said that we have an idea of God or an idea of body, nothing other is to be understood than that we have an idea of the properties by which bodies are distinguished from God or from each other. Whence it is that we nowhere argue about the ideas of substances apart from properties, and deduce no conclusions from the same.[50]

Whatever substance is, whether mental or physical, whether finite or infinite, although we know it exists, its essence is beyond our knowledge, Newton claims. All we may talk of with sense are properties for which we have corresponding ideas. A more Lockian position it would be difficult to imagine. Locke's dualism, although certain, is as cautious as Newton's. Their words are remarkably close and express very similar views:

. . . *the idea* we have *of spirit,* compared with the idea we have of body, stands thus: the substance of spirit is unknown to us; and so is the substance of body, equally unknown to us: two primary qualities, or properties of body, viz. solid coherent parts, and impulse, we have distinct clear ideas of: so likewise we know, and have distinct clear ideas of two primary qualities, or properties of spirit, viz. thinking, and a power of action; i.e. a power of beginning, or stopping several thoughts or motions. We have also the ideas of several qualities inherent in bodies, and have the clear distinct ideas of them: which qualities, are but the various modifications of the extension of cohering solid parts, and their motion. We have likewise the ideas of the several modes of thinking, *viz.* believing, doubting, intending, fearing, hoping; all which, are but the several modes of thinking. We have also the ideas of willing, and moving the body consequent to it, and with the body it self too; for, as has been shewed, spirit is capable of motion.[51]

But whereas Newton's views, mostly unpublished, are largely offered unsupported, Locke reaches his conclusions only after sustained and detailed argument through over twenty pages.

The reverse of this may be seen in another, related, matter. Throughout his active scientific life Newton was intrigued by the problem of the nature of force. In his published work, except in some hints in the *General Scholium*, and several remarks in the Queries of the *Opticks*, he did not develop his ideas. But in his manuscripts there are many relevant papers. In the last Query Newton wrote:

> Seeing therefore the variety of Motion which we find in the World is always decreasing, there is a necessity of conserving and recruiting it by active Principles, such as are the cause of Gravity, by which Planets and Comets keep their Motions in their Orbs, and Bodies acquire great Motion in falling; and the cause of Fermentation, by which the Heart and Blood of Animals are kept in perpetual Motion and Heat; the inward Parts of the Earth are constantly warm'd, and in some places grow very hot; Bodies burn and shine, Mountains take fire, the Caverns of the Earth are blown up, and the Sun continues violently hot and lucid, and warms all things by his Light. For we meet with very little Motion in the World, besides what is owing to these active Principles.[52]

Although Newton never explicitly made the connections in print, it seems likely that he identified these active principles with an immaterial substance, and ultimately with God. To Richard Bentley Newton wrote:

> Tis inconceivable that inanimate brute matter should (without ye mediation of something else wch is not material)

operate upon & affect other matter without mutual contact.[53]

And the answer to which Newton was firmly committed was that the active principles were indeed the manifestation of the direct intervention of God:

> By what means do bodies act on one another at a distance . . . it seems to have been an ancient opinion that matter depends upon a Deity for its laws of motion & it is reasonable to make him the author of the laws of motion. Matter is a passive principle & cannot move it self . . . It receives motion proportional to the force impressing it, And resists as much as it is resisted. These are passive laws & to affirm that there are no other is to speak against experience . . . life and will are active Principles by wch we move our bodies & Hence arise other laws of motion unknown to us.
>
> And since all matter duly formed is attended with signes of life & all things are framed with perfect art & wisdom & Nature does nothing in vain; if there be an universal life & all space be the sensorium of a thinking being who by immediate presence perceives all things in it as that wch thinks in us perceives their pictures in the brain: the laws of motion arising from life or will may be of universal extent.[54]

There are several other manuscript sources indicating Newton's belief that the active principles in nature were immaterial and to be identified directly with the intervention of God. But what of Locke? In one paragraph of the *Essay* we have in a compressed form thoughts so similar to those of Newton that it would be difficult to believe that the two men had not discussed the matter. In fact we know they did, and that Newton claimed his ideas actually came to him whilst in conversation with Locke.[55] The whole paragraph is for this reason worth citing:

> Another idea we have of body, is the power of communication of motion by impulse; and of our souls, the power of exciting of motion by thought. These ideas, the one of

body, the other of our minds, every days experience clearly furnishes us with: But if here again we enquire how this is done, we are equally in the dark. For in the communication of motion by impulse, wherein as much motion is lost to one body, as is got to the other, which is the ordinariest case, we can have no other conception, but of the passing of motion out of one body into another; which, I think, is as obscure and unconceivable, as how our minds move or stop our bodies by thought; which we every moment find they do. The increase of motion by impulse, which is observed or believed sometimes to happen, is yet harder to be understood. We have by daily experience clear evidence of motion produced both by impulse, and by thought; but the manner how, hardly comes without our comprehension; we are equally at a loss in both. So that however we consider motion, and its communication either from body or spirit, the idea which belongs to spirit, is at least as clear, as that, that belongs to body. And if we consider the active power of moving, or, as I may call it, motivity, it is much clearer in spirit than body; since two bodies, placed by one another at rest, will never afford us the idea of a power in the one to move the other, but by a borrowed motion: whereas the mind, every day, affords us ideas of an active power of moving of bodies; and therefore it is worth our consideration, whether active power be not the proper attribute of spirits, and passive power of matter. Hence may be conjectured, that created spirits are not totally separate from matter, because they are both active and passive. Pure spirit, viz. God, is only active; pure matter is only passive; those beings that are both active and passive we may judge to partake of both. But be that as it will, I think, we have as many, and as clear ideas belonging to spirit, as we have belonging to body, the substance of each being equally unknown to us: and the idea of thinking in spirit, as clear as of extension in body; and the communication of motion by thought, which we attribute to spirit, is as evident, as that by impulse, which we ascribe to body.

Constant experience makes us sensible of both of these, though our narrow understandings can comprehend neither. For when the mind would look beyond those original ideas we have from sensation or reflection, and penetrate into their causes, and manner of production, we find still it discovers nothing but its own short-sightedness.[56]

The conjecture that active powers belong only to spirits (roots, perhaps, for Berkeley's speculations) was not one that ever seems to have been strongly held by Locke. It was, after all, only a speculation, an hypothesis. It is evidence for the earlier claim that Locke was in fact less attracted to speculation in matters relating to the physical sciences than Newton was.

HYPOTHESES AND THE SCIENTIFIC ENTERPRISE

Locke was sceptical of the possibilities of scientific knowledge. 'The systems of *natural philosophy* . . . are to be read, more to know the *hypotheses* . . . than with hopes to gain thereby a comprehensive, scientifical, and satisfactory knowledge of the works of nature', he wrote.[57] But he did allow that Newton's *Principia* was a success on a limited front. It had shown 'how far mathematicks, applied to some parts of nature, may, upon principles that matter of fact justifie, carry us in the knowledge of some . . . particular provinces of the incomprehensible universe'.[58]

Hypotheses are uncertain, and hypotheses as speculative explanations should both be recognized as such, and also recognized as essentially an unsatisfactory way of proceeding in matters relating to natural philosophy. Locke's suspicion of hypotheses emerges frequently. The theory of innate ideas is an hypothesis, the view that a man always thinks is 'a confused notion, take up to serve an hypothesis'.[59] Hypotheses too often lead to false explanations, and we are ever tempted to assume our hypotheses to be the truth. The hypothetical method has not proved successful in obtaining true knowledge. 'He that shall consider how little general maxims, precarious

principles, and hypotheses laid down at pleasure have promoted true knowledge', he wrote, including within this
description, no doubt, Descartes and his followers, 'will think
we have reason to thank those who in this latter age have
taken another course and have trod out to us, though not an
easier way to learned ignorance, yet a surer way to profitable
knowledge'.[60] Here Locke would certainly have Boyle and
Sydenham in mind, and probably Bacon as well. However
Locke was careful not totally to rule out hypotheses from
science. The danger was always that we too readily accept
an hypothesis because we are eager for explanation . . . 'We
should not take up any one [hypothesis] *too hastily* . . . till we
have very well examined particulars and made several experiments in that thing we would explain by our hypothesis, and
see whether it will agree to them all'.[61]

An almost identical attitude is to be found in Newton's
writings. Thus in his draft queries we find the following:

> Could all the phaenomena of nature be (evidently) deduced
> from only three or four general suppositions there might be
> great reason to allow those suppositions to be true: but if for
> explaining every new Phaenomenon you make a new
> Hypothesis if you suppose y^t ye particles of Air are of such
> a figure size and frame, those of water of such another,
> those of Vitriol of such another, those of Quicksilver of
> such another. . . . If you suppose that light consists in such
> a motion precession or force & that its various colours are
> made by such & such variations of the motion of so of
> other things: your Philosophy will be nothing else than a
> systeme of Hypotheses. And what certeinty can be there in
> a Philosophy wch consists in as many Hypotheses as there are
> Phaenomena to be explained. To explain all nature is too
> difficult a task for any one man or even for any one age.
> Tis much better to do a little with certeinty & leave the
> rest for others that come after, than to explain all Things
> by conjecture without making sure of any thing: And there
> is no other way of doing any thing with certeinty than by

drawing conclusions from experiments & phaenomena untill you come at general Principles & then from those Principles giving an account of Nature. Whatever is certain in philosophy is owing to this method & nothing can be done without it.[62]

There are several points of note which arise in this passage. Newton, like Locke, does not totally dismiss the possibility that there may be some role for hypotheses in explaining nature. But the emphasis is clearly in another direction. Similarly, he is not at all attracted to the Cartesian ideal[63] of a completely deductive physics. Not that Descartes believed we could achieve that ideal. But he did hold it worthwhile to attempt to move as close as we could. Neither Locke nor Newton shared this aspiration. Indeed both saw in it the inherent danger of the temptation to take as certainties matters which were in truth only conjectures.

This hostility to the deductive ideal on the part of the two men did not lead to a position of scepticism. Between the twin dangers of aspiration to deductive science on the one hand and the nihilism of the sceptic on the other, there was a middle course which led to certainty of a kind which was appropriate to the condition of man. The certainty we can expect to obtain is that of inductive certainty, for the principles of natural science 'are deduced from phenomena and made general by induction, which is the highest evidence that a proposition can have in this philosophy'.[64] Universal propositions about the natural world were, for Newton, to be based on inductive evidence. Of course he recognized that their certainty was not guaranteed, but until there was evidence against such a generalization it should be accepted 'as accurately or very nearly true, notwithstanding any contrary hypotheses that may be imagined, till such time as other phenomena occur by which they may either be made more accurate or liable to exceptions'.[65]

Locke never set out any formal principles of method to correspond to those of the *Regulae*, but his position is un-

doubtedly that of Newton's. Mr. Newton's book can be
accepted because it is based on principles 'which matter of
fact justify'.

It is sometimes said that Locke believed that the ultimate
truths of nature were necessary. There is certainly confused
talk on his part about the status of laws of nature. But even
if he does sometimes use language which suggests that he
subscribes to a rationalist view,[66] such a position is totally
inconsistent with a belief which both he and Newton certainly
did hold, namely that the laws of nature were contingent
upon the will of God. Locke makes a special point of con-
trasting the immutability of mathematical truths with truths
about nature. The truths of geometry do not depend on any
arbitrary power,

> But the coherence and continuity of the parts of matter;
> the production of sensation in us of colours and sounds, etc.
> by impulse and motion; nay the original rules and com-
> munication of motion being such, wherein we can discover
> no natural connexion with any *ideas* we have, we cannot
> but ascribe them to the arbitrary will and good pleasure
> of the Wise Architect.[67]

Locke supports this voluntarist position[68] by reference to
miracles, which he points out, by argument *ad hominem*, none
of his readers wishes to deny.[69]

Newton also placed the events of the world not in *necessity*,
but in the *will* of God. The only route to knowledge of the
world must be through experience because there is no other
way whereby we may come to know the will of God in relation
to the world. Thus Newton believed it was necessary to introduce direct intervention by God to account for the fact that
from one original matter there should arise the luminous
sun and the non-luminous earth. This was an event not
'explicable by mere natural causes, but am forced to ascribe
it [Newton wrote] to the counsel and contrivance of a voluntary
Agent'.[70] 'All that diversity of natural things which we find
suited to different times and places could arise from nothing

but the ideas and will of a Being necessarily existing'[71] he wrote in the *General Scholium*.

The emphasis on the contingency of that which was discovered, but nevertheless the possibility of discovery, is fundamental to the empiricist programme of Locke and Newton. In a sense it is its rationale. There is here no hint of Humean scepticism in the rationality of the programme. The contingency of knowledge was not a source of despair. It merely reflected a (contingent) fact about the relationship between man and God. For Locke it was part of the natural order of things. Man's place on the Great Chain of Being, and the knowledge which was thus available to him, was entirely appropriate to his station. For Newton, who, on occasion, saw himself as a child playing on the sea-shore when the whole ocean of truth lay undiscovered before him, was not thereby intimidated. Even if the inductive generalizations of the natural philosopher should turn out to meet with contrary instances, this would not be a hindrance to either knowledge or progress. It is the quiet but powerful confidence of the empiricism of Locke and Newton which takes us some way into an understanding of the Enlightenment.

NOTES

[1] Henry F. May: *The Enlightenment in America* (New York and London, 1976), p. 25.

[2] A point too often overlooked by commentators who have tended to read the *Essay Concerning Human Understanding* as a product, albeit an off-shoot, of Newton's work. For further discussion on this see G. A. J. Rogers, 'Locke's *Essay* and Newton's *Principia*', *Journal of the History of Ideas*, xxxix April, 1978.

[3] Newton suffered a severe mental disturbance in 1693 which led him to abruptly terminate his relationship with Samuel Pepys and to accuse Locke of endeavouring to embroil him with women, and of being a Hobbist. Cf. Frank E. Manuel *A Portrait of Isaac Newton* (London and New York, 1968), p. 213 ff.

[4] For some discussion of this see G. A. J. Rogers, 'Locke, Newton,

and the Cambridge Platonists on Innate Ideas', *Journal of the History of Ideas*, XL April, 1979.

[5] There is as yet no proper study of their theological connections but there are pertinent discussions in H. McLachlan: *The Religious Opinions of Milton, Locke and Newton* (Manchester, 1941) and Frank E. Manuel *The Religion of Isaac Newton* (Oxford, 1974).

[6] Newton's political views, including the rationale of political power, appear to have been very similar to Locke's. See here Newton's letter to the Vice-Chancellor of Cambridge University, when Newton, as Member of Parliament for the University, advised that the oaths to be taken to the new monarch William III were legal. *The Correspondence of Isaac Newton* (Cambridge, 1959–60), III, pp. 12–13, hereafter cited as *Correspondence*. See also L. T. More: *Isaac Newton. A Biography* (London, 1934), ch. x.

[7] Though basic, these facts have been too rarely heeded by commentators. On this see Rogers, cited in Note 2 above.

[8] We know this from Locke's correspondence with Edward Clarke, to whom Locke sent his completed script in 1686. There is further support in a draft manuscript of the *Essay* (the third and latest extant draft, although only of the first and second books), which closely resembles the published work. For further discussion and references see Rogers (Note 2), Note 11.

[9] The earliest extant reference to Newton's *Principia* in Locke's manuscripts is a series of notes dated September 1687. Bodleian Library MS, Locke C. 33, ff. 19–20.

[10] In the *Regulae Philosophandie* at the beginning of Book III. The clarity of presentation is, however, deceptive. The interpretation of these Rules is full of difficulties. For recent discussions of some of these difficulties see A. Koyré: *Newtonian Studies* (London, 1965), Ch. VI 'Newton's Regulae Philosophandi'; J. E. McGuire 'Transmutation and Immutability: Newton's Doctrine of Physical Qualities', *Ambix*, XIV, 1967; J. E. McGuire: 'The Origin of Newton's Doctrine of Essential Qualities', *Centaurus*, 12, 1968; J. E. McGuire: 'Atoms and the Analogy of Nature: Newton's Third Rule of Philosophizing' *Studies in the History and Philosophy of Science*, I, 1970; M. A. Finocchiaro: 'Newton's Third Rule of Philosophizing: A Role for Logic in Historiography,' *Isis*, 1974.

[11] Locke's copy, which is in Trinity College, Cambridge, appears hardly to have been opened. It is true that Locke was already familiar with many of Newton's optical discoveries.

[12] Newton's more speculative thoughts were contained in the Queries added to Book III.

[13] Whilst Newton's epistemology seems largely to have been empiricist, his ontology is very similar to that of the Cambridge

Platonist, Henry More. His commitment to absolute space and time, for example, was a view shared with More, and may have been derived from him. There are also similarities in their conception of spirit as an active principle.

[14] See, for example, the discussions in the following: J. A. Lohne: '*Experimentum Crucis*', *Notes and Records of the Royal Society* 23 (1968); R. S. Westfall: 'Newton and the Fudge Factor' *Science* 179 (1973); D. T. Whiteside, 'Newton's Lunar Theory: From High Hope to Disenchentment', *Vistas in Astronomy*, **19** (London, 1976).

[15] On the other side, he was often well aware that his own conjectures were *not* supported with sufficient evidence to justify their publication to the world, or even to be held as firm opinion by himself.

[16] Both Locke and Newton probably owed as much to Descartes as they did to any thinker. Both also reacted critically to his stimulus and it is Cartesian views that both of their major works most strongly attack.

[17] For discussions of Newton's speculations see J. E. McGuire: 'Force, Active Principles and Newton's Invisible Realm' *Ambix* 15, 1968; R. S. Westfall: *Force in Newton's Physics. The Science of Dynamics in the Seventeenth Century* (London, 1971), ch. VII, cf. also Query 28 of Newton's *Opticks*.

[18] Locke became deeply interested in both medicine and chemistry whilst still an undergraduate, as his notebooks for that period testify. For a survey of his activities see Kenneth Dewhurst: *John Locke (1632–1704) Physician and Philosopher. A Medical Biography* (London, 1963), ch. I.

[19] See *An Essay Concerning Human Understanding*, II. I. 1–5. All quotations will be taken from the *Clarendon Edition of the Works of John Locke*, edited by Peter H. Nidditch (Oxford, 1975). This edition is based on the fourth edition of the *Essay*, and will be cited by Book, Chapter and Section numbers. Unless otherwise cited all Locke references are to the *Essay* in this edition.

[20] I. IV. 24.

[21] I. IV. 22.

[22] I. IV. 18.

[23] II. I. 9.

[24] II. I. 18.

[25] II. I. 21.

[26] I. I. 2.

[27] For discussion of this draft Rule see Koyré *op. cit.* and I. B. Cohen: *Introduction to Newton's Principia* (Cambridge, 1971), pp. 30–31.

[28] University Library, Cambridge (U.L.C.) MS, Add. 3965.13, f. 419^r.

[29] II. VIII. 4.

[30] II. VIII. 11.

[31] II. VIII. 13.

[32] See A. D. Woozley's Introduction to his abridged edition of the *Essay*, Fontana Library (London, 1964), pp. 26–8, and John W. Yolton: *Locke and the Compass of Human Understanding* (Cambridge, 1970), p. 134. Locke's *An Examination of P. Malebranche's Opinion of Seeing All Things in God* was posthumously published in 1706.

[33] IV. IV. 3.

[34] IV. IV. 4.

[35] IV. XI. 3.

[36] *Opticks* (4th edition, London, 1730 Dover reprint, 1952), p. 15.

[37] Newton to William Briggs, September 12 1682. *Correspondence* II, p. 383.

[38] U.L.C. Add MS. 3970.9 f. 621^v.

[39] U.L.C. Add MS. 3970.9 f. 620^r.

[40] An example taken from a list of phenomena in Newton's manuscripts, now published in *Unpublished Scientific Papers of Isaac Newton*, ed. by A. R. Hall and Marie Boas Hall (Cambridge, 1962), pp. 378–85.

[41] From Newton's paper to the Royal Society, published in the *Philosophical Transactions of the Royal Society* No. 80 (1672). Reprinted in *Isaac Newton's Papers and Letters on Natural Philosophy*, ed. by I. B. Cohen (Cambridge, 1958), p. 47.

[42] As well as the letter already quoted see also the paper published in David Brewster's *Memoirs of Sir Isaac Newton* (2nd edition, Edinburgh, 1860), I, pp. 395–8.

[43] For a description of this notebook see A. R. Hall: 'Sir Isaac Newton's Note-Book', *Cambridge Historical Journal*, 9, 1948, pp. 239–50. The notebook's entries were made between 1661 and 1665, when Newton was an undergraduate.

[44] U.L.C. Add MS. 3996, f. 130.

[45] *Ibid.* f. 102.

[46] *Ibid.* f. 131.

[47] *Ibid.* f. 130.

[48] Hall and Hall (*op. cit.* Note 40), p. 138.

[49] *Principles of Philosophy* Part II, Principle V.

[50] U.L.C. Add MS. 3965, ff. 361–2. Published in Hall and Hall (*op. cit.* Note 40), p. 361.

[51] II. XXIII. 30.

[52] *Opticks, ed. cit.*, p. 399.

[53] *Correspondence* III, pp. 253–4½.

[54] U.L.C. Add MS. 3970.9, f. 619.

[55] Newton's claim was made to Pierre Coste, as reported in a

footnote to Coste's French translation of Locke's *Essay* (3rd edition, Amsterdam, 1735, p. 521). The footnote refers to *Essay*, IV, X, 18. On this see Koyré: *Newtonian Studies*, p. 92. See also the remark of David Gregory: 'Mr. C. Wren says that he is in possession of a method of explaining gravity mechanically. He smiles at Mr. Newton's belief that it does not occur by mechanical means, but was introduced originally by the Creator.' *Correspondence* IV, p. 267.

⁵⁶ II. XXIII. 28.

⁵⁷ *Some Thoughts Concerning Education*, in *The Educational Writings of John Locke*, edited by James L. Axtell (Cambridge, 1968), p. 305.

⁵⁸ *Ibid.* p. 306.

⁵⁹ II. I. 18.

⁶⁰ IV. XII. 12.

⁶¹ IV. XII. 13.

⁶² U.L.C. Add MS. 3970, f. 479.

⁶³ This ideal was expressed in a letter to Mersenne in 1640 thus: 'I would think I knew nothing in Physics if I could only say how things could be, without proving that they could not be otherwise. This is perfectly possible once one has reduced everything to laws of mathematics; I think I can do it for the small area to which my knowledge extends. But I did not do it in my essays because I did not want to present my Principles there, and I do not yet see anything to persuade me to present them in future.' Descartes, *Philosophical Letters* translated and edited by Anthony Kenny (Oxford, 1970), pp. 70–71. The *Principles* were in fact published four years later.

⁶⁴ In a letter to Roger Cotes. *Correspondence*, V, p. 397. See also the draft letter to Cotes (pp. 398–9):

Experimental Philosophy reduces Phaenomena to general Rules & looks upon the Rules to be general when they hold generally in Phaenomena. It is not enough to object that a contrary phaenomenon may happen but to make a legitimate objection, a contrary phenomenon must be actually produced. Hypothetical Philosophy consists in imaginary explications of things & imaginary arguments for or against such explications, or against the arguments of Experimental Philosophers founded upon Induction. The first sort of Philosophy is followed by me, the latter too much by Cartes, Leibniz & some others.

⁶⁵ Rule IV *Regulae Philosophandi*, *Principia* Book III. The translation is that in Andrew Motte's translation, revised by Florian Cajori (Berkeley and Los Angeles, 1962), p. 400.

⁶⁶ R. S. Woolhouse in his *Locke's Philosophy of Science and Knowledge* (Oxford, 1971) attributes rationalism to Locke, which he defines as the view 'that in natural science we have to do with synthetically

necessary propositions which are not by us knowable *a priori*' (p. 25).

[67] IV. III. 29.

[68] On the voluntarist tradition in this context see Francis Oakley: 'Medieval Theories of Natural Law: William of Ockham and the Significance of the Voluntarist Tradition', *Natural Law Forum*, 6, 1961.

[69] Locke expresses a similar position in his *A Discourse of Miracles*, published posthumously in 1706.

[70] *Correspondence*, III, p. 234. Newton to Richard Bentley, 1692.

[71] *Principia (ed. cit.,* Note 65), p. 546.

2

HUME, NEWTON AND 'THE HILL CALLED DIFFICULTY'

Christine Battersby

In a celebrated passage in 'Of the Standard of Taste', Hume tells us that those readers who prefer Bunyan's writings to Addison's are merely 'pretended critics' whose judgment is 'absurd and ridiculous'; this is 'no less an extravagance, than if he had maintained a mole-hill to be as high as TENERIFFE, or a pond as extensive as the ocean' (GG, iii, p. 269).[1] Hume shows a decisiveness and vehemence in his judgment against Bunyan that has greater significance than that of being a mere reflection of his aesthetic principles. Hume does, after all, wish to make 'durable admiration' the foundation of his standard of taste, and both the number of eighteenth-century reprints of *The Pilgrim's Progress* and Johnson's comment that this work has as 'the best evidence of its merit, the general and continued approbation of mankind' testify to the lasting popularity of Bunyan's work (GG, iii, p. 271).[2] Hume's critical judgment on Bunyan is not merely a consequence of a mechanical application of his standard of taste, but is rather a reflection of what I will term Hume's 'epistemology of ease'.

For Bunyan there are many possible paths through the world; but there is only one path that man *ought* to take. He should not choose any of the easy paths – the 'Crooked, and Wide' paths. The path to salvation is the 'straight and narrow' path which leads up 'the Hill called *Difficulty*' and which man must follow '*against Wind and Tide*'. Bunyan's traveller through the world must be prepared to forsake family, friends and human society for the sake of his convictions. He must also be prepared to renounce all thoughts of immediate ease and comfort for the sake of future salvation. The ways of the common people are not his ways; and he must not follow 'Master *Worldly-Wiseman's*' advice and seek ease from the gentleman called '*Legality*' in the village called 'Morality'. The way to 'Morality' is the way to damnation.[3]

On his way to the wicket-gate from whence starts the straight and narrow path of difficulty, Bunyan's pilgrim, Christian, falls into the '*Slough of Dispond*': an area where all the 'fears, and doubts, and discouraging apprehensions' that arise in the soul 'get together, and settle in this place'.[4] Hume's philosophical inquiries also lead him to a place that could be called a '*Slough of Dispond*' – except that Hume's metaphor is that of a ship-wrecked man clinging to a bare rock in the middle of the ocean. Hume, the sceptic, is reduced 'almost to despair', and is resolved 'to perish on the barren rock' rather than to venture out 'upon that boundless ocean, which runs out into immensity' in the 'leaky weather-beaten vessel' that is his human frame (*T*, pp. 263, 264).

Hume is in despond over the 'wretched condition, weakness, and disorder of the faculties' of man. He is 'affrighted and confounded with that forelorn solitude' in which he is placed by his philosophy, and (like Bunyan's pilgrim) sees himself as an outcast from society. 'Expell'd all human commerce, and left utterly abandon'd and disconsolate', Hume feeds his despair 'with all those desponding reflections, which the present subject furnishes' (*T*, p. 264). Hume is indeed deep in the slough. But whereas Christian requires the help of another to escape from the slough and follow his difficult and uneasy path through the world, it is 'nature herself' who cures Hume's 'philosophical melancholy and delirium' (*T*, p. 269). Furthermore, the path that Hume starts along when emerging from the slough is not one of struggle; but rather one of relaxation and playfulness:

I dine, I play a game of back-gammon, I converse, and am merry with my friends; and when . . . I wou'd return to these speculations, they appear so cold, and strain'd, and ridiculous, that I cannot find in my heart to enter into them any farther. (*T*, p. 269.)

Christian's way out of the slough leads away from his family, his friends and human society. Hume's way leads back into society and into an 'indolent belief in the general maxims of the world'. Christian has to struggle '*against Wind and Tide*'; Hume, on the contrary, will acquiesce to the 'current of nature, which leads me to indolence and pleasure', resolving no more to 'torture my brain with subtilities and sophistries' and to 'no more be led a wandering into such dreary solitudes, and rough passages' (*T*, pp. 269, 270).

In this paper I wish to explore the notion that it is a pseudo-Newtonian 'current of nature' that rescues Hume from the '*Slough of Dispond*', and that it is also a pseudo-Newtonian current that draws him into the slough in the first place. I wish to suggest that Hume's solution to scepticism is not an arbitrary and *ad hoc* 'naturalism' introduced simply to solve his sceptical dilemma, but rather a logical consequence of Hume's Newtonian 'science of man'.

It has long been recognized that Hume attempted to model what he calls his 'moral' philosophy on Newton's 'natural' philosophy. Whereas, however, a certain respectability has been granted to Hume's attempt to model his *methodology* on that of Newton, Hume's attempt to model the *content* of his own account of mental motion on Newton's account of physical motion has generally been regarded as incongruous, incomplete and inconsistent with his naturalism.[5] In this paper I will not attempt to determine the ultimate success or failure of Hume's Newtonian analogue; but I wish to suggest that with regard to content the analogue is more complete than has generally been supposed, and that it contributes to, rather than conflicts with, Hume's 'naturalism'.

Hume draws an analogy between the three associative

forces that operate on mental objects and the force of gravity that operates on physical objects in Newton's system. Passmore is amongst those who have objected to this analogy on the grounds that association is a force that does not operate universally in the way that gravity does.[6] Hume does indeed claim that the imagination is 'free', despite the laws of association (*T*, p. 10). It is, however, only necessary to consider Hume's account of freedom to realise that 'free' and 'not law-governed' are not equivalents for Hume. (*T*, pp. 399 ff.) 'We may imagine we feel a liberty within ourselves'; but nevertheless an observer could predict our actions if he knew 'the most secret springs of our complexion and disposition' (*T*, pp. 408, 409). Hume admits no 'medium betwixt chance and an absolute necessity', and dismisses the former as 'directly contrary to experience': 'what the vulgar call chance is nothing but a secret and conceal'd cause' (*T*, pp. 171, 407, 130). To say that the imagination is more 'free' than any other faculty is not to say that there are occasions on which it is not law-governed; it is only to point to the complexity of the 'secret causes' that must be taken into account in explaining its operation.

If, however, it is the existence of these 'secret causes' that Passmore is objecting to when he claims that Hume's Newtonianism is 'a mere pretence', then the objection is still not valid. Gravity is not the only attractive force in Newton's system: magnetism and electricity are likewise 'Attractions', and it is said to be 'not improbable but that there may be more attractive Powers than these'.[7] Newton's system is not closed; so that when Hume suggests that there are other secondary forces in addition to resemblance, contiguity and causation, 'the only *general* principles, which associate ideas', he is not stepping outside his Newtonian paradigm (*T*, pp. 92–93). In another lecture in this volume, D. D. Raphael indicates that Adam Smith did not regard Newton's system as depending on a single causal factor – gravity.[8] Hume seems to have made the same, quite justifiable, observation. It is only some of our modern commentators who have failed to notice the

complexity of Newton's account, and thus suppose that Hume's
account is rendered non-Newtonian by his admission of other
possible secondary forces and even by the fact that 'sometimes
contiguity operates, at other times resemblance'.[9]

It is not the uniqueness of gravity as an attractive force
that enables Newton's science to be predictive, but rather his
three laws or 'axioms' of motion. Neither is gravity the force
that Newton makes essential to bodies; essential is only the
'inertia' or 'force of inactivity' that gives sense to Newton's
first law of motion.[10] In an earlier lecture G. A. J. Rogers
points out that it is only *bodies*, not minds or spirits, that
Newton sees as possessing this inherent inactivity: the limits
of the laws of motion are revealed by the existence of 'active
Principles by wch we move our bodies & Hence arise other
laws of motion unknown to us'.[11] In Hume's attempt to model
the forces of mental attraction on Newton's forces of physical
attraction, we find an implicit denial of Newton's restriction
of the laws of motion to matter. Indeed, hidden in Hume's
account, we find analogues not only for Newton's three
attractive forces, but also for the laws of motion themselves.
In what I term Hume's 'Newtonianism' lies Hume's opposition
to Newton's own view of the 'active' power of the mind, the
soul and God.

Despite this paradox, the completeness of Hume's mental
analogue entitles him to the title 'Newtonian'. Thus where
Newton's first law of motion instructs us that bodies are
essentially inactive and will maintain their initial state of rest
or rectilinear motion unless impinged upon by external forces,
for Hume,

> the imagination, when set into any train of thinking, is
> apt to continue, even when its object fails it, and like a
> galley put in motion by the oars, carries on its course
> without any new impulse. (*T*, p. 198)

Change in thought and feelings occurs only because, 'any
new object naturally gives a new direction to the spirits'

(*T*, p. 99), and

> nature has bestow'd a kind of attraction on certain impressions and ideas, by which one of them, upon its appearance, naturally introduces its correlative. (*T*, p. 289)

Which particular direction the spirits will 'naturally' follow depends on analogues for Newton's second and third laws of motion. According to the second law '*change in motion is proportional to the motive force impressed*', thus 'If any force generates a motion, a double force will generate double the motion.'[12] Hume's initial definitions of 'ideas', 'beliefs' and 'impressions' in terms of the respective amounts of 'force' or 'vivacity' that they possess, seems designed to enable him to apply the Newtonian model to the mental universe. And indeed we are told that 'If I diminish the vivacity of the first conception, I diminish that of the related ideas' (*T*, p. 386), and 'The vivacity of the idea is always proportionable to the degrees of the impulse or tendency to the transition' (*T*, p. 130). And in matters of feeling too, where a passion 'has a double task to perform, it must be endow'd with double force and energy' (*T*, p. 291).

According to Newton's third law '*an equal reaction*' must be assumed for every observed action: where X attracts Y and dominates, Y is also attracting X. The stronger force will prevail; but this does not mean that there is not also a weaker force exerting pressure. Equilibrium is not a state where no forces are exerted, but one where 'being equally attracted' by opposing forces, bodies 'will sustain each other's pressure, and rest at last in an equilibrium'.[13] Similarly, for Hume, 'To every probability there is an opposite possibility' (*T*, p. 136). Belief is a 'compounded effect' that results from balancing the force of the probability against its opposite possibility: 'their influence becomes mutually destructive, and the mind is determin'd to the superior only with that force, which remains after subtracting the inferior' (*T*, pp. 137, 138). Since belief is proportional to force, the analogue for this third law is of crucial importance in balancing one idea against another and forming 'a kind of system' which 'we are pleas'd to call a *reality*' (*T*, p. 108).

The third law also plays an important role in Hume's account of the passions and of morality. Passions are classed as 'impressions of reflexion' and impressions are seen as possessing more force than ideas. Hume then builds Newtonian conceptions of opposition and equilibrium into his account of the passions: 'Nothing can oppose or retard the impulse of passion, but a contrary impulse' (*T*, p. 415), and

> To excite any passion, and at the same time raise an equal share of its antagonist, is immediately to undo what was done, and must leave the mind at last perfectly calm and indifferent. (*T*, p. 278)

If the contrary impulse must be of equivalent force to attain equilibrium, then the checks that morality provides to the passions must stem from moral impressions, not moral ideas. Hume's thesis that 'Reason is, and ought only to be the slave of the passions' is consistent with his Newtonian system, despite Kemp Smith's claims that it must be traced back to a purportedly anti-Newtonian Hutchesonian influence.[14]

For Newton bodies proceed passively along the line of least resistance; for Hume minds proceed passively along the easiest path. Indeed the terms 'easy', 'facility', 'naturally' echo through the *Treatise*. Association provides us with the 'natural' relation amongst ideas, on which all other relation is founded (*T*, pp. 13 ff.), and

> The very nature and essence of relation is to connect our ideas with each other, and upon the appearance of one, to facilitate the transition to its correlative. The passage betwixt related ideas is, therefore, so smooth and easy, that it produces little alteration on the mind, and seems like the continuation of the same action. (*T*, p. 204)

'Easy transition' is also elsewhere described as 'the effect, or rather essence of relation' (*T*, p. 220).

Since Hume teaches that belief is a matter of response to,

and balancing of, the associative forces or natural relations, it is hardly surprising that 'ease' determines belief for Hume, as well as relation itself. Furthermore, since what we call 'reality' is constructed out of our beliefs, Hume's ' "principle"' of natural order' is not, as Stuart Brown suggests in his lecture, the *logical* 'principle of parsimony', but rather its *psychological* equivalent – 'the principle of ease'.[15] Man believes not that which is most correct, nor even that which is most simple, but rather that which is easiest – and it is thus the latter that determines reality. Hume is not being inconsistent when he criticises 'that love of *simplicity* which has been the source of much false reasoning' in natural philosophy. (*ENQS*, p. 298) Neither is Hume being inconsistent when he develops a discriminatory scepticism alongside his radical scepticism, and distinguishes between the 'wise' and the 'vulgar' man. (*T*, p. 150.)[16] The wise man is no more determined by correctness than the foolish man; but he is more far-sighted than the foolish man and can better calculate when the acceptance of the *prima facie* easier hypothesis will, in the end, introduce inconsistency into the system and unease into the mind. The wise man is more successful in building a coherent system of reality on the 'principle of ease'.

Hume allows that a number of factors affect the 'ease' with which an idea enters the mind and the consequent belief: including, the *force* of the original impression, the *type* of associative forces at work, the *number* of associative forces tending towards the same end, the *quantity* of each individual force, and the strength of the forces acting in *opposition* to the dominant force. I will here be concerned, however, only with the factor that might be termed the resistance of the medium in which the forces act.

In his pseudo-scientific language Hume claims that,

> the conviction, which arises from a subtile reasoning, diminishes in proportion to the efforts, which the imagination makes to enter into the reasoning, and to conceive it in all its parts. Belief, being a lively conception, can never be

entire, where it is not founded on something natural and easy. (*T*, p. 186)

Where 'The labour of the thought disturbs the regular progress of the sentiments . . . The idea strikes not on us with such vivacity', and consequently cannot produce belief (*T*, p. 153). But for Hume there are whole areas of inquiry where 'The attention is on the stretch: The posture of the mind is uneasy', and where, 'the spirits being diverted from their natural course', ideas have insufficient vigour to sustain belief (*T*, p. 185). In such areas percepts lose vigour by encountering the resistance of the imagination in a not dissimilar way to the loss of momentum of bodies passing through a resistant medium. Inertia, or the maintaining of momentum, is for Hume (as it is for Newton) only the ideal of a non-resistant medium. Metaphysics is given as an example of an area of great imaginative resistance:

> The same argument, which wou'd have been esteem'd convincing in a reasoning concerning history or politics, has little or no influence in these abstruser subjects, even tho' it be perfectly comprehended; and that because there is requir'd a study and an effort of thought, in order to its being comprehended: And this effort of thought disturbs the operation of our sentiments, on which the belief depends. (*T*, p. 185)

It would seem to be a Newtonian current of nature that rescues Hume from the '*Slough of Dispond*'. In his sceptical inquiries Hume has ventured into topics of metaphysics that provide great imaginative resistance; the associative trains of ideas are slowed down and lose force with the consequent prevention of conviction. We do not have to step outside Hume's Newtonian framework to understand Hume's 'naturalistic' solution to his sceptical doubts: the 'easy' paths of the imagination, analogues for the paths of least resistance followed by bodies in Newton's science, can adequately account for Hume's appeal to mental indolence for his cure. Neither, however, need we step outside the Newtonian framework to understand the sources of Hume's scepticism. According to Hume the balancing of one force against another produces belief, and by balancing one belief against another we construct a system which we call reality. This constructed reality is not, however, necessarily an accurate reflection of the external world: it mirrors our mental indolence and tendency to believe that which it is easiest to believe, rather than any objectively existing fact. Once mental indolence becomes Hume's analogue for the 'force of inactivity' of bodies, there is no wonder that Hume lapses into the slough when contemplating the nature and limits of the human mind.

There is one aspect of Hume's Newtonian path into despond that remains puzzling, however, even after the analogue for the Newtonian notions of 'inertia' and 'least resistance' has been detected. If the mind for Hume always follows the easiest path, how could it ever be led into metaphysics – an area of great imaginative resistance and where the spirits are 'diverted from their natural course'? To understand this we need to understand the role that 'ease' and its converse 'unease' play in Hume's account of the passions.

We have already seen that there are analogues for Newton's second and third laws of motion in Hume's account of the passions, and (despite Hume's celebrated contrast between the 'active' passions and the 'inert' reason (T, pp. 457, 458)), Hume does not believe that the passions are any less subject to the law of inertia than the imagination. Hume's passions are 'active' in the sense that they are the direct causes of actions; they are not self-caused or spontaneous, but are moved only when some other force impinges. This other force is another impression – generally an 'impression of sensation' which has itself been forced into being and proceeded 'from the constitution of the body, from the animal spirits, or from the application of objects to the external organs' (T, p. 275).

Hume claims that it is the pleasurable or painful sensations that arise from the perception of good and evil that causally determine passion (*T*, p. 438). But 'unease' seems to be a synonym for 'pain' in Hume's usage. Thus, as well as being 'founded on pain and pleasure', passions are often described as 'being always agreeable or uneasy', with 'uneasiness' frequently used as an antithesis to 'pleasure' (*T*, pp. 438, 439, 297, 298, for example). Hume claims that it is probable that 'uneasiness' is the 'very nature and essence' of vice, and thus transmutes questions concerning the 'pain' distinguishing the vicious act to questions concerning 'uneasiness' (*T*, pp. 296, 475). We learn that 'every thing, which gives uneasiness in human actions, upon the general survey, is call'd Vice' (*T*, p. 499). Passion is not simply determined by the principle of pleasure and pain, but also by the equivalent principle of satisfaction and unease.

In Book I of the *Treatise* 'easy' is used as a synonym for 'without difficulty', 'naturally', 'with facility'. Man's passions are guided by the imagination to a great extent, and we therefore find the same cluster of terms in Book II of the *Treatise*. To this extent the message of the two Books is identical: 'ease' is the essence of relation, and man's mind follows the 'easiest' path. But where the passions are not guided by the imagination, they are guided not by the principle of 'ease', but by a principle of 'unease'; and 'unease' is not a synonym for 'difficulty', but for 'pain'. The paths of the imagination and passions diverge; for each there is an analogue for Newton's 'force of inactivity' and path of least resistance, but the analogues reveal an inner dynamism of the mind. Whilst obeying the principle that the mind always follows the easiest path, the mind is pulled in two directions at once – along the least difficult and least painful paths. It is this inner dynamism which explains Hume's excursus into the 'dreary solitudes, and rough passages' of metaphysics (*T*, p. 270).

The paths of the passions and the imagination do not simply fork; they can lead in precisely contrary directions. This can be seen most easily in Hume's analyses of the passions for truth and for novelty. The imagination prefers that which is familiar: the broad paths of 'natural' relations established by constantly repeated experience. At first sight, it would seem that the passions have the same preference:

> 'Tis a quality of human nature . . . common both to the mind and body, that too sudden and violent a change is unpleasant to us, and that however any objects may in themselves be indifferent, yet their alteration gives uneasiness. (*T*, p. 453)

Custom is said to produce 'facility' – 'an infallible source of pleasure, where the facility goes not beyond a certain degree' (*T*, p. 423). Hume's principle of inactivity seems to have been transposed into a principle of conservatism.

As this last quotation indicates, however, there are limits to the pleasure derived from facility: 'as facility converts pain into pleasure, so it often converts pleasure into pain' (*T*, p. 423). Familiarity can pall, and novelty can give pleasure. This palling occurs because although new actions or conceptions are still seen to encounter 'a certain unpliableness in the faculties, and a difficulty of the spirit's moving in their new direction', we are now told that a moderate degree of opposition 'inlivens the mind', and 'is in itself very agreeable' (*T*, pp. 422–3).

> Whatever supports and fills the passions is agreeable . . ., what weakens and infeebles them is uneasy. As opposition has the first effect, and facility the second, no wonder the mind, in certain dispositions, desires the former, and is averse to the latter. (*T*, p. 434)

The passions lead us to seek out an opposition of forces; the imagination to avoid opposition. Imagination leads us down the easy and obvious paths; but for the passions, when not modified by the imagination, 'What is easy and obvious is never valu'd' and that which is 'without any stretch of thought or judgment, is but little regarded' (*T*, p. 449). It is passion, and in particular the passion that Hume calls 'love of truth', that leads away from the broad and familiar paths of common sense into the 'rough passages' of metaphysics and religion.

It is ironic to note that whereas it is Book II of the *Treatise* that has generally been regarded as Hume's most Newtonian work, it is here that Hume's analogue is stretched almost to breaking point.[17] In Newton's system where one force is opposed by another, the stronger force dominates but is slowed by the pull of the opposing weaker force. In Hume's system the same proportionality applies for ideas or for passions determined by the imagination. But for unmodified passions, opposition does not decrease but augments 'the predominant passion, and encreases its violence, beyond the pitch it wou'd have arriv'd at had it met with no opposition' (*T*, p. 421). It does this because of a generally unremarked difference between passions and ideas in Hume's system. Hume compares *ideas* to 'the extension and solidity of matter'; *impressions* to colours which 'may be blended so perfectly together, that each of them may lose itself, and contribute only to vary that uniform impression, which arises from the whole.' As such they are completely different in nature from ideas which 'never admit of a total union, but are endow'd with a kind of impenetrability, by which they exclude each other, and are capable of forming a compound by their conjunction, not by their mixture' (*T*, p. 366). Hume has not abandoned the analogues for Newton's three laws of motion; but the application of these laws has become infinitely more complex with the admission that one object may absorb another into itself. The laws of motion merely provide the skeleton structure for the laws of emotion, as they do for Newton's account of colour in his *Opticks*. Book II of the *Treatise* seems more intrusively Newtonian only in as far as Hume has to strain his Newtonian paradigm in order to encompass the inner dynamism of the mind.

Kemp Smith has suggested that the inner dynamism of Hume's man is a tension between Hutchesonian instinct and Newtonian forces of attraction, and the blending of the passions is picked out as one of a number of 'survivals from a time when Hume still held strictly to Hutcheson's teaching'.[18] What I am suggesting is that Hume never steps outside his

Newtonian model: the tension is simply between the effect of forces on penetrable and impenetrable objects. In emphasizing the extent and completeness of Hume's Newtonian metaphor I do not intend to suggest, however, that Hutcheson had no influence on Hume, nor that Hume's only inspiration to write the *Treatise* was his reading of Newton. Hume's attractive forces are supposed to be no more ultimate as causes of motion than Newton's forces of gravity and inertia.[19] Both authors are providing merely phenomenological descriptions of motion; but whereas the justification for Newton's principles lies in his mathematical results and method, Hume's principles allow of no such justification. Hume is working from a basic Newtonian metaphor, rather than from a deep comprehension or extensive knowledge of Newton's system. It seems likely that Hume, having grasped the basic outline of Newtonian science, received the actual impetus to write the *Treatise* from moral rather than from natural philosophy.

Hutcheson had, no doubt, his own special role in inspiring Hume to write the *Treatise*. In his *Abstract* Hume suggests that it is because he makes the association of ideas the 'cement' of the mental universe that he is entitled 'to so glorious a name as that of "inventor" ' (*I*, p. 198). Similar claims about the centrality of association are made in the *Treatise*: it binds together words, imaginings, passions and thoughts and provides the foundation of language. (Compare *I*, p. 198 with *T*, pp. 10–13.) But Hutcheson had, in his unsystematic way, also expressed this insight:

> 'all our *Language* and much of our *Memory* depends upon it:' So that were there no such *Associations* made, we must lose the use of *Words*, and a great part of our Power of *recollecting past Events*; beside many other valuable *Powers* and *Arts* which depend upon them.

Hutcheson does not develop this notion; but places it in an essay which is prefaced by the hope that,

> some Person of greater Abilities and Leisure apply himself

to a more strict Philosophical Inquiry into the various *natural Principles* or *natural Dispositions* of Mankind.[20]

The immodest tone of Hume's Introduction to the *Treatise* and his youthful letters to Hutcheson suggest that Hume may have seen himself as this 'Person of great Abilities'. Hutcheson may well have influenced Hume; but there is no need to suppose that this influence was *in conflict* with Hume's Newtonian associationism. This observation is reinforced by the fact that Hutcheson's colleague, William Leechman, characterizes Hutcheson's enterprise as an attempt to apply the new methods of natural science to the discovery of 'a true scheme of morals'.[21] Hutcheson himself had Newtonian pretensions.

Hutcheson is an important influence on Hume; but he is not the only influence. The thesis that 'Reason is, and ought only to be the slave of the passions' that Kemp Smith traces to Hutcheson's influence, could equally well have been inspired by Mandeville's comment that even when following reason all human creatures are 'Slaves to their Passions'.[22] Hume's doctrine of the supremacy of passion is not original; what is new is his synthesis of scattered insights into a systematic account of the origin of emotion to explain the supremacy of passion. Indeed, the five moral philosophers listed by Hume as precursors in the Introduction to the *Treatise*, all offer an account of human motivation, and all make some use of the pair of concepts 'ease' and 'unease' – what is new in Hume's treatment is not the subject-matter, but the tying of the central concepts to a Newtonian framework.

The five precursors listed are Locke, Shaftesbury, Mandeville, Hutcheson and Butler (*T*, p. xxi n.). Of these five, Locke makes the most use of the notion of unease, claiming 'the chief if not only spur to humane Industry and Action is uneasiness' and ' 'tis *uneasiness* alone determines the will'. Like Hume, Locke treats 'Delight and Uneasiness' as synonyms for '*Pleasure* and *Pain*', and asserts 'Things then are Good or Evil, only in reference to Pleasure or Pain.'[23] Shaftesbury, Hume's second author, opposes Locke and dissociates himself from 'the

C

easy philosophy of taking that for good which pleases me';
but he does not thereby abandon the notion of ease altogether.
His main complaint against 'the easy philosophy' is that it is
short-sighted: 'The tutorage of fancy and pleasure . . . will in
time give me uneasiness sufficient.' Goodness is still seen as
'natural', although now it is connected not directly with
pleasure but with the notions of balance, equilibrium, harmony
and proportion.[24] An excess of passion is indicative of a loss
of equilibrium; Shaftesbury's continued concern with ease can
be seen from Hume's approving quote of the lesson that
Shaftesbury claimed: 'Nature herself . . . dictated to the clown,
that he who had the better of the argument would be easy,
and well-humoured' (*GG*, iii, p. 117 n.).

Mandeville claims that 'two Systems cannot be more
opposite' than Shaftesbury's and his own, and opposes his
predecessor's view that man can 'govern himself by his Reason
with as much Ease and Readiness as a good Rider manages
a well-taught Horse by the Bridle.' On the contrary, says
Mandeville,

> Man's natural Love of Ease and Idleness, and Proneness
> to indulge his sensual Pleasures, are not to be cured by
> Precept: His strong Habits and Inclinations can only be
> subdued by Passions of greater Violence.

As this last quotation indicates, the notion of ease is of the
greatest importance in Mandeville's own account of motivation:
all creatures – even 'the most savage and most industrious' –
are said to be 'furnish'd, more or less, with a Love of Ease';
and man's love 'for his Ease and Security, and his perpetual
Desire of meliorating his Condition' are made the sufficient
causes of his apparent benevolence towards other men.[25]

Hutcheson's influence on Hume has already been established.
Here it is only necessary to mention that he directs several of
his writings against Mandeville, and develops the distinction
between passions and affections to counter Locke's account of
motivation. This distinction is dropped by Hume, indicating
a distancing from Hutcheson's claim,

'THAT no Desire of any Event is excited by any view of removing the *uneasy Sensation attending this Desire itself*.'[26]

Hume and Hutcheson share the vocabulary of 'ease' and 'unease', however, as does the final author on Hume's list – Joseph Butler.

Butler asserts that man does not 'desire things, and be uneasy in the want of them, in proportion to their known value'. He allows that to 'keep free from uneasiness' should be one of man's aims in his 'passage through this world', and that, in general, 'less uneasiness, and more satisfaction' will flow from following a virtuous life. Butler insists, however, that the elimination of unease cannot be the final explanation of every action or every good: there is 'such (a) thing as delight in the company of one person, rather than another', and this is seen to conflict with the thesis that 'what is called affection, love, desire, hope in human nature, is only an uneasiness in being at rest'.[27] Butler, like Hutcheson, opposes Mandeville's reduction of benevolence to a principle of ease.

In using the terms 'ease' and 'unease' Hume is joining a philosophical tradition and ongoing debate. From each of these authors he takes something that is synthesized into his pseudo-Newtonian system of mental motion. From Mandeville and Locke comes the insistence on the appropriateness of 'ease' and 'unease' to encompass human motivation. From Shaftesbury comes the concern with balance and maintaining an 'easy' disposition – although for Hume the balance is no longer a function of rationality, but of the opposing of one force of passion or belief against another in accordance with Newtonian laws of motion. From Hutcheson and Butler comes the belief that 'ease' and 'unease' cannot provide the final causes of human behaviour. Like Newton, Hume is only giving a phenomenological description of motion. However appropriate the categories of 'ease' and 'unease', and however much they might be ultimates in our phenomenological descriptions of the universe, they are not thereby rendered final causes. Thus although hatred of pain (unease) is described as 'an ultimate end, and is never referred to any other object' (*ENQS*, p. 293), it is only an ultimate in explanation, not an ultimate cause:

> . . . the utmost effort of human reason is to reduce the principles, productive of natural phenomena, to a greater simplicity, and to resolve the many particular effects into a few general causes, by means of reasoning from analogy, experience and observation. But as to the causes of these general causes, we should in vain attempt their discovery . . . These ultimate springs and principles are totally shut up from human curiosity. (*ENQS*, p. 30)

In recent years there has been much debate as to whether or not Hume was really a sceptic or a naturalist. By abandoning our still current category of the 'natural', and concentrating instead on the eighteenth-century category of the 'easy', we can synthesise Hume's so-called 'naturalism' and his so-called 'scepticism' into one consistently Newtonian system. Some previous commentators have, of course, noticed that ease and inertia play an important role in Hume's philosophy, without recognizing their important synthesizing role for Hume's Newtonian analogue. Thus, Passmore, for example, has complained that 'associationism comes to be a special example, only, of a much more general principle, the principle that the mind moves in whatever direction will bring it most ease'; but he uses this observation only to show that Hume was not a consistent associationist. He does not notice that he might have proved Hume a consistent Newtonian instead. More recently, Duncan Forbes has noted the centrality of inertia in Hume's system, commenting 'which makes a rigidly mechanistic interpretation of the principle of association inadequate'. Again there is no recognition that Hume may have been aiming to be a consistent Newtonian, rather than a consistent associationist.[28]

Concentration on the category of 'ease' shows up the failings of some of Hume's eighteenth-century commentators, as well as his twentieth-century critics. These shortcomings are amusingly illustrated by James Beattie's use of the John Bunyan metaphor to indicate Hume's penchant for the difficult and the abstruse:

> Now I saw in my dream, as John Bunyan says, and behold, as we advanced, the road grew gradually more intricate and laborious; precipices appeared on either hand; and we were much annoyed by the stones, brambles, and underwood that beset our way. The sky grew misty, and the sun of the colour of blood; screams were heard at a distance . . . Yet many of my fellow-travellers still went on . . . Certain grave persons among us remarked, that this twilight or rather darkness was much better for the eyes than broad day-light, that the continual screams tended to produce firmness of mind in the hearers; that the bad smell and rough road were the occasion of much wholesome exercise both to the mind and body . . .; in a word, it was generally allowed, that this region, which they named *The Paradise of Perplexity*, was infinitely more delightful, and a much better school of discipline, than the azure skies, fresh gales, and sunny places we had left behind.[29]

Hume's *'Castle of Scepticism'* is seen to be located in the midst of this *'Paradise'*, and Beattie supposes that Hume delighted in obscurity, perplexity and rejecting common sense – to enter Hume's castle it is said to be necessary to make an offering of 'a very small parcel neatly wrapt up, and inscribed *Common Sense*'[30]. Beattie does not recognize that far from venturing willingly into the 'dreary solitudes, and rough passages' of metaphysics, Hume does so reluctantly and only when compelled by passion. Hume does not defend or recommend the path that leads up 'the Hill called *Difficulty*', as does John Bunyan. Rather, he resolves he 'will no more be led a wandering into such dreary solitudes' (*T*, p. 270). Straying from the broad path of common sense is not considered a virtue by Hume, as it is by Bunyan: Hume says it is 'from my very weakness I must be led into such enquiries' (*T*, p. 271). Whereas Bunyan exhorts others to follow him along his difficult

way, and to deny common sense and see the world as a huge
'*Vanity-Fair*', Hume has only admiration for the 'honest
gentlemen' of England who are not impelled by passion to
carry their thoughts 'beyond those objects, which are everyday
expos'd to their senses.'[31] 'They do well to keep themselves in
their present situation'; Hume wishes not that the honest
gentlemen should be changed by the model of philosophy,
but that they could communicate to philosophers 'a share of
this gross earthy mixture' (*T*, p. 272).

Bunyan's pilgrim strides eagerly through the difficult and
dangerous, and claims his path to be virtuous. Hume, on the
contrary, is dragged reluctantly into the dreary solitudes by
his passions which make him despise the familiar; his path is
one of weakness. Once away from the broad and easy paths
of common sense, we ought, says Hume,

> to deliberate concerning the choice of our guide, and
> ought to prefer that which is safest and most agreeable.
> And in this respect I make bold to recommend philosophy,
> and shall not scruple to give it the preference to super-
> stition of every kind or denomination. (*T*, p. 271)

Not only does Hume differ from Bunyan in his unwillingness
to recommend the dreary solitudes, he also differs from him
in the choice of a guide through the solitudes. The religious
path is seen to arise more 'naturally and easily from the
popular opinions of mankind' with a consequent ability 'to
disturb us in the conduct of our lives and actions' that philosophy does not possess (*T*, pp. 271–2).

To understand Hume's objection to religion we have to
bear in mind the double sense of Hume's principle of ease.
The world that we construct and call reality is a product of
the imagination receiving data from the senses which, through
constant repetition, gradually form the 'natural' paths of
association which determine belief. In the case of God we have
no data to synthesize; here the 'natural' paths of the mind
will be established not by experience and imagination, but
by the passions. Metaphysics is in the same predicament as

religion; but its conclusions do not have the same inherent appeal to the passions as those of religion. Religion panders to the weakness of man's passions – a story that Hume will tell again elsewhere, most notably in *The Natural History of Religion*. The path of philosophy is preferable because it allows a way back to the broad and easy path of common sense, the ideal path pursued by the honest gentlemen of England.

Hume and Bunyan are both writing for the reader who has started to question everyday notions; but Bunyan hopes to turn his reader into a puritan, and lead him away from human society, Hume hopes to change his reader into a sceptic and lead him back to human society via the paradoxes of scepticism. Hume's hope is that he will be followed in his 'future speculations' by readers in 'the same easy disposition' as himself – where the passions that draw man into metaphysics are balanced by a concern with ease (*T*, p. 273). Despite the desire for an 'easy disposition' or a 'serious good-humour'd disposition', however, and the conviction that the sceptical problems will all disappear with its arrival, it is clear that much of the final chapter of Book I of *A Treatise* reflects a time in Hume's life when such a disposition eluded him (*T*, pp. 270, 273). The chapter resonates with terms like 'spleen', 'melancholy', 'disease', 'delirium', 'cloud', 'splenetic humour' and 'despair', and takes the mind back to a letter that Hume drafted to a doctor five years prior to the publication of the *Treatise*.

In this letter Hume writes about a disease that keeps recurring and that has been brought on by his philosophic labours. He compares his 'Coldness & Desertion of the Spirit' to that of certain of 'the French Mysticks' and some of 'our Fanatics here', commenting

> I have often thought that their Case & mine were pretty parralel, & that their rapturous Admirations might discompose the Fabric of the Nerves & Brain, as much as profound Reflections, & that warmth or Enthusiasm which is inseperable from them. (*L*, i, p. 17)

In his despair at his condition Hume, like the religious fanatics, indulges

> in peevish Reflections on the Vanity of the World & of all humane Glory: which, however just Sentiments they may be esteem'd, I have found can never be sincere, except in those who are possest of them. (*loc. cit.*)

Instead of resting in this state of despair, Hume's letter shows him to be working towards a cure for his disease that parallels the cure in the *Treatise* – by abandoning philosophy and study for 'a more active life' with 'Business & Diversion' as the medicine.

According to Hume's 'epistemology of ease', both he and the fanatic Bunyan have been led into despair by passion or 'warmth'. The cases are indeed parallel; but even in this early letter a Bunyan-type solution is dismissed. Seeing the world as a large '*Vanity-Fair*' is 'peevish' and involves an element of insincerity – an insight developed most fully many years later in *The Natural History of Religion*, where Hume claims that in 'the obscure, glimmering light afforded in those shadowy regions' of religion, there is nothing 'to equal the strong impressions, made by common sense and experience.' Men cannot believe in God, although the strong passions of fear and hope that guide men in these shadowy regions lead men to 'disguise to themselves their real infidelity' (*NHR*, p. 74). Without belief, Hume has no good reason to lurk in these 'shadowy regions', and neither, he claims, has any other man.

Hume's path, though parallel to Bunyan's in that he has deserted the realms of common sense, leads in a contrary direction to that of Bunyan. It is hardly surprising that Hume should make such a scathing judgment on Bunyan in 'Of the Standard of Taste'. As for Beattie's supposition that Hume was recommending that man should follow him into 'the obscure, glimmering light', this can be seen to be absurd. Although Hume differed radically from the common sense school of philosophers in placing religion beyond the jurisdiction of common sense, his Newtonian system leads him to value common sense more than his contemporary critics supposed. Hume ventures into the 'dreary solitudes', but he does not remain there long. Like 'Master *Worldly-Wiseman*' Hume asks '*why wilt thou seek for ease*' by following the directions of the '*Evangelist*' and by '*meddling with things too high*' for man.³² Hume does not set up home in the '*Castle of Scepticism*' in '*The Paradise of Perplexity*', but hastens back along the 'natural paths' of association to found his 'Village of Morality' far away from the 'shadowy regions' of religion.

NOTES

¹ In-text references to Hume's writings have been provided using the following abbreviations: *ENQS – Enquiries concerning Human Understanding and concerning the Principles of Morals*, ed. L. A. Selby-Bigge, rev. P. H. Nidditch (Oxford, Clarendon Press, 3rd edition, 1975); *GG – The Philosophical Works of David Hume*, eds. T. H. Green and T. H. Grose (London, Longmans, Green & Co., 1874–5); *I – An Inquiry concerning Human Understanding, with a supplement, 'An Abstract of A Treatise of Human Nature'*, ed. Charles W. Hendel (New York, Liberal Arts Press, 1955); *L – The Letters of David Hume*, ed. J. Y. T. Greig (Oxford, Clarendon Press, 1932); *NHR – 'The Natural History of Religion' and 'Dialogues concerning Natural Religion'*, eds. A. Wayne Colver and John Valdimir Price (Oxford, Clarendon Press, 1976); *T – A Treatise of Human Nature*, ed. L. A. Selby-Bigge (Oxford, Clarendon Press, 1888).
² James Boswell, *Boswell's Life of Johnson*, ed. G. Birkbeck Hill (Oxford, Clarendon Press, 1887), ii, p. 238. Johnson also comments, 'Few books, I believe, have had a more extensive sale' – a sale evidenced by the fact that in 1799 A. Millar was publishing what purported to be 'The hundred and twenty first edition' of the two volumes, and Millar's count was by no means all inclusive.
³ John Bunyan, *The Pilgrim's Progress from this World to That Which is to Come*, ed. James Blanton Wharey (Oxford, Clarendon Press, 2nd edition, rev. Roger Sharrock, 1960), pp. 27–8, 41, 69, 100, 17–22.
⁴ *Ibid.* p. 15.
⁵ Thus, for example, James Noxon argues that the analogue is incongruous in *Hume's Philosophical Development: A Study of his*

Methods (Oxford, Clarendon Press, corrected edition 1975); John Passmore that it is also incomplete in *Hume's Intentions* (London, Duckworth, rev. edition 1968); Norman Kemp Smith that it is also inconsistent with Hume's 'naturalism' in *The Philosophy of David Hume* (London, Macmillan, 1941). These judgements have begun to be undermined by the work of Nicholas Capaldi in *David Hume: The Newtonian Philosopher* (Boston, Twayne, 1975), and Nelly Demé, 'La Méthode Newtonienne et les Lois Empirique de l'Anthropologie dans *Traité II*', *David Hume: Bicentenary Papers*, ed. G. P. Morice (Edinburgh University Press, 1977). However, neither of these authors discuss the central role played by 'ease' and 'unease' – the topic of this paper.

⁶ Passmore, p. 108.

⁷ Isaac Newton, *Opticks: Or a Treatise of the Reflections, Refractions, Inflections & Colours of Light* (New York, Dover, 1952; based on the 4th London edition of 1730), p. 376: Query 31.

⁸ D. D. Raphael, 'Adam Smith: Philosophy, Science, and Social Science', *below* pp. 87 f.

⁹ Passmore, p. 108.

¹⁰ Isaac Newton, *Principia: Sir Isaac Newton's Mathematical Principles of Natural Philosophy and his System of the World*, trans. Andrew Motte (1729), rev. Florian Cajori (1934), (University of California, 1966) i, pp. 2 (Definition III), 13 (Law I); ii, p. 400 (Rule III).

¹¹ G. A. J. Rogers, 'The Empiricism of Locke and Newton', *above* pp. 5, 15, 19–20. Rogers quotes Newton: University Library, Cambridge, Add. MS. 3970.9, f. 619.

¹² *Principia*, i, p. 13.

¹³ *Principia*, i, pp. 13–14 (Law III), 25–6 (Scholium).

¹⁴ Kemp Smith, pp. 45, 550, for example, and see *T*, p. 415.

¹⁵ Stuart Brown, 'The "Principle" of Natural Order: *Or* What the Enlightened Sceptics did not Doubt', *below* pp. 70 ff.

¹⁶ The consistency of the two scepticisms justifies my treatment of the two *Enquiries* as mere extensions of the argument in the *Treatise*, and my concentration on the eventually repudiated youthful work. If time permitted I would explain here how Hume's own philosophical development could be traced to his attempt to render his own writings consistent with his 'principle of ease', where 'ease' does not only affect style but also subject-matter.

¹⁷ Kemp Smith, p. 72; Richard Kuhns, 'Hume's Republic and the Universe of Newton', *Eighteenth-Century Studies Presented to Arthur M. Wilson*, ed. Peter Gay (University of New England, 1972), pp. 86, 88, for example.

¹⁸ Kemp Smith, p. 49 n.

[19] Compare Newton *Opticks*, pp. 401–2 with *ENQS*, pp. 30–31, and see p. 73 n., and *T*, p. 224.

[20] Francis Hutcheson, *An Essay on the Nature and Conduct of the Passions and Affections* (London, 3rd edition (1742)), pp. 11, xi–xii.

[21] William Leechman, 'Life of Hutcheson', prefixed to Francis Hutcheson, *A System of Moral Philosophy in Three Books: published by his son Francis Hutcheson* (Millar, 1755), p. xiv, and see pp. xiii–xv, xxi.

[22] Bernard Mandeville, *An Enquiry into the Origin of Honour and The Usefulness of Christianity in War* (London, Frank Cass, 1971; based on 1732 edition), p. 31.

[23] John Locke, *An Essay concerning Human Understanding*, ed. Peter H. Nidditch (Oxford, Clarendon Press, 1975), pp. 230: II, XX, 6; 254: II, XXI, 37; 229: II, XX, 2; and for the synonymity see, for example, 232: II, XX, 15.

[24] Anthony, Earl of Shaftesbury, *Characteristics of Men, Manners, Opinions, Times*, ed. John M. Robertson (Indianapolis, Bobbs-Merrill, 1964), ii, p. 280: 'Miscellaneous Reflections', IV, I; on goodness see, for example, i, pp. 237 ff.: 'An Inquiry concerning Virtue or Merit'.

[25] Bernard Mandeville, *The Fable of the Bees: Or, Private Vices, Publick Benefits*, ed. F. B. Kaye (Oxford, Clarendon, 1924), i, p. 324; i, p. 333; ii, p. 176; ii, p. 180.

[26] Hutcheson, *Essay*, p. 16; and see Henning Jensen, *Motivation and the Moral Sense in Francis Hutcheson's Ethical Theory* (The Hague, Nijhoff, 1971), pp. 10–25.

[27] *The Whole Works of Joseph Butler* (London, 1843), ii, p. 157: 'Sermon XIV'; ii, p. 63: 'Sermon VI'; i, p. 33: 'The Analogy of Religion', I, III; ii, p. 148: 'Sermon XIII'.

[28] Passmore, p. 122. Duncan Forbes, *Hume's Philosophical Politics* (Cambridge University Press, 1975), p. 10. In a footnote Forbes connects 'inertia' with Malebranche's influence on Hume. He is certainly right to make this connection – one that cannot be explored in the confines of this lecture. It is not only the scattered insights of British philosophers that Hume synthesizes into a comprehensively Newtonian science of man.

[29] 'Beattie's "The Castle of Scepticism": An Unpublished Allegory against Hume, Voltaire and Hobbes', ed. E. C. Mossner, *University of Texas Studies in English*, xxvii (1948), pp. 121–2.

[30] *Ibid.* p. 123, and see pp. 124, 127, 133.

[31] For the *Vanity-Fair* metaphor see Bunyan, pp. 88 ff.

[32] Bunyan, pp. 19, 18.

3

THE 'PRINCIPLE' OF NATURAL ORDER: OR WHAT THE ENLIGHTENED SCEPTICS DID NOT DOUBT

Stuart Brown

My title advertizes a paradox. The characteristic complaint of the sceptic is that others make assumptions they are not entitled to make. A philosophical sceptic is committed to a systematic refusal to accept such assumptions in the absence of the kind of justification they think is required. A sceptic who, none the less, helps himself to such an assumption, seems to be caught in a paradoxical position. This is the kind of situation in which, it seems, certain eighteenth-century sceptical philosophers were placed in relation to the 'principle' of natural order. They did not doubt that there *is* such a principle, that there *is* a source or ultimate cause of the order to be found in the universe. And yet, on their own terms, is not the existence of such a principle something we should expect them to have doubted? What I shall try to do in this lecture is to bring out why they did not doubt the existence of such a principle and how serious their failure to do so is for their sceptical position.

I

Firstly, it is incumbent upon me to explain what I mean by

the phrase 'enlightened sceptic' and to what purpose I have adopted it. My reason for adopting this phrase is that it seems to me that there is a quite distinct form of scepticism which characterizes certain philosophers of the Enlightenment period. I do not, of course, wish to imply that all the sceptical philosophers of this period are, in my sense, enlightened sceptics, still less do I want to insist that only those philosophers of the period who were sceptics of some sort should be accounted 'enlightened'. I shall not indeed attempt to assess how extensive a phenomenon enlightened scepticism was. But I shall claim that some philosophers, including Condillac, d'Alembert and Hume, were definitely enlightened sceptics in my sense. If others, such as Voltaire, were also enlightened sceptics so much the better.

I shall begin, then, with a short profile of enlightened scepticism. It is a moderate form of scepticism which is not concerned to deny that men can have real knowledge of the natural world. The enlightened sceptics were what is sometimes called 'scientific realists'. They believed, that is to say, that true scientific laws and principles correspond to laws and principles which operate in the physical world. They believed, moreover, that progress in the sciences was not merely possible but had actually taken place and that this progress involved an increased correspondence between what was put forward in scientific theories and what actually happened in the world. Their confidence in such progress reflected not simply their acceptance of the achievements of figures such as Copernicus and Newton but also their belief in a method. It is partly because of their confidence in the availability of a method for advancing enquiry that they dismissed, as rash and pretentious, the claims of metaphysician and mere sceptic alike.

If this confidence in the methodical advancement of human knowledge is what makes such a sceptic 'enlightened', what makes him a 'sceptic' at all? An enlightened sceptic is, as I intend the phrase, someone who believes that there are necessary limits to the advancement of human knowledge. He is someone who thinks it is not possible to know the ultimate causes or principles which govern the operations of nature. He is therefore opposed to attempts at producing systems of the world, after the manner of Descartes or Leibniz, in which certain fundamental principles are established *a priori* and deductions about the nature of the world made from them. He does not accept that reason can tell us anything about the world without the aid of experience. Broadly, then, he is an empiricist, an admirer of Newton and perhaps a follower of Locke. He looks for accounts which conform to experience and are not merely consistent with it. What makes him enlightened is his rejection of gratuitous hypotheses and his corresponding belief that there is a surer path to the advancement of knowledge. What makes him a sceptic is his belief that, for one reason or another, there are limits to how far we can go in making a system of nature. Ultimately, for the enlightened sceptic, the world is a mystery. Human knowledge may best be advanced, not by speculation or *a priori* reasoning, but by building carefully on experience. The man imbued with a spirit of intellectual modesty is to be preferred to the man who is imbued with a spirit of system.

This emphasis on modesty takes a rather particular form amongst the 'enlightened sceptics'. The reason for this is, so far as I can see, not that they formed any kind of cohesive 'school', but that they saw a kind of modesty as a prime virtue of Newton. Here, for example, is how one such sceptic, Jean d'Alembert (1717–83), writes about Newton in his *Preliminary Discourse*:

Anything we could add to the praise of the great philosopher would fall far short of the universal testimonial that is given today to his almost innumerable discoveries and to his genius, which was at the same time far-reaching, exact, and profound. He has doubtless deserved all the recognition that has been given him for enriching philosophy with a large quantity of real assets. But perhaps he has done more by teaching philosophy to be judicious and to restrict within reasonable limits the sort of audacity which Descartes had been forced by circumstances to bestow upon it. His Theory of the World (for I do not mean his System) is today so generally accepted that men are beginning to dispute the author's claim to the honour of inventing it (because at the beginning great men are accused of being mistaken, and at the end they are treated as plagiarists). To the people who find everything in the works of the ancients I leave the pleasure of discovering gravitation of planets in those works even if it is not there. But supposing that the Greeks had had the idea of it, what was only a rash and romantic system with them became a demonstration in the hands of Newton. That demonstration, which belongs exclusively to him, constitutes the real merit of his discovery. Without such support, the theory of attraction would only be an hypothesis like so many others . . . . Newton, who had studied Nature, did not flatter himself that he knew more than the ancients concerning the first cause which produces phenomena. . . . He contented himself with proving that the vortices of Descartes could not reasonably explain the movements of the planets, but phenomena and the laws of mechanics unite in overthrowing the vortices, that there is a force through which the planets tend toward one another, whose principle is entirely unknown to us. (Library of Liberal Arts Edition, p. 81 f.)

The enlightened sceptics made a virtue out of what Newton's critics took to be a defect in his theory of gravitational attraction. Where the critics insisted that Newton's 'attraction' could only be measured and not be explained, the enlightened sceptics responded by crediting Newton with – as d'Alembert puts it – 'disabusing us of our ridiculous confidence that we know everything' (*Preliminary Discourse*, p. 83).

This way of thinking finds a very full expression in the writings of Hume. It is expressly linked with the name of Newton in a much quoted passage in the *History of England*:

While Newton seemed to draw off the veil from some of the mysteries of nature, he shewed at the same time the imper-

fections of the mechanical philosophy; and thereby restored
her ultimate secrets to that obscurity in which they ever
did and ever will remain. (ch. lxxi)

In his first *Enquiry* Hume remarks that 'No philosopher,
who is rational and modest, ever pretended to assign the
ultimate cause of any natural operation, or to show distinctly
the action of that power, which produces any single effect in
the universe.'[1] The 'ultimate springs and principles' which
produce natural phenomena are 'totally shut up from human
curiosity and enquiry'. The same limitations as are found
with natural philosophy are to be found also with moral
philosophy. Hume, having cited Custom or Habit as the
principle which determines all inferences from experience,
goes on to insist that 'we pretend not to have given the ultimate
reason' for our making these inferences in the way we do. He
goes on:

> Perhaps we can push our enquiries no farther, or pretend
> to give the cause of this cause; but must rest contented with
> it as the ultimate principle, which we can assign, of all our
> conclusions from experience. It is sufficient satisfaction,
> that we can go so far, without repining at the narrowness of
> our faculties because they will carry us no farther. (*op. cit.*
> p. 43)

II

The enlightened sceptics, then, were sceptical about the
extent to which human knowledge could be advanced. They
did, at the same time, share certain assumptions concerning
the object of human knowledge. They conceived of nature
as an entirely orderly system, undisturbed by miraculous
intervention, which was governed by unfailing laws. They
conceived of laws which were already known as explicable in
terms of more fundamental principles. And, if they believed
that no further account could be given of these principles,
they none the less supposed that there must be further principles
which accounted for them. The advance of science, at a

theoretical level at least, was conceived as the discovery of more fundamental principles from which less fundamental ones could be derived. These principles thus formed a kind of hierarchy. They formed, to put it metaphorically, a pyramid whose summit was, from a human point of view, perpetually enshrouded in mist. It is because of this that the full pyramid, i.e. the full system of nature, cannot be brought into view. They saw the shape of the lower part of the pyramid, i.e. they saw that the advance of science involved an advance towards a smaller number of principles. It may have seemed a logical projection from what they did know to conclude that the entire system of nature must be derived from a single principle.

Here, for example, is how Condillac defines a 'system' in his Dictionary of Synonyms:[2]

> A body of knowledge with mutually dependent parts, which is derived from a single principle, so that a good system is simply a principle successfully expanded. I know that many people take this word in bad part, believing that every system is a gratuitous hypothesis or something worse, like the dreams of metaphysicians. Nevertheless, this universe is nothing but a system, that is to say, a multitude of phenomena which, being related to one another as causes and effects, all spring from a first law.

Again, here is how Voltaire writes in his *We must take sides*: or *The principle of action*:[3]

> . . . the unvarying uniformity of the laws which control the march of the heavenly bodies, the movements of our globe, every species and genus of animal, plant, and mineral, indicates that there is one mover. If there were two, they would either differ, or be opposed to each other, or like each other. If they were different, there would be no harmony; if opposed, things would destroy each other; if like, it would be as if there were only one – a twofold employment.

I am encouraged in this belief that there can be but one principle, one single mover, when I observe the constant and uniform laws of the whole of nature.

Both Condillac and Voltaire were to identify this first law or principle or mover with a transcendent being and indeed, in Condillac's case, with the God of Christianity. Neither d'Alembert nor Hume made any such identification. D'Alembert took it as 'undeniable that all the bodies of which this universe is made up form a single system, whose parts are interdependent and whose interrelations derive from the harmony of the whole'.[4] In his *Preliminary Discourse to the Encyclopedia of Diderot* he seems to acknowledge the requirement that, if the universe is to be a system, it must have a 'primary cause'. Here he seems to identify the principle of natural order with something which could be known in an ideal state of scientific advancement:

> Electrical bodies, in which so many curious but seemingly unrelated properties have been discovered, are perhaps in a sense the least known bodies, because they appear to be more known. That power of attracting small particles which they acquire when they are rubbed, and that of producing a violent commotion in animals, are two things for us. They could be a single one if we could reach the primary cause. The universe, if we may be permitted to say so, would only be one fact and one great truth for whoever knew how to embrace it from a single point of view. (*op. cit.* p. 29)

Those who remember Hume first and foremost as the arch sceptic about induction might expect him to have pressed his sceptical doubts far enough to call in question the existence of a principle of natural order. But Hume was no more a Pyrrhonian sceptic than Descartes was a solipsist. The 'mitigated' scepticism which he professed is by no means subversive of the belief that nature is an orderly determined system. It seems to me indeed that Hume himself did believe that the universe was such a system, if not in precisely the sense of

Condillac and d'Alembert. In his essay *Of Miracles*, Hume is mainly concerned to provide an 'everlasting check' against the attempt to found a system of religion upon the supposed evidence of miracles. But it is evident also that he believes that any apparent breaches of laws of nature will be found, on further examination, not to be the disruptions of the natural order that they might appear at first sight. Hume is, I believe, committed to the view that the universe is entirely orderly and is therefore committed to taking seriously the problems which this admission poses. It is, indeed, difficult on any other assumption to explain Hume's apparent interest in the topics he discusses in his *Dialogues Concerning Natural Religion*. I do not think that he is by any means unsympathetic to the view he puts in the mouth of Philo in a passage towards the end of Part VI:[5]

> How could things have been as they are, were there not an original, inherent principle of order somewhere, in thought or in matter? And it is very indifferent to which of these we give preference. Chance has no place, on any hypothesis, sceptical or religious. Everything is surely governed by steady, inviolable laws. And were the inmost essence of things laid open to us, we should then discover a scene, of which, at present, we can have no idea. Instead of admiring the order of natural beings, we should clearly see, that it was absolutely impossible for them, in the smallest article, ever to admit of any other disposition.

There are points in the *Dialogues* where it seems that Philo is moved by such considerations, as Condillac and Voltaire were, to identify the principle of natural order with a transcendent God. I think, however, that he consistently refuses to do this. At one point he says: 'Were I obliged to defend any particular system of this nature (which I never willingly should do), I esteem none more plausible than that which ascribes an eternal, inherent principle of order to the world.' (*Op. cit.* p. 174.) And this fits in with the enlightened scepticism expressed in an earlier passage:

It were better, therefore, never to look beyond the present material world. By supposing it to contain the principle of its order within itself, we really assert it to be God; and the sooner we arrive at that divine being so much the better. When you go one step beyond the mundane system you only excite an inquisitive humour, which it is impossible ever to satisfy. (*op. cit.* p. 162)

In Part XII of the *Dialogues*, Philo suggests that the issue between theist and atheist is, in the end, something of a verbal one. The atheist can be made to concede that 'the principle which first arranged, and still maintains, order in this universe, bears . . . some remote inconceivable analogy to the operations of nature, and among the rest to the economy of human mind and thought'. The theist for his part allows that the original intelligence which he identifies with the original principle of order is very different from human reason. Whether or not there *is* an original principle of order is a subject which is not on the agenda in the debate between theist and atheist. In that sense I think the *Dialogues* are not so much a debate about the existence of God but, as Pamphilus advertizes in the Prologue, only a debate about his nature. The same assumption is made in the section of Hume's first *Enquiry* where the argument for design is considered within a much briefer compass.

I am not suggesting that Philo in the *Dialogues* should be taken throughout to be the spokesman for Hume. Nor am I suggesting that Hume was in any interesting sense a theist. What I am suggesting is that, if what is meant by 'God' is just the principle, whatever it is, which secures order in the universe, Hume's scepticism was reserved for claims about the nature of such a 'God' not for claims as to the existence of such a 'God'. In other contexts Hume uses the word 'nature' for the same purpose. For example, in the first *Enquiry* (Section V, Part II) Hume remarks on the 'kind of pre-established harmony' which exists 'between the course of nature and the succession of our ideas'. He concludes this section – his sceptical solution to his earlier doubts concerning the operations of the understanding – by admitting the existence of something, which we cannot know anything about, but which underwrites the harmony or correspondence between the course of nature and the succession of our ideas:

> As nature has taught us the use of our limbs, without giving us the knowledge of the muscles and nerves, by which they are actuated; so has she implanted in us an instinct, which carries forward the thought in a correspondent course to that which she has established among external objects; though we are ignorant of those powers and forces, on which this regular course and succession of objects totally depends. (*Enquiries*, p. 55)

Hume's thesis is, of course, that custom is 'that principle, by which the correspondence has been effected' but, as we have already seen, he holds only that we must 'rest contented with it as the ultimate principle', not that it is the 'ultimate principle' which determines our inferences from experience. Custom is simply 'a principle of human nature, which is universally acknowledged, and which is well known by its effects' (p. 43). People have a propensity, upon the repetition of any particular act or operation, to renew the same act or operation. In using the word 'Custom' and saying that this propensity is the effect of custom, Hume insists that 'we pretend not to have given the ultimate reason of such a propensity'.

III

I have suggested that Hume, and other enlightened sceptics, assumed that nature was a system and that, therefore, there was a principle of natural order. Why is it that they were willing to make such an assumption when they were sceptical about the project of making a system of nature or finding out about the principle of natural order? I do not imagine that there is one simple explanation which would do for even one of the enlightened sceptics, still less for them all. At the same time I think it is a little too easy to opt for explanations of a rather extraneous sort. In the case of Condillac, for example, it is no doubt at least partially true that he found in a principle of natural order a way of reconciling his philosophical views with his commitment to religious orthodoxy. I have already tried to bar the way to that kind of explanation in the case of Hume. For I have argued that Hume actually accepts a principle of natural order. It thus becomes a hypothetical question whether, if he had not accepted it, he would have pretended to do so in order preserve some appearance of religious orthodoxy. My hypothesis is that the assumption of a principle of natural order was needed to underwrite other philosophical commitments of the enlightened sceptics. In particular, I want to suggest, it was necessary to underwrite the principle of parsimony, i.e. the principle in accordance with which simpler theories are preferred to more complicated ones. This principle appears as the first of Newton's 'Rules of Reasoning in Philosophy' in Book III of his *Principia*:

> *We are to admit no more causes of natural things than such as are both true and sufficient to explain their appearances.*
> To this purpose the philosophers say that Nature does nothing in vain, and more is in vain when less will serve; for Nature is pleased with simplicity, and affects not the pomp of superfluous causes.

As Newton states this rule there is a clear dichotomy between the rule as it applies on the side of thought, viz. the principle of parsimony, and the principle which underwrites it on the side of Nature – Nature does nothing in vain. Expressed in terms of such a dichotomy this rule immediately raises a sceptical doubt. How do we know that the principle of parsimony is indeed underwritten by Nature? And, if the answer is that we do not know, there is the further question: How do we know that simpler theories are better than more complicated ones?

For philosophers imbued with the 'spirit of systems' there are short-cuts to be taken from the order of thought to the order of Nature. Thus Leibniz, for example, could first establish the existence of a wholly perfect being who would choose to create that world which contained the greatest amount of perfection. Leibniz is able to arrive within his system at the conclusion that, since the world contains the maximum amount of perfection, it must contain 'as great a variety as possible, along with the greatest possible order' (*Monadology*, Section 58). The principle of parsimony, for Leibniz, is simply a corollary of this particular conclusion.

As Newtonian philosophers, the enlightened sceptics would have attached a particular importance to the principle of parsimony. But they did not have the option, if they were to remain sceptics about such systems as that produced by Leibniz, of taking the kind of high road to a justification for the principle which had been trodden by Leibniz before them.

It would be inconsistent for an enlightened sceptic to help himself to the principle of parsimony as an *a priori* require-ment. It is a principle which, from his point of view, needs to be justified by the evidence of experience. It would need at the same time to be a justification for taking a principle of natural order to operate on the side of nature. There are, for this reason, ways of defending the principle of parsimony which may commend themselves to some empiricists but which could not commend themselves to the enlightened sceptics. One solution, which is at least hinted at in the philo-sophy of Berkeley, is to cut the Gordian Knot and attempt to justify a principle of parsimony without any parallel justifica-tion for the principle of natural order. It is, I think, illuminating to see how such an anti-realist account must stand in the eyes of an enlightened sceptic. Here it is particularly relevant to consider the status of the principle of parsimony in Berkeley's philosophy.

On Berkeley's account, that a true theory or hypothesis is just the one which accommodates the facts in the simplest way is a matter of definition. It is part of what is *meant* by calling it 'true'. The facts, on a Berkeleian account, are the various ideas which we are given, which depend in no way

on our will. There are different levels of theory which relate
to these facts. There are, for example, philosophical theories,
such as that of materialism, according to which real ideas
are caused in us by bodies existing without the mind. We
can explain the facts without appealing to this theory, according to Berkeley. He rejects the theory partly on the ground
that it implies that the whole of nature has been made in
vain. But, as is well known, his account makes quite ordinary
statements about the world, such as 'There is a table in the
next room', hypothetical or theoretical in character. Such
statements are true if they are the simplest way of accommodating the ideas which we are given. Indeed the meaning
of such statements is given by spelling out what claims they
make about the order in our ideas. By the same token, ideas
are to be accounted 'real' precisely insofar as they are part
of an orderly pattern of ideas, namely, the simplest or most
orderly which we can arrange out of the ideas we are given.
The principle of parsimony is, on Berkeley's account, absorbed
into a coherence theory of truth and is thus promoted from
being a *test* of a theory being true to being part of what is
meant by talking about 'truth'.

The principle of parsimony has, in Berkeley's philosophy, a
secure status. But it is not grounded in nature, nor does it
imply the corresponding principle on the side of nature, that
nature does nothing in vain. Berkeley does at one point invoke
this principle as a supplementary argument against the hypothesis of matter, but only in a guarded way. It did have a
spokesman in the *Three Dialogues*. Philonous is made to remark:

> . . . if it pass for a good argument against other hypotheses
> in the sciences, but they suppose Nature, or the Divine
> Wisdom, to make something in vain, or to do that by
> tedious roundabout methods which might have been per-
> formed in a much more easy and compendious way, what
> shall we think of that hypothesis which supposes the whole
> world made in vain? (Library of Liberal Arts, 1954, edition,
> p. 57)

Berkeley does want to infer the goodness of God from the orderliness of our ideas. He could not therefore, without begging that question, invoke the doctrine that Nature or the Divine Wisdom does nothing in vain to underwrite the principle of parsimony. Nor does he need to. Where, on a realist account, the principle that Nature does nothing in vain appears most readily as a metaphysical principle, it is built into the fabric of an idealist epistemology.

There are a number of features of Berkeley's philosophy which would make it difficult for enlightened sceptics who read him to disregard him entirely. But their realist predilections stood in the way of his finding much support from them. D'Alembert was appalled at the elimination of ordinary efficient causes in Berkeley's system and, because it makes God the efficient cause of all our ideas, was inclined to dismiss it as being so close to 'sheer Malebranchism that you would need to have been a metaphysician to notice the difference'.[6] As to Berkeley's way of distinguishing real ideas from ideas of the kind we have in dreams, d'Alembert held that we 'noticed' the difference. 'Actions preceding sleep are distinguished by causal connexion, and upon waking we notice the gap made by sleep.' On both these points d'Alembert's response to Berkeley is a realist one.

For all his admiration of Berkeley the same is true of Hume. In a well-known footnote to his first *Enquiry* (Section XII, Part I), Hume writes of Berkeley that 'all his arguments, though otherwise intended, are, in reality, merely sceptical'. It is clear from the context that the argument which Hume had in mind is Berkeley's argument for the view that 'all sensible qualities are in the mind, not in the object' (*Enquiries*, p. 155). What makes such arguments 'merely sceptical' in Hume's eyes is '*that they admit of no answer and produce no conviction*'. Here Hume the Pyrrhonian sceptic is better remembered by philosophers than Hume the enlightened sceptic. For Hume does not deny the force of Berkeley's argument and it is not surprising that he should allow that this argument admits of no answer. But he also wants to say, and this appears to be his main point against such 'merely sceptical' arguments, that they 'produce no conviction'. If Hume thought that the argument for saying that all sensible qualities are in the mind and not in the object was incredible he cannot himself have believed it.

There are other possible anti-realist accounts of the principle of parsimony which are not idealist, e.g. that later offered by Mach. But, since the principle of parsimony applies only to theories, any such account which is to avoid idealism must make a sharp distinction between theories and facts. I think that one will be unsympathetic to such a view to the extent that one perceives the advancement of knowledge as involving the upgrading of theories into facts. Such an upgrading is only intelligible on a realist interpretation of the principle of parsimony, i.e. one which sees it as corresponding on the side of thought to a principle which operates in nature itself. It is possible, with philosophical consistency, to insist that it is not a fact that the earth goes round the sun but only the simplest theory which is consistent with the facts. But it is tempting to accept that, in this case, as in others, what was once a theory has become a fact. Copernicus himself had professed to believe that one should only expect 'hypotheses' from astronomy. Hume's Philo, in the *Dialogues*, is so far from that modest expectation that he can say: 'One great foundation of the Copernican system is the maxim, that nature acts by the simplest methods, and chooses the most proper means to any end.' (*Op. cit.*, p. 214.) If all one could expect from astronomy were hypotheses the Copernican system could have no such foundation.

Hume himself not only understood the principle of parsimony in a realist way but invoked it in favour of the system which he himself proposed in the *Treatise*. In Book II he laments the *status quo* in moral philosophy or, at any rate, the *status quo ante* Hume, by likening the condition of the subject in his time to the state of astronomy before the time of Copernicus. Here is how he writes:

Here, therefore, moral philosophy is in the same condition as natural, with regard to astronomy before the time of *Copernicus*. The antients, tho' sensible of that maxim, *that nature does nothing in vain*, contriv'd such intricate systems of the heavens, as seem'd inconsistent with true philosophy, and gave place at last to something more simple and natural. To invent without scruple a new principle to every phaeno-menon, instead of adapting it to the old; to overload our hypotheses with a variety of this kind; are certain proofs, that none of these principles is the just one, and that we only desire, by a number of falsehoods, to cover our ignorance of the truth. (Clarendon Press edition, p. 282)

It is noticeable in this passage that Hume associates a simple system with one which is natural and an intricate system with one which is contrived. A contrived system will serve only to disguise ignorance, so, presumably, a natural system will be, if not the true one, at all events one which is not obviously a mere cover for ignorance.

It seems that the best kind of support available to Hume for his belief that nature is an orderly determined system and that there is a principle of natural order is inductive support. This kind of support, however, is not strong enough for the kinds of purpose to which Hume wants to put the principle of parsimony. If his commitment to the principle of parsimony were inductively based it could not be used to dismiss intricate-looking theories in advance of further investigation. Yet it is just this which Hume seems to propose. In accepting a principle of natural order he seems to have helped himself to the benefits of a metaphysical system without having enough argument to entitle him to those benefits.

IV

I have attempted to make the commitment of enlightened sceptics to a principle of natural order intelligible by repre-senting it as corresponding, on the side of nature, to the epistemological principle of parsimony. I have suggested that it is difficult for someone who accepts a realist view of scientific theory to avoid commitment to a principle of natural order. Such a commitment is, however, problematical, given the non-acceptability of rationalist or idealist justifications for the principle of parsimony in the eyes of enlightened sceptics and in view of the insufficiency of inductive support to licence the kind of use to which the principle of parsimony is put. Is there any way out of these difficulties which can be found on terms satisfactory to an enlightened sceptic? I think that any solution involves some retrenchment from a thorough-going scientific realism. It would involve identifying the principle of parsimony as a meta-theoretical principle and offering an account of it and other such principles which is different from the realist account of empirical theories and laws. One such solution, which perhaps involves too great a dilution of scientific realism, is that proposed by Kant. Another, less compromising solution is at least hinted at in the writings of d'Alembert though, so far as I know, is not fully developed by him. In many ways Kant's credentials for being included as an enlightened sceptic are impeccable. But, in retrospect, his position is at least ambiguous. For whilst he eagerly sought to produce refutations of idealism and would have dissociated his own position entirely from that of Berkeley, it is by no means obvious that his own idealism leaves nature sufficiently independent of the mind. His account of the principle of parsimony is, however, independently interesting. Kant saw that it was difficult to give a rationale for the principle which did not make it too metaphysical to be acceptable to an enlightened sceptic or too subjective to be acceptable to a realist. Kant thought that the principle of parsimony was a requirement of reason but argued that it could not be justified merely as 'an economical requirement' (*Critique of Pure Reason*, A 650). Like the enlightened sceptics he thought that 'parsimony in principles . . . is one of Nature's own laws'. Hume's difficulty, to put it in Kantian terms, is that he found himself committed to a position of transcendental realism in respect of a principle of natural order. Kant's own solution is to propose that the principle of parsimony be grounded in a regulative principle. Kant suggests that the idea of a God is a speculative idea, i.e. one which 'seeks only to formulate the command of reason, that all connection in the world be viewed in accordance with the principles of a systematic unity – *as if* all such connection had its source in one single all-embracing being, as the supreme and all-sufficient cause' (A 686). Kant, perhaps following Hume, insisted that 'it must be a matter of complete indifference to us, when we perceive such unity, whether we say that God in his wisdom has willed it to be so, or that Nature has wisely arranged it thus' (A 699). It must be a matter of 'complete indifference' because the unity required by reason in phenomena is a merely regulative principle and not a constitutive one.

It is a moot point whether a Kantian solution of the problem of providing a rationale for the principle of parsimony is one which could be accepted by an enlightened sceptic. I think it should be acceptable to the extent that Kant succeeds in combining his transcendental idealism with an empirical realism.

D'Alembert knew more about the physical sciences than any of the other enlightened sceptics that I have mentioned. Perhaps it is not surprising, therefore, that we can find some hint of a solution in his writings to the problem of justifying the principle of parsimony without invoking a principle of natural order. At one point in the *Preliminary Discourse*, d'Alembert writes:

. . . it is not at all by vague and arbitrary hypotheses that we can hope to know Nature; it is by thoughtful study of phenomena, by the comparisons we make among them, by the art of reducing, as much as that may be possible, a large number of phenomena to a single one that can be regarded as their principle. Indeed, the more one reduces the number of principles of a science, the more one gives them scope, and since the object of a science is necessarily fixed, the principles applied to that object will be so much the more fertile as they are fewer in number. (*op. cit.* p. 22)

D'Alembert goes on to indicate that this reduction does, moreover, make the principles easier to understand. But he is far from believing that the principle of parsimony could be satisfactorily justified on such a subjective basis. This passage contains the more interesting suggestion that by minimizing principles used in an explanatory system one maximizes their scope. The fewer the principles, assuming the phenomena to be constant, the greater the consequences of accepting them.

It is not clear just why d'Alembert thinks it is a virtue in an explanatory system to reduce the number of principles. He remarks that the principles will be 'so much the more fertile as they are fewer in number', and the suggestion here seems to be that they will aid the discovery of subsidiary principles or hypotheses. One example of such fertility, perhaps, is the application of the theory of universal gravitational attraction to explain the behaviour of tides. What d'Alembert did not explicitly do, so far as I know, is to link the satisfaction of the principle of parsimony with the quest for truer theories. He might, however, have done so without any great modification. For the more a principle generates hypotheses that themselves seem to be confirmed by what is observed the more the principle establishes itself as the right one to have chosen. Simplicity, on such an account, becomes a mark of objectivity. This, as Popper was to point out in *The Logic of Scientific Discovery*, cuts both ways. If a simpler principle, because of its fertility, can more objectively be claimed as true, it is also clear that the more consequences a principle has the more its chances of being found false. Popper held it to be a particular merit of his account of the nature of a scientific claim that it explains why simplicity is desired so much in science.

> To understand this there is no need for us to assume a 'principle of economy of thought' or anything of the kind. Simple statements, if knowledge is our object, are to be prized more highly than less simple ones *because they tell us more: because their empirical content is greater; and because they*

are better testable. (London, Hutchinson, 1968 Edition, p. 142)

Popper's account of the principle of parsimony is consistent with a realist theory but it does not commit him to a principle of natural order. D'Alembert was not far from the beginnings of an account which could equally dispense with the requirement of a principle of natural order. The fact that the principle of natural order was just as much assumed by d'Alembert as the other enlightened sceptics shows that he was still some way from grasping the implications of an adequate rationale for the principle of parsimony. The principle of parsimony thus became, as Hume's Philo admitted, a 'strong foundation of piety and religion'. It is thus perhaps not surprising that the less philosophically sophisticated of the enlightened sceptics, such as Voltaire, should have believed in a God and that even the more sophisticated, such as Hume, still regarded the argument from design as one which deserved careful examination. On some views of the principle of parsimony we do not, as we have seen, need to assume a principle of natural order. It is that assumption which makes the argument for design an impressive argument. That is why, at least in part, the enlightened sceptics were impressed by the argument. They could, I have been suggesting, have been a little more sceptical without ceasing to be enlightened and then they need not have been impressed by the argument for design at all.

NOTES

[1] *Enquiries concerning Human Understanding and concerning the Principles of Morals,* ed. L. A. Selby-Bigge, rev. P. H. Nidditch, (Oxford (Clarendon Press), 3rd edition, 1975), p. 30. Other references to this work will also be to this edition.
[2] *Oeuvres Philosophiques de Condillac,* ed. G. LeRoy (Paris, 1947–51), **3**, p. 511 f.
[3] *Selected Works of Voltaire,* trans. by Joseph McCabe (London (Watts & Co.), 1935), p. 9.

[4] In his article '(Qualités) Cosmiques' in the *Encyclopédie*.

[5] Library of Liberal Arts edition, ed. N. Kemp Smith, Indianapolis (Bobbs-Merrill), p. 174 f.

[6] In his article in the *Encyclopédie* on 'Corps', quoted by Ronald Grimsley in his *Jean d'Alembert* (Clarendon Press, 1963), p. 278.

4

ADAM SMITH: PHILOSOPHY, SCIENCE, AND SOCIAL SCIENCE

D. D. Raphael

What darkness was the 'Enlightenment' supposed to have removed? The answer is irrational forms of religion. Most of the 'enlightened' took the view that revealed religion was irrational and that natural religion could be rational; but some were sceptical about natural religion too. Hume was the most honest and the most penetrating thinker of the latter group. His biographer, Professor E. C. Mossner, is not alone in believing that the *Dialogues concerning Natural Religion* is 'his philosophical testament'.[1]

Among Hume's friends no-one understood and appreciated his personal beliefs better than Adam Smith. Yet Smith was unable to share Hume's view of natural religion. On this cardinal issue Smith belonged to the moderate and not to the radical Enlightenment. Indeed there are a couple of passages in Smith's early work which express an adherence to revealed religion and so lead one to ask whether Smith belonged to the Enlightenment at all.

One of these passages is particularly relevant to that question, for it ascribes the very idea of enlightenment to revelation:

. . . as ignorance begot superstition, science gave birth to the first theism that arose amongst those nations, who were not enlightened by divine Revelation.

D

It comes from a fragmentary essay on the History of Ancient Physics (§9), written in Smith's youth but published only after his death, in *Essays on Philosophical Subjects*, edited by his executors. If Smith could have brought himself in his later years to complete and publish the work for which it was intended, he might well have altered or struck out that phrase about being 'enlightened by divine Revelation'. This seems probable from the history of the second passage in which he referred to revealed religion. I have recounted this history elsewhere,[2] but since it will not be known to most members of my present audience I shall repeat the gist of it briefly.

The passage was published in the first edition of *The Theory of Moral Sentiments* (1759) and came from the lectures that Smith delivered, in the years preceding that date, as Professor of Moral Philosophy at Glasgow. In one of the chapters of TMS (II.ii.3), Smith criticizes the view that our approbation of justice arises from utility. He argues that the thought of social utility often reinforces but is not the original ground of our sentiment of justice. He supports his opinion with several examples, one of which illustrates the striking contrast that can sometimes arise between justice and utility. Smith then ends the chapter with an argument from theology. Our sense of justice leads us to thoughts of divine retribution, and moral feeling is seconded by religious doctrine: 'Nature teaches us to hope, and religion authorises us to expect,' that virtue and vice will be rewarded and punished in and after life if not in this one. In the original version there followed a paragraph that might have been written by a 'high-flying' clergyman. Before the infinite perfection of God, man appears to be a 'vile insect' whose past conduct requires 'repentance, sorrow, humility, contrition'. Even that is not enough; the penitent imagines that 'some other sacrifice, some other atonement,' is needed, 'beyond what he himself is capable of making'. These 'original anticipations of nature' coincide with 'the doctrines of revelation' which teach us 'that the most powerful intercession has been made, and that the most dreadful atonement has been paid for our manifold transgressions and iniquities'.

Towards the end of his life Smith revised the book extensively for the sixth edition (1790). In that edition the whole paragraph about repentance and the Christian doctrine of the Atonement was simply deleted. Instead the chapter ended with a single sentence added to the preceding paragraph:

> In every religion, and in every superstition that the world has ever beheld, accordingly, there has been a Tartarus as well as an Elysium; a place provided for the punishment of the wicked, as well as one for the reward of the just.

Smith died a few weeks after the sixth edition of TMS appeared. It seems that one of his friends may have asked him why he had omitted the Atonement paragraph, and there is a report that he said it was because the paragraph had been 'unnecessary and misplaced'. The report followed an amusing incident. Some twenty years after Smith's death, his adherence to the Christian doctrine of the Atonement was noted in a book on the subject by William Magee, Archbishop of Dublin. Magee quoted from Smith's paragraph and was naturally glad to cite the support of a leading philosopher, especially since that philosopher had been a friend of Hume. But then some unkind person pointed out to Magee that Smith had withdrawn the passage in a later edition of his book, so that his final opinion must have been adverse to Magee's case. Magee had his answer: the change in Smith must have been due to 'the infection of David Hume's society'. Magee's suggestion was ridiculed by Smith's biographer, John Rae, but I think that it needs to be taken seriously. The disputed paragraph had concluded a chapter in which Smith argued against a utilitarian view of justice. Although Smith's original criticisms of that position in his lectures had been directed against a general tradition, by the time he wrote the book they had come to be directed especially at Hume as the most powerful advocate of a utilitarian account of justice. The proper arguments to use against Hume were those taken from human nature. In the circumstances the addition of an argument resting on revealed religion was certainly 'unnecessary and misplaced'. After Hume's death it must have seemed to Smith unutterably out of place, and so he substituted for it a sentence that might have been written by Hume himself: 'every religion and . . . every superstition' has a Tartarus and an Elysium.

There is a good deal of evidence to support the view that Smith in later life was unwilling to endorse specifically Christian doctrine, at any rate as it was commonly presented by many Christian clerics, and some of that evidence does seem to reflect the influence of Hume. For example, both in the *Wealth of Nations* (1776) and in the sixth edition of the *Moral Sentiments* Smith appears to echo Hume's dismissal of 'penance, mortification, . . . and the whole train of monkish virtues' (*Enquiry concerning the Principles of Morals*, IX.i). In WN (V.i.e.29) he attacked the moral philosophy which is subservient to theology and which teaches that 'heaven was to be earned only by penance and mortification, by the austerities and abasement of a monk', and in the sixth edition of TMS (III.2.35) he poured scorn on 'the futile mortifications of a monastery' and the idea that heaven is reserved 'for monks and friars, or for those whose conduct and conversation resembled those of monks and friars'.

So I think we can take it that the isolated passages endorsing revealed religion are characteristic of Adam Smith only in his youth and that his mature thoughts were much nearer to those of Hume on this issue, though not on natural religion.

When the thinkers of the Enlightenment criticized irrational forms of religion, their paradigm of acceptable belief was natural science. The process which they initiated has gone on ever since and continues to dominate our own intellectual horizon. A great many issues in present-day philosophical debate – not only about religion, of course, but about epistemology, metaphysics, psychology and the philosophy of mind, ethics, and the social sciences – turn on the immeasurably greater confidence that we have in natural science than in any other set of ideas. In the eighteenth century, however, there was far less of a distinction between science and philosophy: the paradigm was the success of 'natural philosophy', especially in the system of Newton, but it was generally assumed that the other branches of 'philosophy' were on the same road and could be classed together with natural science. Certainly Adam Smith uses the two terms 'science' and 'philosophy' almost interchangeably. Professor T. D. Campbell, in his admirable book on *Adam Smith's Science of Morals* (p. 27), says that Smith sometimes contrasts philosophy, as more abstract and theoretical, with science, as more practical and immediately useful; but the passages that he cites do not in fact contain the term 'science' at all. At any rate Professor Campbell agrees that in general Smith uses the two terms indifferently.

There is, however, one place in WN (V.i.g.14) where Smith appears to imply a distinction between the two. He writes of 'the study of science and philosophy'. It is not clear just how he understands the distinction, but he goes on in the same paragraph to say that 'Science is the great antidote to the poison of enthusiasm and superstition'. He has been talking about religion and religious ethics. His strong phrase, 'the poison of enthusiasm and superstition', means religion; this is another place where one sees the influence of Hume. I suppose that Smith is forced to distinguish between science and philosophy here because he has told us earlier in the same chapter that much post-Christian moral philosophy has pandered to absurd doctrines of religion. And so I think that by 'science' in this paragraph he means the kind of inquiry which conforms to empirical fact: in the case of moral philosophy, to the facts of human nature. This does approach the modern sense of science, in which it may be (though it does not have to be) distinguished from philosophy.

At any rate that sentence, 'Science is the great antidote to the poison of enthusiasm and superstition', epitomizes the spirit of the Enlightenment. By 1776 Adam Smith was fully caught up in it.

Smith wrote two books for publication. Most people think

that his reputation depends simply on the second of these, the *Wealth of Nations*. In his own day, however, Smith achieved fame even with his first book, the *Theory of Moral Sentiments*. A delightful letter from Hume to Smith (No. 31 in *The Correspondence of Adam Smith*, ed. E. C. Mossner and I. S. Ross) gave him 'the melancholy news' that his book was an instant success, as much with 'the foolish people' as with 'the mob of literati', with prelates as with peers, to say nothing of the publisher, whose bragging of his sales showed him to be 'a son of the earth' who valued books 'only by the profit they bring him'. Hume was far too generous-hearted to be jealous but he must have reflected ruefully on the difference between this and the reception of his own first book, the *Treatise of Human Nature*. The *Theory of Moral Sentiments* soon became popular in France and Germany too. When Smith gave up the Chair of Moral Philosophy at Glasgow in 1764, the University's regret is recorded in a resolution which says that 'his elegant and ingenious *Theory of Moral Sentiments* [had] recommended him to the esteem of men of taste and literature throughout Europe'. The word 'throughout' is an exaggeration, but the book did undoubtedly win for Smith an international reputation as a moral philosopher.

The *Wealth of Nations* established his renown as a great economist. Anyone who reads the whole of that work, however, will be aware that it ranges well beyond economics to general sociology and cultural history. In WN Smith made his mark not simply as an economist but as a social scientist.

It would be a mistake to emphasize a difference in aim between the two books, as if TMS were philosophy and *not* social science. Professor T. D. Campbell has good reason to describe Smith's ethical theory as a '*science* of morals', and others have equally good reason to praise TMS mostly for its contribution to psychology. For all that, the two books belong to different genres. TMS does not have the wealth of solid empirical evidence that supports the theories of WN. Despite its character of social science, TMS remains primarily a work of philosophy. That is certainly not true of WN.

Nevertheless, it is true of both books that Smith made his way to their final form by moving from philosophy to social science. He did it through the medium of cultural *history*. Smith usually found it helpful to approach a subject historically and then developed his own ideas as a result of the historical survey. His study of the history of astronomy suggested to him that a leading feature of Hume's philosophy could be adapted to produce a philosophical theory of science. His distinctive ideas in ethics seem to have come after he had engaged in critical discussion of the history of ethical theory. Here again the influence of historical study took concrete form only when joined to the influence of Hume's philosophy. In this instance, however, Smith did not take over a Humean thesis but rather reacted against it. His economic and social theories likewise are the result both of historical study and of advancing (sometimes by development, sometimes by criticism) upon the work of contemporaries – Montesquieu, Hutcheson, Hume, and the French Physiocrats. In this case the historical study was the history of law and government: the *Wealth of Nations* arose from Smith's lectures on jurisprudence, which were in the first instance largely historical. Smith himself would not have seen any *essential* difference in his various investigations. For him they were all philosophy. Philosophy includes as a matter of course a critical treatment of the history of philosophy. Moral philosophy in the Scottish Universities of the eighteenth century included as a matter of course a discussion of 'jurisprudence', that is to say, ideas about justice and a comparative treatment of legal systems. The latter led naturally to the theory of government, and that to political economy.

Smith's long essay on the History of Astronomy (published posthumously in *Essays on Philosophical Subjects*) deserves to rank with TMS and WN as the work of an outstanding mind. It is one of the originators of the history and philosophy of science. On the historical side it is remarkably well informed and in general pretty accurate. But it is also genuinely philosophical, both in the pattern which it draws out of the historical facts and even more in its explanation of the changes from one type of scientific theory to another. Smith starts off with the traditional view of Plato and Aristotle that philosophy (or science) begins in wonder. But he immediately elaborates this into a psychological theory of intellectual discomfort with the unfamiliar leading to the removal of that discomfort when we can find connections with the familiar again. A modern scholar might describe the situation with the statement that an apparently unusual event is explained by showing it to be, not an isolated individual, but an instance of a general law. Smith concentrates on the psychological effects, first of surprise at the oddity, and then of relief at assimilating it with the familiar after all. A scientific theory (in astronomy or anything else) satisfies by removing intellectual discomfort at oddity. But oddity is not the only reason for intellectual discomfort. If we are to feel at ease with a recurring pattern, it must be relatively simple. Once it becomes complex, the recurrences are less easy to grasp, less familiar, and so less comfortable. When a scientific theory (for instance, the Ptolemaic account of astronomy) has grown very complex in order to accommodate all the observed phenomena, we are dissatisfied once more and are prepared to welcome a different sort of theory (like the Copernican) that is simpler. But of course the simplicity may have to be bought at a price. In the case of the Copernican theory we have a simpler pattern but we must adjust ourselves to a new suggestion that is exceedingly unfamiliar, namely that the Earth is in motion. So we need a development of theory which will remove our discomfort, indeed our shock, at *that* unfamiliarity.

This psychological explanation of the development of science or philosophy is itself, for Adam Smith, a piece of philosophy. It is in line with the interpretation of philosophy that he learned from Hume. At the heart of Smith's explanation is an account of the functions of the imagination, which comes straight out of Hume but is adapted from Hume's theory of our belief in a persisting external world and is used instead to show how scientific theory builds a framework to fit on to observed phenomena. Roughly it goes like this. Hume said that the imagination fills in the gaps between observed impressions so as to produce the supposition of a permanent object; Smith said that the imagination fills in the gaps between observed phenomena so as to produce the supposition of a great 'machine' (such as a system of crystalline spheres revolving round the Earth).

We are inclined to say that such psychological explanations are themselves attempts at scientific theory rather than philosophy. That is not the view of Adam Smith, nor is it the view of Hume. Like Professor Barry Stroud in his recent book, *Hume*, I think it is a mistake to regard the psychological explanations in Hume as an aberration from his supposed true purpose of giving logical analyses of concepts after the manner of modern analytic philosophy. We can as a matter of fact derive from Hume some admirable suggestions for logical analysis, but that was not Hume's purpose. Hume stated expressly, in his sub-title to the *Treatise*, that his book was 'an attempt to introduce the experimental method of reasoning into moral subjects'. By 'experimental' he meant empirical, and by 'moral subjects' he meant the study of the human mind and human behaviour. His sub-title was derived, I think, from part of the full title of the first edition of Francis Hutcheson's *Inquiry into Beauty and Virtue* – 'with an attempt to introduce a mathematical calculation in subjects of morality'. Both of them had in mind an imitation of Newton, a transfer of Newton's method from 'physicks, or natural philosophy' to 'ethicks, or moral philosophy' (Smith writes in these terms, in WN V.i.f.23, of the traditional Greek classification of knowledge into three branches, logic, physics, and ethics). In fact Hume's original intention in the *Treatise* was to amalgamate the two, to show that the philosophy of man was part of the philosophy of nature. This is, in modern terms, *both* a scientific *and* a philosophical enterprise. It is scientific because it aims to give a genetic (psychological) explanation of various puzzling things like our belief in the objective existence of causation, material bodies, minds, virtues and vices. It is also philosophical because it achieves its scientific aim by a rearrangement of categories, by extending the concept of nature so as to include what others had contrasted with it, by breaking down the concepts of substance and identity so as to make mind and matter equally dependent on elements common to both.

Adam Smith was not the great *philosopher* that Hume was. His work does not propose to us a radical rearrangement of fundamental categories. Nevertheless, there is, in him as in Hume, a combination of science and philosophy. His psychological theory of the development of science is, like the psychological theorizing of Hume's *Treatise*, an attempt at genetic explanation. So is the psychological theory of moral judgment in TMS, with its elaborate, and on the whole persuasive, account of the formation of conscience, the imagined impartial spectator or 'man within the breast', an account derived from reflection upon the social function of moral feelings. These theories therefore fall into the realm of science or would-be science. But they have a philosophical character, too. The psychological explanation of the development of science implies, as Smith explicitly recognized, that scientific theories are products of the human imagination, not the discovery of objective truths. The doctrine of the impartial spectator implies that moral judgments about oneself have a more complex structure than moral judgments about other people.

I said earlier that WN differs from TMS in not being primarily a work of philosophy, and my remark just now about the combination of science and philosophy in Smith's work does not apply to WN. In writing WN Smith had turned away from philosophy, as we understand that term, and was engaged mainly in social science. Here too there is an analogy with Hume, who turned away from philosophy to write history. But this does not mean that they had abandoned their interest in philosophy. Hume was working on the *Dialogues concerning Natural Religion* right up to the end of his life; Smith made huge additions to TMS in the last years of *his* life. It is also proper to say that both Hume's history and Smith's economics have an *underlying* philosophical character, first by way of large-scale generalizations, and secondly by way of implied value judgments. In the case of WN all the references to a kind of natural law in economics – the 'natural price', the system of 'natural liberty', the working of the 'invisible hand' that makes self-interested behaviour contribute to the general good – show the permanent influence on Adam Smith of Stoic philosophy with its belief in cosmic harmony. But here, as elsewhere, Smith probably recognized no essential difference between philosophy and science. The cosmic harmony which he thought he had found in economic life was like the cosmic harmony displayed in Newton's 'natural philosophy'.

For Smith, a 'philosopher' is a reflective observer, who can think of connections that allow theoretical explanation or practical invention. He gives a virtual definition in WN I.i.9, where he writes of some inventions being made by

> those who are called philosophers or men of speculation, whose trade it is, not to do any thing, but to observe every thing; and who, upon that account, are often capable of combining together the powers of the most distant and dissimilar objects.

'Philosophers or men of speculation' are not just armchair speculators, although they are contrasted with men of action. James Watt, no less than Sir Isaac Newton, is a 'philosopher', as Smith uses the term. In corresponding passages of earlier versions of this thought (LJ(A) vi.43,49; LJ(B) 221; ED 19), Smith refers to the 'philosopher' who invented the 'fire engine' or 'fire machine'. Scientists and technologists, no less than philosophers in the modern sense of the word, are 'men of speculation' who have the leisure to observe widely and to make connections which would not occur to others. The connections may be physical, metaphysical, or social. In WN IV.ix.28 Smith refers to Quesnay as 'a physician, and a very speculative physician,' because he thought of 'the political body' after the analogy of the human body. In TMS III.3.4 Smith imagines what our reaction would be if the whole of

China were destroyed by an earthquake: after initial sympathy
with the widespread distress, a 'man of speculation' might
'enter into many reasonings concerning the effects which this
disaster might produce upon the commerce of Europe, and
the trade and business of the world in general'. If it were
Voltaire thinking about the Lisbon earthquake, he would
reflect on the implications for theology. If it were Adam
Smith, he would reflect on the implications for the world
economy.

Philosophy, science, and social science, then, were all the
same sort of activity for Smith. In the manuscript that has
been called 'An Early Draft of Part of *The Wealth of Nations*'
(§20), Smith has a list of different kinds of 'philosophers' –
'mechanical, chymical, astronomical, physical, metaphysical,
moral, political, commercial, and critical' (by this last word
he means writers on literary theory and aesthetics). His
Lectures on Jurisprudence (LJ(A) vi.43) contain a similar
list, omitting the 'physical, political, commercial, and critical'
philosophers, but adding 'theological'.

Like so many thinkers of his day, Smith looked upon Newton
as the great exemplar to be followed. In TMS, although there
is no explicit reference to the Newtonian model, Smith clearly
regards sympathy as the gravitational force of social cohesion
and social balance. That is why the work starts off firmly
with the words 'Of Sympathy' as the title of the first chapter.
WN starts in similar fashion by entitling its first chapter 'Of
the Division of Labour' because Smith regards the division of
labour as the primary causal factor in economic growth, the
subject-matter of this book. Governor Pownall of Massachu-
setts, who sent Smith a long and penetrating critique of some
of his doctrines, had no hesitation in drawing the Newtonian
analogy explicitly. He described the *Wealth of Nations* as 'a
system . . . that might become *principia* to the knowledge of
politick operations; as mathematicks are to mechanicks,
astronomy, and the other sciences' (*The Correspondence of Adam
Smith*, p. 337). Smith himself consciously uses a Newtonian
metaphor when he writes (WN I.vii.20) that the market

price is 'continually gravitating, if one may say so, towards the natural price'.

There is one important respect in which Smith seems to have distinguished natural science from moral philosophy and social science. In his History of Astronomy he quite definitely regards scientific theories as imagined structures and not as truths of nature. A theory is preferred, he says, because it suits the propensities of the human mind, not because it is the only one which accommodates the observed phenomena. He was struck especially by the change of attitude among scientists towards Descartes's theory of vortices. As Smith saw the history of astronomy, the Copernican hypothesis scored over its predecessors by its simplicity but faced an enormous psychological obstacle with its implication that the Earth was subject to two sets of motion at a very high speed. The difficulty was not the mere idea that the Earth was in motion, contrary to all appearances of rest. For the learned at least, the trouble was rather that earlier theory had represented any motion of ponderous bodies as slow, while the Copernican hypothesis required us to suppose that the daily rotation of the Earth round its own axis meant, for any point on the equator, a speed of a thousand miles an hour, faster than a cannon ball or even than the speed of sound, and that the orbital motion of the Earth round the Sun was faster still (Astronomy, IV.38). Descartes's theory of vortices became popular because it tried 'to render familiar to the imagination the greatest difficulty in the Copernican system, the rapid motion of the enormous bodies of the Planets' (IV.65). In due course, however, the system of Newton gave a more satisfying account and the theory of Descartes became an 'exploded hypothesis'. Consequently Smith was quite ready to understand that Newton's theory might not be the last word. He ends his essay (IV.76) by recalling, with some difficulty, that his account of science as the work of the imagination must apply to Newton as much as to the rest.

And even we, while we have been endeavouring to represent

all philosophical systems as mere inventions of the imagination, . . . have insensibly been drawn in, to make use of language expressing the connecting principles of this one, as if they were the real chains which Nature makes use of to bind together her several operations. Can we wonder then, . . . that it should now be considered, not as an attempt to connect in the imagination the phaenomena of the Heavens, but as . . . the discovery of an immense chain of the most important and sublime truths . . .?

Since Smith treated science and philosophy alike, one would suppose that he regarded philosophical and economic theories too as 'inventions of the imagination' and not as 'the discovery of truth'. Yet he says in TMS (VII.ii.4.14) that Mandeville's moral philosophy 'in some respects bordered upon the truth', and he writes in WN (IV.ix.38) that the Physiocratic system 'with all its imperfections is, perhaps, the nearest approximation to the truth that has yet been published upon the subject of political economy'.

How are we to take this apparent inconsistency? Had Smith abandoned the relativist theory of the History of Astronomy by the time he came to write TMS and WN? If so, it is surprising that he should have told Hume in 1773 (Letter No. 137) that in the event of his death the essay on the History of Astronomy might merit publication. (Smith does say in the letter, 'I begin to suspect myself that there is more refinement than solidity in some parts of it', but this does not suggest that he had positively abandoned what is a major thesis of the essay.) Or are the references to truth in the later works to be understood as not themselves literally true but simply the natural expression of the common error into which we all fall, as described at the end of the History of Astronomy? Or did Smith think that while theories about the physical world were bound to be inventions of the imagination, theories about man need not be? It is hard to say.

I suspect that originally Smith intended to place a history of moral philosophy alongside a history of natural philosophy and a history of logic and metaphysics. (In his *Essays on Philosophical Subjects* the History of Astronomy is followed by fragmentary essays on the History of Ancient Physics and the History of Ancient Logics and Metaphysics.) My hypothesis is that he then made use of the history of moral philosophy as the starting point of his lectures on ethics at Glasgow, and eventually transferred it, in TMS, to the final part of his treatment of the subject. If I am right, would the originally contemplated work have *compared* or *contrasted* moral philosophy with natural philosophy and metaphysics?

Smith's statement in TMS (at the conclusion of a chapter of vigorous criticism) that there was some truth in Mandeville's moral philosophy introduces a paragraph which draws a distinction between natural and moral philosophy. A writer on natural philosophy, says Smith, is like a traveller who talks of a distant country and 'may impose upon our credulity the most groundless and absurd fictions as the most certain matters of fact'. But a writer on moral philosophy discusses things familiar to us all and so is like one who talks of events in our own parish; although he can deceive us (as Mandeville did), his tales must 'bear some resemblance to the truth, and must even have a considerable mixture of truth in them'. As an example of how far we can be taken in by a system of natural philosophy, Smith refers to Descartes's vortices, which he had discussed at length in his History of Astronomy. But it is worth noting that, despite his account of science in the Astronomy, he writes here in TMS as if a system of natural philosophy *could* be true. He says:

> A system of natural philosophy [such as that of Descartes] may appear very plausible, and be for a long time very generally received in the world, and yet have no foundation in nature, nor any sort of resemblance to the truth.

This seems to imply that other systems of natural philosophy *can* have a foundation in nature and resemble the truth.

I think that Smith could, and should, have distinguished more sharply between theories of the physical world and theories about man. In physical science the postulated causes of phenomena are *unobservable* entities or forces, hypothetical 'machines', as Smith calls them. Crystalline spheres, vortices, gravitational force – all are unobservable and so must be treated by Smith as 'inventions' of the imagination. But in moral philosophy and social science the postulated causes of phenomena need not be unobservable, and are not such in Smith's own theories. Sympathy may or may not have the particular causal function that TMS attributes to it; in itself, however, it is no hypothetical entity but an observable phenomenon. Similarly, the division of labour, or freedom of trade, may or may not have quite the causal functions attributed to them by WN; in themselves, however, they are observable phenomena.

But what about more metaphysical elements in Smith's ethics and economics? What about his suggestion in WN that (observable) market prices 'gravitate' towards the (unobservable) 'natural' price? What about the 'invisible hand' that is supposed to play a causal role in producing general benefit from self-interested actions? What about the argument of TMS (III.5) that the general rules of morality are properly regarded as laws of God?

I think Smith could, and should, agree that these concepts have a status like that of the imagined 'machines' in scientific theories. He does not in fact need them for his causal explanations. To say that market prices 'gravitate towards' the natural price is a metaphor. It does not mean that the hypothetical natural price exercises an actual force; it is simply a way of describing the pattern of price movements. Similarly, the 'invisible hand' is not to be understood literally as the hand of God. This can be seen from the way in which Smith first used the expression in the History of Astronomy (III.2) when talking of early religious ideas. Polytheists, he wrote, attribute irregular events to the agency of the gods, but not regular events; 'nor was the invisible hand of Jupiter ever apprehended to be employed in those matters' (i.e. in the regular events). When Smith talks, in TMS and WN, of self-interested men being led by an invisible hand to benefit a wider circle, he means simply that this is the natural effect, though unintended by the agents. You do not necessarily have to think that the effect was intended by a divine agent. So, too, you do not necessarily have to interpret moral rules, derived inductively from experience, as expressing the commands of God; but if you accept theism, it is legitimate to interpret them in that way.

This seems to imply that theology for Smith was not strictly true but was hypothetical, a construction of the imagination. What now happens to my initial contention that Smith, unlike Hume, accepted natural religion? I do not suppose that Smith recognized the implication which I have described, but it seems to me that if he had done so, he need not have been unduly disturbed. For the conclusion which I have attributed to him gives theology the same status as natural science – not something more elevated, as the unenlightened claimed, nor something less, as the radical Enlightenment argued. For a member of the moderate Enlightenment, what could be better than to put natural religion on the same plane as natural science?

REFERENCES AND NOTES

References to Smith's books, essays, and manuscripts follow the form used in the Glasgow edition of The Works and Correspondence of Adam Smith. The title of a work, often abbreviated to initials, is followed by numerals (and letters) denoting (as relevant) Part, Book, or Volume, section, chapter, sub-section, and paragraph.

1 Ernest C. Mossner, 'Hume and the Legacy of the *Dialogues*', in *David Hume*, ed. by G. P. Morice (Edinburgh, 1977), p. 3.
2 D. D. Raphael, 'Adam Smith and "the infection of David Hume's society" ', *Journal of the History of Ideas*, xxx (1969); reprinted, with revision, as Appendix II of Adam Smith, *The Theory of Moral Sentiments*, ed. by D. D. Raphael and A. L. Macfie (Oxford, 1976).

5

HUME AND THE SCOTTISH ENLIGHTENMENT

Duncan Forbes

The term 'Scottish Enlightenment' annoys some Scottish historians,[1] because to them it seems to suggest that a state of unenlightenment prevailed in Scotland before the mid-eighteenth century, but 'enlightenment' when used by the historian of ideas is simply a technical term to describe certain aspects of eighteenth-century thought. The trouble is in defining precisely what aspects of eighteenth-century thought it is meant to describe. Different people study the eighteenth-century Scottish thinkers for different reasons; for Professor Pocock, for example, they belong to the tradition of 'civic humanism' and constitute one of his Machiavellian moments. But they are more widely known nowadays for the modernity and sophistication of their social theory.

In eighteenth-century Scotland, say from the failure of the '45 to the mid 1770s or 1780s, there was a conjunction of circumstances: politics recessive; economic factors, prospects, opportunities, growth dominant, that forced on the attention of thinkers peculiarly well-fitted and well poised to observe it in a detached and clinical and critical sort of way, the fact of modern commercial civilization, in all its aspects, good and bad. They were mostly university professors, very selfconsciously dedicated Newtonian 'philosophers' whose job, as Adam Smith defined it, was to do nothing but observe everything, but who also in their various ways were moralists and humanists in the classical mode, especially concerned with the social context of morality, peculiarly sensitive to the fact of man's sociality, his existence as a social being, and to anything that appeared to threaten or devalue this. You had the phenomena, that for local reasons were especially compelling and striking, and you had this special type of observer.

When, however, one considers Hume in relation to the Scottish Enlightenment, viewed in this way, one is met at first sight by something of a paradox. It would generally be agreed that Hume was the greatest and most original thinker in eighteenth-century Scotland, but it would also be generally agreed that this is not on account of his social theory. Hume's fame in the twentieth century rests on his philosophy, and anything in his writings that is not philosophy in the narrower modern sense tends to be thrown into shadow. Just as one must rescue Adam Smith from the economists if one is to see him whole and in a historical context, so one must rescue Hume from the philosophers – and indeed one must do the same for Kant and no doubt many other victims of the professional philosophers' ahistorical manner of thinking.

One does not, however, have to rescue Hume from the sociologists and historians of social science,[2] for they have for the most part simply by-passed him on the way to more promising things, such as Adam Ferguson's *Essay on the History of Civil Society*, a work incidentally in which Hume, who was a close friend of Ferguson, could see nothing of value.[3] Compared with Ferguson, who is for some sociologists the founding father of their discipline, and Smith, who seems in fact to have been the seminal mind in many of those things in the Scottish Enlightenment that have attracted the attention of modern social theorists and Marxists, and his pupil and continuator John Millar, in whose *Origin of Ranks* one can see the most sophisticated version of a historical materialism or economic interpretation of history before *The German Ideology* of Marx, Hume's social theory appears backward and hesitant. Smith's study of the progress of civilization involved pushing

historical causation further back more consistently than Hume
was prepared to do, undermining the pragmatic individualism
and the play of chance and historical accident, that is so much
more conspicuous in Hume, who, for example, was anxious
to stress the role of accident, together with the rational pur-
posiveness of a creative minority, in the making of the British
constitution. In Smith, Millar and Ferguson, the Legislators
and Founders of States, that one still finds playing their classical
role in Hume, are more determined than determining, and the
Spartan institutions are no sort of 'prodigy', as Hume calls
them, but the typical product of a certain stage in the progress
of society.

It is this sort of thing that one has in mind when one says
that Hume's thinking is less sophisticated, sociologically,
than that of the others. For example, only in his last essay, of
1774, on the *Origin of Government* does one find Hume abandoning the contract as the probable 'historical' (or pre-historical)
origin of government, and presumably under the influence of
the others, saying that government commences more casually
and imperfectly. In general, in Hume's historical thinking,
the spotlight is on the political foreground of historical causation: political institutions and machinery, political parties,
political opinion – to a much greater extent, anyway, than
the others, presumably because Hume was to such a large
extent using history in the service of political moderation.

Again, Hume was untypically unconcerned with the problem
that obsessed so many of his contemporaries: the great problem
of Machiavellian socio-political science, of social corruption,
loss of national *virtù*, the corruption of 'manners', which, e.g.
plays such an important part in Ferguson's *Essay* and is the
grit in the oyster of so much of his social theorizing. Hume
certainly did not take the fact of civilization for granted: it
was a chancy, precarious achievement, but his view of social
progress is, paradoxically perhaps, the most optimistic, the
most unshadowed, of all the leading Scottish social theorists.
He did not see social progress as inevitably accompanied by
social evils like the ever-increasing division of labour, the loss

of community and the sense of community, what came to be called human alienation. Something of this can be seen in the others, and, owing to the reflected glare from the writings of the young Hegel and the young Marx, it is well enough known these days, even, some might say, apt to be exaggerated.

So there are a number of reasons why Hume does not and should not figure so prominently in the chronicles of sociology and political science as Ferguson, Smith, Millar and the others.

But there is a danger of missing worthwhile things. The prospects that might attract historians of social science to Hume have been traditionally blocked by thick hedges of misconception, congealed abridgement, and generalization. The old view of Hume's scepticism as essentially negative and destructive, something to be refuted, cast a long shadow. And so did the stereotype of eighteenth-century *naturrechtlich* thinking as rationalistic, atomistic, uniformitarian, something from which a more concrete, historical, socially realistic way of thinking had to emancipate itself. The natural jurisprudence taught in the Scottish universities, e.g. by Hutcheson, which was just as important in Scottish university education as the Newtonian science that has become a commonplace of Hume exegesis, was not like that at all. The emphasis was empirical and social. This natural law – the natural law of Grotius and Pufendorf and their followers – was in fact the matrix of the social theory of the Scottish Enlightenment, and seen in this context, Hume's idea of justice is an extension of the social-empirical mode of Hutcheson and the authors recommended by Hutcheson, to meet the needs of an age increasingly secular, and ever more conscious of society as a system of mutual interdependence. Hume agreed that politics should have a foundation in a natural law grounded on the observed facts of human nature, i.e. man's social constitution. But for Hume, a proper empirical foundation meant excluding the 'religious hypothesis', together with piety, as an allegedly fundamental fact of human nature. Piety was the product of men in society, and so were the rules without which any human society is impossible. So here surely is something new in the history of social theory: an exclusively sociological idea of society. By the use of this adjective I simply mean that whereas one can presumably talk of a Kantian kingdom of ends, an idea of pure reason, or the Stoic cosmopolis as a 'society', a 'society' of rational men as such, it would be perverse to talk of 'sociology' in such contexts. For Hume, society is one-dimensional, and outside that any bonds or intercourse between men are inconceivable: an absolute state of nature would be absolutely atomistic, solipsistic. Hume has no need for the 'mere' hypothesis of social bonds, obligation and justice prior to the rules men make for their own convenience in the earthly societies we know or can imaginatively reconstruct or assume to have existed in the absence of written records.[4]

This attempt to give natural law a proper empirical foundation in the observed principles of human nature, the operative word being 'proper', can be seen as an example of the modernization and need to adapt to changing circumstances that eighteenth-century Scotsmen, especially of Hume's class, would be peculiarly sensitive to. Men like Kames, the most influential and active of the improving lairds and a kinsman and close friend of Hume at the time of the publication of the *Treatise*, were acutely conscious of Scotland's backwardness. It is in this light that the backward-looking, inward-looking, increasingly reactionary 'Tory' Hume of the traditional interpretation, no less than the more recent and sophisticated version of Hume as country gentleman, subscriber to Bolingbroke's 'politics of nostalgia', suspicious of the men of finance and commercial civilization generally, seems so improbable, though one can gather evidence to support these interpretations. Hume's thought is not seamless, as those who have tried to view it synoptically know to their cost.

Views of Hume's politics have been too circumscribed. The Tory view, in whatever guise, is too narrow, and one suspects that it is an English view, the view of those who do not mentally cross the Tweed when they study and write about Hume, and still think of him as an Englishman, even if they do not, though many have done, actually describe him as one. Hume was a forward-looking, outward-looking Scotsman, and his science of politics was an education for contemporaries in the realities of modern European politics and the meaning of political civilization, breaking down the parochial prejudices, especially of Whiggism, which made an intellectually respectable theory of political obligation and science of politics impossible.

So powerful were these prejudices that one can find examples in Hume himself, for example, when he talks of French 'slavery'. In the light of Hume's philosophical or scientific politics such things appear like rust on shining metal. Nor in spite of all his polishing and revising and correcting did he ever get rid of them all. Perhaps he thought it expedient to make some use of the fashionable rhetoric, perhaps he was just inconsistent, but the corrections in the successive editions of the *Essays* and *History* suggest a conscious effort to rid himself of these powerful stereotypes; they show one not merely the stylist and the scholar who has learnt more and changed his mind, but also the 'philosopher', whose task is to observe in ice-cold detachment, critically watching the 'man', who participates, 'mixing and bustling with men'[5] in society.

In fact one must be careful how one interprets Hume's well-known and much-loved maxim, which Mossner, for example, placed on the title page of his biography: 'Be a philosopher, but amidst all your philosophy, be still a man'. Viewed technically and narrowly, this refers to those aspects of Hume's philosophy that represent his conscious distancing of his science of man from Cartesianism or for that matter, from extreme scepticism. But most men are very far from being capable of the 'moderate scepticism' that is the essence of Hume's philosophy, and one aspect of that is a disjunction of 'man' and 'philosopher' such as one finds in *La Recherche de la Vérité* of Malebranche, one of the greatest of the Cartesians, a book which Hume himself recommended in one of his earliest letters as one of the best ways into the philosophy of the *Treatise*. In *La Recherche de la Vérité*,[6] which is a *science de l'homme*, that most necessary, but not the most cultivated of all sciences whose subject is *l'esprit de l'homme tout entier* (20), the philosopher is warned to be continuously on guard against those aspects of life in society that breed illusion and error. Men as creatures of sense and bodily need are dependent on one another and to this end are tightly knit together in a *union sensible* (378), i.e. an interdependence in the things that concern bodily self-preservation, not by rational benevolence, *une charité fondée sur la raison*, which is too weak a principle for the purpose, but by a *disposition du cerveau* to imitate those with whom they converse and enter into their sentiments and passions, that is, by *liens naturels, qui subsistassent au défaut de la charité et qui interessassent l'amour propre* (321). For this reason, men of strong imaginations, *imaginations fortes*, who are ordinarily not seekers after truth (330), have a powerful influence over others, even when they are not in positions of authority. Not even the wisest of men can altogether escape *la communication contagieuse de l'imagination* (335) – *les hommes mêmes les plus sages se conduisent plutot par l'imagination des autres, c'est-a-dire par l'opinion et par la costume, que par les regles de la raison* (373) – but the philosopher, unlike most men, is aware of this as a weakness to be corrected (180, 312, 340). He knows that the search for truth means consciously dividing oneself in two: the man *qua* philosopher who knows clearly and distinctly, for example, as all men do in the silence of their senses and passions, that virtue is to be preferred to wealth, ever watchful and critical of the man of sense, the conforming animal, prone to social contagion, who pursues wealth *pour obtenir dans l'esprit des autres une place honorable* (322), because he sees that wealth is what everyone esteems (489–90).

The same sort of dichotomy of 'philosopher' seeking truth and 'man' active in society is seen in Adam Smith's *Theory of Moral Sentiments*, in so far as the detached observer sees that the 'race for wealth, honours and preferments' is a deception practised by nature on men, by means of their passions, because it is necessary for the preservation and welfare of the species. There are striking affinities, in fact, between *La Recherche de la Vérité* and Smith's teaching, which my quotations from the former will have suggested to those who know the latter not simply from the *Wealth of Nations*.

Seen in this light, a phrase Hume used in a letter of March 1763 anent the mistakes that he was correcting in his *History* that had 'chiefly proceeded from the plaguy Prejudices of Whiggism' (*Letters*, I, 379) has more or less conscious overtones of what we would call social psychology, that the 'Tory' as opposed to 'philosophical' approach to Hume is certain to miss. It may be a far cry to Malebranche, but certainly social contagion is a very prominent feature of Hume's science of politics. Perhaps this will be thought to be making too much of what may be regarded in this letter as simply a term of abuse, in which case one would need to know whether Hume was given to using 'plaguy' as such. I get the impression that he does not use empty terms of abuse in his letters. But even if 'plaguy' is there merely for emphasis, the emphasis may be on 'prejudices' rather than 'Whiggism': they are prejudices which Hume is confessing had infected his interpretation of English history. *Qua* 'philosopher', above party, he is distancing himself from the 'man', and the emphasis is on 'prejudices', *la communication contagieuse de l'imagination*.

Be that as it may, *qua* philosopher Hume set himself against the chauvinism and limitation of outlook of vulgar Whig prejudices – the 'matchless constitution' and 'despotism begins at Calais' syndrome. It is a leitmotif of all his political, social and historical thought, from the *Treatise*, in which the theory of political obligation expounded in Book III is such that it can accommodate the absolute monarchies of the continent, as Locke's and the 'fashionable system' of contract, could not; to the *Essays*, in which one can make out the outlines of a science of comparative politics, weighing the advantages and disadvantages of the British constitution against the republics and monarchies of modern Europe; and to the History, in so far as its standpoint is not Anglocentric, but Europocentric.

Political civilization, Hume, in effect, told his insular compatriots, was not a birthright of ancient or Germanic freedom which the English alone had managed to maintain, and which was lost in the absolute monarchies, since the essence of it is the liberty and security of the individual under the rule of law. The English prided themselves on their government being a government of laws, not men, but for all practical purposes this was the mark of what Hume called the 'civilized monarchies' of the continent. They too were governments of laws, not men, enjoying the liberty that in Hume's political philosophy is the end of government as such, and which is epitomized in the word 'regular': regular liberty, regular monarchy. No doubt the European civilized monarchies were inferior in political civilization, but there was no qualitative difference between the two types of government.

The fundamental sort of liberty that matters is the end-product of the progress of civilization; the ability to grasp the idea of a general rule is a late development in the history of man and presupposes a very high level of civilization, as Hume says in the essay *Of the Rise and Progress of the Arts and Sciences*, and also the growth of commerce and manufactures and a middling rank of men that was largely absent in the states of classical antiquity, who 'covet' equal laws, and for whom regularity of government, regularity of expectation and security are essential.

Liberty in this sense was a modern European achievement. The progress of political civilization was a European theme. To those who argued or took it for granted that you could not have liberty in the fundamental sense of security and the rule of law without liberty in the sense of a parliament representing the nation etc., Hume pointed out these facts and this historical development. Comparative politics showed that liberty, in the sense of the rule of law, was a property both of what were called the 'free' and what were called the 'absolute' or 'despotic' governments of modern Europe.

The English political system did represent a kind of political perfection: a degree of regularity such as the world had never seen before was necessitated by the type of government in which the republican element was powerful, but not all-in-all, so that the monarch could be allowed no discretionary powers. In that it was unique: the 'most perfect system of liberty'. On the continent, not only the absolute monarchies, but the governments of the republics had at their disposal, and were able to exercise, considerable discretionary powers, for reasons explained by Hume in his essay on the liberty of the press. That was one reason why the 'most perfect system of liberty' was not the 'best system of government', to use Hume's own terms: no government hitherto known in the world had managed to function with so little discretionary power as that of modern Britain. There was an element of danger therefore in its very perfection and uniqueness, and moreover the mixed monarchical-republican government of Britain which went along with this unique degree of liberty had certain necessary disadvantages without which it could not function as such: for example, a system of adversary politics, that is a court and country party whose normal functioning had been disturbed by the Whig-Tory division of parties, which was a historical contingency caused by the disputed succession to the throne; a system of parliamentary dependence, attacked by the opposition as corruption, and so on.

England was thus politically ultra-civilized to a dangerous degree. The absolute monarchies of Europe were less advanced in political civilization, but they were catching up fast, and their disadvantages, for example, the French system of taxation, were remediable. In Britain, on the other hand, liberty was such that it was difficult to remedy its abuses without endangering its very existence. The national debt, for example, was a much more fatal disease in a free than in an absolute government. Considerations of this sort lie behind the notorious remarks in Hume's letters in the late 1760s and early 1770s about the English having enough liberty already and perhaps too much.

A comparative politics made possible by the breaking down of parochial vulgar Whiggism was at the same time a lesson in political moderation, not only in domestic politics, but in foreign politics too, in so far as the anti-French chauvinism which was so prevalent and which Hume detested, was self-defeating in commerce and war.

It is worth looking more closely at Hume's concept of regularity as the distinguishing mark of modern governments, for it does not seem to have attracted the attention of historians of political science as much as it deserves. The civilized absolute monarchy was an especially remarkable phenomenon and a sign of an advanced state of civilization because as Hume said in the essay on *The Progress of the Arts and Sciences*, 'monarchy when absolute contains even something repugnant to law'. The civilized or regular monarchy was something new in political experience; it makes nonsense of the cyclical view of civilization that one finds in a well known passage in the *History*. It means that in the ancient world there was no true knowledge of liberty, and in fact Hume says as much. It means that modern governments of all sorts are more highly civilized than any in classical antiquity.

In the opening paragraphs of the essay on *Civil Liberty*, Hume makes a point of being struck by the fact that political science is in its infancy because most of what we have is out of date. For one thing, economic science and the state's concern with economic matters is modern; 'there scarcely is any ancient writer on politics who has made mention of it. Even the Italians have kept a profound silence with regard to it . . .' But economic science apart, Machiavelli's reasonings on politics, he says, have been found extremely defective, 'especially upon monarchical government.' Because he 'lived in too early an age of the world, to be a good judge of political truth', he did not understand the role of ministers in the state. He thought that if the king relied on many, he would not know whose advice to take, if he relied on the capacity of a single minister, he would almost certainly be dispossessed by him. This is the example of Machiavelli's erroneous reasoning that Hume singled out, and he has been criticized for doing so. But Hume's criticism of Machiavelli should be seen in connection with his notion of regular monarchy: the point he is making is that a prime minister like Fleury who 'though ever so vicious could not, while in his senses, entertain the least hopes of dispossessing the Bourbons', is a characteristic feature of civilized monarchy. Civilized monarchy is a new phenomenon in politics and one which Machiavelli did not know, which is why Machiavelli's political science is mostly out of date, in spite of the fact that Machiavelli was a 'great genius.' This would have been great heresy for all those eighteenth-century political thinkers for whom Machiavelli's concern with the moral health and corruption of states was of central importance and relevance. As against this, Hume was centrally concerned with something that Machiavelli had no knowledge of, viz: the 'civilized', 'regular' monarchy. This is another example of what is forward-looking in Hume's science of politics.

The civilized absolute monarchies were not as regular as free governments. In the essay on the *Science of Politics* Hume says that it is one of the 'great inconveniences' of all absolute governments that they 'must very much depend on the administration', whereas the checks and controls in a republican and free government make it in the interest of even bad men to act for the public good. This is the intention of such governments, and this is their effect when properly modelled. Hume then goes on to say that politics can be a science in so far as the action of rulers or the governing part of the state is predetermined by the laws and form of the constitution.[7]

Elsewhere (*Rise and Progress of the Arts and Sciences*) Hume says that whereas, in a despotic government, there is a 'want of laws' and full delegation of powers to every petty magistrate, the latter being unrestrained 'by any methods, forms, or laws', as in Turkey, 'in a civilized monarchy the prince alone is unrestrained in the exercise of his authority', but 'every minister or magistrate, however eminent, must submit to the general laws which govern the whole society, and must exert the authority delegated to him after the manner which is prescribed.' And in the essay on *Civil Liberty*, he says that 'almost all the princes of Europe are at present governed by their ministers'.[8]

In fact, the prime feature of civilized government is that the state runs itself and is not 'wholly sustained by the abilities of the sovereign' (*History I*, 186).[9] In the *History*, Hume says that the kingdom of Scotland in the fifteenth century 'had not yet attained that state which distinguishes a civilized monarchy, and which enables the government by the force of its laws and institutions alone, without any extraordinary capacity in the sovereign to maintain itself in order and tranquility' (*History IV*, 91–2). And the 'office of a prime minister', it seems, is a distinguishing mark of all 'regular monarchies' (*id*, III, 23). Surely it is not too fanciful in the light of such remarks to see in Hume's idea of regular monarchy a remote ancestor, in a general sort of way, of Max Weber's essentially bureaucratic modern state? As we have seen, the personality of the ruler hardly matters, the kings are governed by their ministers who in turn must keep to the rules and forms, as in Hegel whose *Philosophy of Right*, properly understood, is a much less remote ancestor of Weber's bureaucratic state, and where the constitutional monarch merely dots the i's and sovereignty is the normally unnoticed functioning of the whole.

Montesquieu does not seem to have such a clear and distinct idea of regularity as such as the distinguishing mark of the modern state. He insists that political liberty depends on the citizens' feeling of security, and especially on the goodness or badness of the criminal laws, and says that this is a question of time and a long development. His distinction between monarchy and republic in fact implies a progress in civilization and law, provided one forgets or treats as recessive the Machiavellian moment in his thought, i.e. the idea of monarchical 'honour' as a degree of corruption of republican 'virtue'. But the latter, i.e. selfless *amor patriae* was possible only in the small, economically primitive republics of antiquity and is out of place in large, socially unequal and complex modern monarchies where political liberty or the rule of law is guaranteed by the separation of executive and judicial powers and supported by the *corps intermédiaires*.

But 'modern' in Montesquieu is contrasted with Greek and Roman, not medieval. It includes, and some interpreters would say centres on and looks back to 'medieval'. In any case, even if one plays down the feudal seigneurial side of Montesquieu, his emphasis is on social and structural heterogeneity as the guarantee of liberty, or, as in two recent American authors, on commerce and the necessary implications of commerce[10] rather than the regularity, as such, of the modern state. And ministers, in *De L'Esprit des Lois*, means men like Richelieu and Louvois, who are the villains of the drama of the centralization of power.

The contrast present to Hume is that between modern regular government and medieval irregular government, where the personality of the king was all-important and respect for the rule of law, as such, weak or non-existent. In such circumstances men who would have made excellent kings in a modern monarchy were bad kings. Thus Henry III, Hume says in the *History* (III, 350), would have been a 'proper pageant of state in a regular monarchy, where his ministers could have conducted all affairs in his name and by his authority; but too feeble in those disorderly times to sway a sceptre, whose weight depended entirely on the firmness and dexterity of the hand which held it.'[11] This aspect of the progress of civilization is not to be found in Montesquieu.

It may seem to be rather stretching a point to talk of a science of comparative politics in Hume. But it is not so much the weight of the contents that matters. Hume's essays and *History* are packed with thought, but he does not get down to the detail of the laws and institutions of the republics and civilized monarchies of Europe, and so far as the latter are concerned, it seems to be France that he has in his sights most of the time. What matters is not the deployment of information, but the breaking down of the insular prejudices that made a comparative science of politics impossible. This allowed Hume to balance the pros and cons of the free and absolute governments of his day in a manner that, however rudimentary, is that of comparative politics, and to grasp the central feature of the modern state in the broadest possible perspective.

But if one persists in thinking of Hume's *History* and politics as 'Tory', and looks at them through the keyhole of English party politics exclusively, one is likely to miss these dimensions. See Hume in the context of the Scottish Enlightenment and its concern with modernity and the progress of society as it concerns Europe as a whole; and one is in a better position to be able to appreciate his contribution to social and political science.

NOTES

¹ See, for example, Gordon Donaldson, *Scotland: the shaping of a nation*, p. 245.

² With the notable exception of Comte, who in the *System of Positive Polity* saluted Hume as 'the founder of the law of the Temporal or Active Evolution', meaning the declension of the military and rise and ultimate supremacy of the industrial regime. (See *System of Positive Polity*, Vol. III (London, 1876), p. 51.)

³ For this see Hume's *Letters*, ed. J. Y. T. Greig, Volume II (Oxford, 1932), pp. 11–12, 133. Writing in February 1766 to Hugh Blair, Hume says that he does not think Ferguson's *Essay on the History of Civil Society* is fit to be given to the public, 'neither on account of the style nor the reasoning; the form nor the matter'. He begs Blair and Robertson to read the ms again with more severity, because publication may damage Ferguson's reputation and that of his class (in the university). In April 1767 he writes that he is pleased with the success of the book on account of his 'sincere friendship for the author', but re-reading does not make him alter his original judgment, 'to his mortification and sorrow'. 'We shall see, by the Duration of its Fame, whether or not I am mistaken.' It is perhaps relevant in this context to notice that Hume then goes on to damn another sociologically epoch making book with rather faint praise. *L'Esprit des Lois* has considerably sunk in vogue and will probably sink further, but will probably never be totally neglected. It has 'considerable merit'.

⁴ This is a long and complex story which I have written about elsewhere and summarized in a lecture for the Hume Conference

in Edinburgh in August 1976. See *Hume, Bicentenary Papers* (Edinburgh U.P., 1977).

[5] This is not a Humean phrase but comes from Sir Walter Scott.

[6] The references are to *Oeuvres Complètes de Malebranche*, Tome 1 (Paris, 1972).

[7] One of the disadvantages of the English constitution is the need for a system of dependence and crown patronage and this is at the discretion of the monarch, so that in this important instance, his personality and the strength or weakness of his character does matter.

[8] Contrast the anonymous writer in the *Political Register* quoted by John Brewer. 'Absolute monarchs choose their ministers as they govern their kingdoms; that is for themselves and their own pleasure: but the Kings of England reign for their people.' *Party Ideology and Popular Politics at the Accession of George III*, 119.

[9] The references to Hume's *History of England* are to the edition of 1808–10 (London) in ten volumes.

[10] See T. Pangle. *Montesquieu's Philosophy of Liberalism*, and M. Hulliung, *Montesquieu and the Old Regime*.

[11] Henry VI in my *Hume's Philosophical Politics* in this context is a mistake. It should be Henry III. This has been corrected in the second impression of 1978.

E

6

CONDORCET: POLITICS AND REASON

Ian White

From the time of its clearest origins with Pascal, the theory of probabilities seemed to offer means by which the study of human affairs might be reduced to the same kind of mathematical discipline that was already being achieved in the study of nature. Condorcet is to a great extent merely representative of the philosophers of the seventeenth and eighteenth centuries who were led on by the prospect of developing moral and political sciences on the pattern of the natural sciences, specifically physics. The development of economics and the social sciences, from the eighteenth century onwards, may be said in part to have fulfilled and in a manner to have perpetuated these ambitions. In so far as the new sciences have been susceptible of mathematical treatment, this has not been confined to the calculus of probabilities. But there is a temptation at every stage to ascribe fundamental significance and universal applicability to each latest mathematical device that is strikingly useful or illuminating on its first introduction. It is the theory of games that enjoys this position at present, and shapes the common contemporary conception of the very same problems that preoccupied Condorcet.

But from the very start, the development of probability theory was motivated and shaped by an interest in its immediate application to the problems of human life. Pascal proposed an astonishing fusion of ideas from very different sources when he saw the deepest questions of religion and morality in terms of the arithmetic of gambling. Leibniz became a pioneer in the philosophical and mathematical foundations of probability theory, as a result of his early interest in jurisprudence, and the problems of analysis and proof in law.

There are two aspects of probability theory that made it seem very promising in this way. The first is the fact that a theory of gambling is a theory about how to make decisions, because it considers not only the odds, but the values of the stakes and the prizes: it calculates, not only the likelihood of a certain outcome, but its degree of desirability, and it evaluates a risk or an advantageous chance as the product of these two magnitudes. In the subsequent development of economics, the problem of calculating utilities, the measure of goodness or badness, has come to be investigated independently of the question of likelihood with which it was originally associated. The second attractive aspect of probability theory was that the calculus of chances seemed to correspond in structure to the arithmetic of combinations and permutations. To work out, for example, the chance of getting two sixes, or the chance of getting a total score of seven, when tossing two dice together, we have to consider the number of ways that situation can come about, as against the number of all possible different outcomes. That encourages us to think that the probability of a fact would be given by breaking it down into its simplest constituents, analysing it as a conjunction or disjunction of atomic facts, and then comparing the number of equally possible cases it covers with the number of all equally possible cases. Just as Pascal gave prominence to the idea of the wager, so on the other hand Leibniz developed the idea of subjecting propositions to an atomistic logical analysis. From the clearer understanding of the issues that he thought such an analysis could give, as well as from the application of a new logic of probability to the results of it, Leibniz hoped to have a method for resolving controversies and disputes. Men of science and men of law could turn to their pencils and paper, and say 'Let us calculate!'

Condorcet was profoundly influenced both by Pascal and by Leibniz in his most important work, which makes him more than just a representative of eighteenth-century Enlightenment, and more than just a fore-runner of Comte and nineteenth-century sociology.

In 1785, Condorcet published under the auspices of the French Academy, his *Essay on the application of analysis to the probability of decisions taken by a majority of votes*, the first, and still the greatest, major work in the theory of collective decisions. As the title indicates, he approached this subject from the standpoint of an existing branch of the theory of probability. The same subject has been approached again, in this century, from the quite different standpoint of welfare economics, and more recently, from the standpoint of the theory of games. Some of Condorcet's points have been rediscovered, or set in a new light. The points at which he arrived after long inquiry, are often the points from which a modern investigation sets out. Condorcet's theory has always seemed somehow conceptually unsatisfactory, puzzling and even bizarre; and yet he is much closer, or so it seems to me, to an adequate account of the subject, than any modern investigators.

A modern analysis of collective choice takes the following form. There are a number of alternative courses of action, any one of which might be taken by or for a collection of persons. The wishes and interests of these persons are diverse; the various courses of action satisfy the various persons to a greater or lesser extent; and this may be expressed by constructing, for each person, an order of preference among the options. The problem is then to find a way of combining the various orders of preference in a single, collective, order of preference. There are two conceptions of this. The first is the conception of a welfare judgment, which purports to be a judgment of fact (made by officials deputized to make it and act on it) as to which of the alternative courses of action would be most in the interests, or most in accordance with the wishes, of most people. The second may be called the market conception. On this view, the procedure of collective decision is thought of as a sort of game, in which, with the help of bargaining and other kinds of tactic, individuals deploy their voting power, partly competitively, partly collaboratively, to secure their various interests as far as they can. Such a procedure is thought to be justified by the fact that its effective outcome accords with the result of a welfare judgment, without requiring the existence of officials designing social policy.

The essential problem over welfare judgments, is what rule to fix for passing from an aggregate of diverse individual orders of preference to a single collective order. Various rules seem plausible in various situations, but it has been shown, by Kenneth J. Arrow, that no rule will satisfy certain intuitively plausible requirements, for all possible combinations of individual orders of preference. The difficulty here is by no means confined to welfare theory; it is a general difficulty for all theories of collective choice: Given individual choices, by what rule or on what principle, do we derive a collective choice? The nature of the difficulty may be brought out by considering the familiar problem of an election of one out of a number of candidates. Different electoral systems will lead to different results. Which most truly represents the collective view? Suppose, for example, that there are three candidates, *A*, *B*, and *C*, and nine voters. On a single-vote simple majority system, 4 vote for *A*, 3 for *B*, and 2 for *C*. A has most votes, but not an over-all majority, and he may owe his precedence only to the division of the opposition to him between his rivals. If *C* were not standing, *B* might defeat him. Borda, in a paper read to the French Academy some years before Condorcet's *Essay*, introduced the device from which people still hope to derive a resolution of the problem: that is, to consider the second and third preferences of the voters. Borda then proposed a system of points. For each first preference he gets, let a candidate receive 3 points, for each second preference 2, and for each third preference 1. That candidate wins who receives the highest total of points. This candidate's claim may be supported by various kinds of reasoning, which are applicable to welfare judgments in general. Borda's points may be taken to represent the amount of satisfaction which the selection of each candidate would give to each voter: the totals represent the total amounts of satisfaction of all the voters together. This argument assumes that we can give a cardinal, interpersonal, and aggregative measure of utilities: that we can say that a certain option will give twice or three times as much satisfaction to a given voter as another option, that a certain option will give the same amount of satisfaction to this voter as it gives to another voter, or twice as much, or three times as much, and that the satisfaction which an option will give to this voter is equal to, or twice as much as, or half as much as, the satisfaction which it gives to these two or three voters together. The intelligibility of all this has been questioned. But another argument for the same system depends only on a purely ordinal scale of preferences: in statistical theory, Borda's method will give the answer to the question: Which candidate stands on the average highest in the voters' orders of preference? His marks reduce the problem to the mathematics of rank-ordering.[1]

An alternative approach is the one first proposed by Condorcet, for complex reasons of his own, from which however it can be detached: that is, to consider how each of the candidates would fare in a straight contest with each of the others separately. We take the candidates in pairs, *AB*, *BC*, and *CA*, and have a simple majority vote between each pair: if any candidate succeeds in defeating each of the others separately, he is taken to have defeated both (even though in a three-cornered contest he would not get an absolute majority, nor necessarily any majority, over both together). He therefore has a claim to be the one elected. (A convenient way of recording each voter's view on the preferability of the candidates taken in pairs, is simply to ask him for a complete order of preference of the three candidates, and then to analyse the data on the ballot papers. Thus, a voter who puts *ABC* in that order would vote for *A* against *B*, *A* against *C*, and *B* against *C*.)

There are plausible grounds for adopting either of these principles. My present point is that they can yield different results. Suppose 4 voters put the candidates in the order *ABC*, 2 voters put them in the order *BCA*, 1 in the order *BAC*, 1 in the order *CAB*, and 1 in the order *CBA*. Then *A* will receive 19 points, *B* 20 points, and *C* 15 points: so *B* seems to win. But in a straight vote between *A* and *B*, *A* would receive 5 votes, *B* 4 votes, and in a straight vote between *C* and *A*, *A* would receive 5 votes, and *C* 4 votes: so *A* seems to win. The system of pairwise majorities seems plausible, but suppose there are four candidates, *A*, *B*, *C*, and *D*, and seven voters or equal groups of voters, and that three put the order *DABC*, two the order *BACD*, and two the order *CABD*. Then the candidate who would defeat each of the others separately is *A*, whom no voter puts first; and the candidate *D* who gets the greatest number of first preferences, and only one short of an absolute majority, is actually in the position that a majority would prefer each of the others to him in a straight contest, so by Condorcet's principle the majority is for putting him below all the others, as it is for putting *A* above all the others. On the other hand, if we now favour Borda's system, consider this case. Suppose that, with three candidates and nine voters once again, 5 voters put the candidates in the order *ABC*, 3 in the order *BCA*, and 1 in the order *CBA*. Then *A* has an absolute majority of first preferences, and in a straight three-cornered contest he would defeat both the other candidates together. Yet, on Borda's system, *A* receives 19 points, *B* receives 21 points, and *C* receives 14 points. So *B* has the highest average placing. Before we revert to the contrary conclusion that it is majorities that ought to be considered, we have finally to reckon with another sort of case, which Condorcet is chiefly famous for discovering. Suppose that (with three candidates and nine voters once again), 4 voters put *ABC*, 3 put *BCA*, 1 puts *CAB*, and 1 puts *CBA*. Then in a straight vote between *A* and *B*, *A* would defeat *B* by 5 votes to 4; in a straight vote between *B* and *C*, *B* would defeat *C* by 7 to 2; and in a straight vote between *C* and *A*, *C* would defeat

A by 5 to 4. The majorities are cyclical. *B*'s majority over *C* is indeed the biggest, but on the other hand *A* is nearest to getting an over-all majority.

How, given a set of various individual judgments, do we discern the collective judgment that they constitute? The interest of Condorcet's work is that it offers a principle for doing so, and an argument for the principle. Part of the argument is given in another work, the *Essay on the Constitution and Functions of Provincial Assemblies*, published in 1788 on the eve of the summoning of the States General and the ensuing Revolution. In this *Essay* he proposed the establishment of a system of elected regional bodies, and he was at that time opposed to a general assembly for the whole of France, since he had confidence rather in the use of enlightened royal authority, directed by men like the great reforming minister Turgot, his admired and regretted patron and friend. His interest in the principles and practice of majority decision did not result from any commitment to democratic theory, but from a concern for political education and for wise and effective administration.

> What [he asks] do we mean by being elected? Is it not being judged preferable to competitors? Why do we make this judgment depend on the opinion of the majority? It is because we regard a proposition declared true by, say, fifteen persons, as more probable than its contradictory declared true by only ten. So, the one who has really got the will of the majority in an election must be the one whose superiority is most probable, and consequently the one who has been judged by the majority to be superior to each of the others.

Condorcet's idea is that we can decide which candidate ought to be considered as elected, in cases, like those I have raised above, where the answer is not clear, by considering the reason why we submit questions to majority vote at all, indeed why we submit questions for collective decision by a number of persons, rather than having them decided by single individuals. Condorcet's answer is that the whole practice is justified by the fact that the judgment of a greater number of persons is more likely to be correct; and that consequently, when we have to decide which opinion is to be counted as having most support, we must ascertain this by considering which opinion is made most probable by the support it has. If there are two candidates, *A* and *B*, and *A* receives more votes then *B*, then *A* is chosen rather than *B*, not simply by the preponderance of voting strength, but because more people have judged *A* to be preferable to *B* than have judged *B* to be preferable to *A*, and that makes it more probable that *A* is preferable to *B* than that *B* is preferable to *A*. We shall see later how Condorcet applies the same idea to the case of three or more candidates.

Before I examine this argument, I should draw attention to the great difference between Condorcet's approach and that of modern welfare or market theories, in respect of the conception it is based on, of the questions submitted to collective decision. The latter theories cannot serve for a general account of collective decision, since they depend on a limiting assumption about the kind of issue to be decided, and the class of persons admitted to participate in deciding it. That is why they figure entirely in the context of the theory of political democracy: they are concerned with aggregating or reconciling the wishes and interests of all those affected by the decision. But the fact that this is a limitation is evident as soon as we turn to two other sorts of case, which are undeniably species of collective decision, but where it would be both absurd and immoral either to measure utilities or to indulge in the tactical deployment of voting power. The first case is of a board of examiners, jointly engaged in assessing the candidates; the second case is that of a jury or a bench of judges, jointly engaged in arriving at a verdict on the accused, or a judgment between plaintiff and defendant. It cannot simply be because many people are affected by the decision, that many people should participate in making it. Being affected does not generally give one the right to be consulted. A body of persons can be taking a decision about their own joint action, or about the exercise of an authority that they share, which will affect the interests of others who are not members of the body: for example, a parliament legislating, members of a trades union deciding whether or not to go on strike, or the fellows of a college deciding whether or not to admit women. No doubt in these cases they ought to consider the effects of their decisions on other people, as ought a single individual deciding what to do. But this does not mean that they are in any way bound to admit the general public to voting participation in the decision. And in the cases of the board of examiners and of the court of law, they are actually subject to a rule quite contrary to the democratic rule that a man whose interests are affected by a decision has a right to be consulted as to those interests in the making of it. That the candidates or the parties to the case are vitally affected by the decision, so far from constituting reason why they should be admitted to voting participation in the decision, constitutes reason why they should be utterly excluded from it. This is in virtue of the principle at least as deserving of respect as the principles of democracy, that no man should be judge in his own cause.

The kinds of collective decision which modern discussions of the subject disregard, are the kinds on which Condorcet concentrates. In the great *Essay* of 1785, he was primarily concerned with judicial decisions, and his account of the rationale of majority voting is set in the context of a general discussion of the role of judgments of probability in civil and criminal jurisdiction. It will be retorted that this, too, is a limiting assumption; and it is indeed true that his analysis applies only to questions the answers to which can be considered as susceptible of truth and falsehood, or rightness and wrongness, not, perhaps, in the same way as theoretical questions of science, but in the same way as practical questions of morality or law. He thought that political issues ought to be regarded in the same way: but he did not simply assume this view, he elaborated an argument for it.

To return to the argument of Condorcet's that I quoted:

even if we grant for the present that we accept a collective decision rather than an individual decision, and a majority decision rather than a minority one, for the reason that it is more likely to be correct, we may dispute that it follows that what counts as the collective decision, or the majority view, is determined by what decision is most probable in the light of the support for it. For it can be argued that the general justification of a practice need not provide the appropriate rule for detailed decisions made in the course of it. I have in mind a distinction drawn by Professor H. L. A. Hart, in connexion with the justification of punishment.[2] He holds that the grounds for having the institution of punishment at all may be different in nature from the grounds on which we decide what kinds of action to penalize, who is to be liable, and how much punishment to inflict in each case. He argues that the institution is generally justified as a whole on purely utilitarian grounds – the benefit of society or the prevention of harm – but that in deciding who to penalize and how much, we may attend to considerations of just desert. Otherwise we might find ourselves apparently justified, by our utilitarian view of the general aim of punishment, in inflicting unpleasant treatment on individuals who are not at fault, because society will gain some benefit or avoid some harm in consequence of our doing so. Likewise it might be argued that the reason for submitting questions to collective and indeed majority decision is that on the whole they are more likely to be correctly decided in that way than in other ways, but that there may still be particular cases in which what is clearly the collective decision is also clearly not the one that is most probably correct. This argument would have force, if there were some reason why we had to follow a general procedure for decision, and were not allowed to change the procedure in exceptional cases. It might be like this situation: there are circumstances in which it would have been safer to have the rule of driving on the right, and also circumstances in which it is safer to have the rule of driving on the left; the risks arising in the long run from both rules may be compared; but it is clear all along that not having a fixed rule, or having either rule according to circumstances, would be even more unsafe than sticking to the less safe of the two rules.

A radical objection to Condorcet's argument (with many other penetrating criticisms) was offered in a valuable but forgotten *Memoir on Elections by Ballot*, read by a member of the French Institute, P. Cl. F. Daunou, to the class of moral and political sciences in 1803. Condorcet purports to be offering, not just a reason for following a certain course of action, given a certain pattern of individual votes over the alternatives, but a criterion for what counts as the collective judgment. But, insists Daunou, the concept of what, in the light of the individual choices, is most probably the correct choice, is a different concept from the concept of what, in the light of the individual choices, is effectively the object of collective choice. To give reasons for following the collective judgment is not to define what the collective judgment consists in, and to propose other grounds for acting, such as ascertaining what is most probably the right thing to do, is simply to set aside the question of what the collective judgment favours, and to consider another question.

Let me turn now to the premise of Condorcet's argument: that we accept the judgment of the greater number because it is more likely to be true. His great *Essay* of 1785 is a formal analysis of this claim. There was already a branch of probability theory which Condorcet was able to apply to the problem. One of the earliest applications of the calculus of chances was to the assessment of testimony. This was of interest in connexion with religious belief based on miracles and revelation, and in connexion with judicial evidence.

Suppose that there are a number of independent witnesss, who testify on a question to which there is a simple yes-or-no answer. Suppose that we know the degree of reliability of each witness, that is, the probability that he will testify truly rather than falsely, and suppose that our judgment on the question has to be based entirely on the evidence of these witnesses. It is possible to calculate the probability of either answer, on this evidence, by plausible principles. (Condorcet adopted the commonest, or standard, method, though this is by no means the only method, and James Bernoulli had already offered an alternative, which is intuitively more satisfactory in some ways, though it is at odds with the mathematics of the calculus.)

Suppose that all the witnesses have an equal probability of testifying truly, namely v, and an equal probability of testifying falsely, namely e. ($v + e = 1$.) And suppose that the witnesses are all independent in the sense that the fact that one witness has testified a certain way makes no difference to the probability that another witness will testify the same way or the probability that he will testify to the contrary. Now if there are only two witnesses, the probability that they will agree in testifying truly is v^2; the probability that one will testify truly, the other falsely, is $2ve$ (there being two cases, the first testifying truly, the second falsely, and the first testifying falsely, the second truly); the probability that both will agree in testifying falsely is e^2. If we know that the witnesses agree, then only the first and last case are considered. The ratio of the probability that the agreed testimony is true to the probability that it is false is $v^2 : e^2$; so the values of the two probabilities are given by $\dfrac{v^2}{v^2 + e^2}$ and $\dfrac{e^2}{v^2 + e^2}$. A similar calculation can be performed for any number of witnesses, n. If they all agree, the probability that their agreed testimony is true is $\dfrac{v^n}{v^n + e^n}$. Now if v is greater than e, that is, if each witness is more likely to testify truly than falsely, then not only is the probability that the agreed testimony is true greater than the probability that it is false: the probability that it is true is greater than the probability that the testimony of a single witness is true. And as n, the number of witnesses, increases, the probability of the truth of their testimony, given that they agree, also increases, and tends to 1, or certainty.

If there are, say, 10 witnesses, then it is possible for them to disagree, and to be divided in various ways, say 6 against 4.

One can calculate the probability that such a division will occur, and that the 6 rather than the 4 will be the ones that are testifying truly. The ratio between the probability of getting such a division with the majority in favour of the truth, and the probability of getting such a division with the majority in favour of falsehood, yields the probability, given that there is a 6–4 division, that the majority testimony is true. It is actually $\dfrac{v^6e^4}{v^6e^4 + v^4e^6}$, which reduces to $\dfrac{v^2}{v^2 + e^2}$. The probability that a majority of 2 (6 against 4) is testifying truly, is the same as the probability of the truth of a unanimous judgment of two witnesses if only two are available. Generally, if there are $m + n$ witnesses, divided m against n, where m is greater than n, the probability that it is the m rather than the n who are testifying truly is $\dfrac{v^{m-n}}{v^{m-n} + e^{m-n}}$. This means that the probability depends only on the difference between m and n, that is, the margin of majority, not on the sum of m and n, or the total number of witnesses.

More complicated calculations give the probability of truth in the testimony of the majority, given only that it is *at least* a certain size, say at least a simple majority of 1, or at least a two-thirds majority, and so forth. To do this we take account of the various numbers of ways the various combinations of voters, giving various divisions into a majority and a minority, can arise, as well as the probability of so many true testimonies, and so many false testimonies, for each kind of division in question. And generally, the greater the majority, the greater the probability, given that each witness is more likely to testify truly than falsely.

But conversely, if e is greater than v, that is, if the witness is more likely to testify falsely than truly, the multiple or majority testimonies are correspondingly even more improbable than the individual ones.[3]

This manner of arguing can be carried over simply to Condorcet's problem. Instead of independent witnesses, who have a certain individual probability of testifying truly, we have independent judges of the truth or falsehood of a simple proposition, who have a certain individual probability of judging correctly, and on whose judgment we have to rely.

Condorcet derived many novel and interesting results by calculation. They have to be treated with caution. For one thing, unless stated carefully, they can give rise to misapprehension as to their implications. One of Condorcet's famous results is that if we have an assembly with an odd number of voters, deciding by simple majority on a simple yes–no question (when there is bound to be a majority one way or the other), then given only that the members are individually more likely to be right than wrong in their judgment (by however small a margin), then the probability that the majority judgment is correct tends to 1 as the number of voters increases. It might seem that we could ascertain the truth on any question simply by holding a vote in a sufficiently large assembly of minimally qualified people. But this result only gives the probability of truth in the majority judgment in the case where one does not know the actual size of the majority. An increase in the total number of voters only raises the probability of the majority judgment, because of the possibility of having greater and greater majorities. A known majority margin of only 1 gives the same probability as the judgment of a single individual judging alone, whatever the size of the assembly. It is also clear that the assumptions or conditions on which the calculation depends have to be stated carefully. It is assumed either that we are given the individual's probability of judging correctly prior to the voting on this issue, or that we have no reason to assign one probability rather than another to the individual judgment, and assume only that it is over $\frac{1}{2}$. Without these assumptions, the results given would be very paradoxical. For it seems obvious that we should place much more confidence in a decision passed by a majority margin of 15 in a group of 25, that is, by 20 against 5, than in a decision passed by the same majority margin of 15 in a group of 1025, or by 520 against 505. We should naturally place equal confidence, other things being equal, in the judgment of a majority which bore the same ratio to the total number of voters. Condorcet makes clear the source of this paradox. If the majority margin obtained is small in proportion to the total number of voters, that is a reason for thinking that, in respect of that particular question, the probability of truth in each individual judgment was not much above $\frac{1}{2}$: indeed, it will most likely be close to the ratio which the number of votes on the winning side bears to the total number of votes, or $\frac{520}{1025}$. This is much less than $\frac{15}{25}$. So probability of the majority judgment will be reduced accordingly. The probability of an individual's judgment is not constant from one issue to another: all we know at most is the average. Condorcet adds to these considerations the remark that the larger the number of judges it is proposed to have, the more difficult it will be to find enough highly qualified people, so that the average individual probability will probably diminish anyway as the number of judges is increased. On many subjects and for many people, he even believes that prejudice and ignorance will make the average individual probability fall below $\frac{1}{2}$. Members of very numerous assemblies are then more likely to be wrong than right, and the method of majority decision will make things even worse. The larger the majority, the further the probability of its decision will fall below the probability of an individual voter's judgment. Condorcet is thus led to the conclusion that democracy is unsuited for any nation actually in being, though he hopes that the expansion and diffusion of enlightenment will one day make it possible. In the course of the Revolution his views became more democratic, but largely because of the hopes he placed in the scheme of national education that he pioneered. Experience before the Revolution had suggested to him that hopes of liberal reform in legislation and administration would be difficult to reconcile with a popular form of government.

The larger the body that is taking the decisions, the further the average individual probability of judging correctly is likely to fall, even if it continues to remain above $\frac{1}{2}$. On the other hand, the smaller the body, the smaller the majorities it is possible to obtain. The probability of the collective judgment can be increased, either by increasing the size of the required majority, or by raising the level of the individual probabilities. Condorcet favours the latter. In principle, so long as the individuals are merely more likely to judge truly than falsely, we can require a sufficiently large majority (assembling a large enough body for such a majority to occur) to get a probability in the collective decision equal to any that can be obtained by setting up a smaller assembly of more enlightened voters. But here we encounter a difficulty. If we only require a simple majority in an assembly with an odd number of voters, we are certain to get this majority one way or the other. But if we require a higher majority (say a constant margin of at least 10, or a proportional majority, such as two-thirds of the total number of voters) then we may not succeed in obtaining this majority either for or against the proposition at issue. Condorcet calculates for different kinds of special majority not only the probability that a given decision is correct, but also the probability of getting a correct decision, the probability of getting an incorrect decision, and the probability of getting a decision at all. He shows how all these probabilities are affected by greater or lesser probabilities in the individual judgment. Assuming that the individual is more likely to judge truly than falsely, then an increase in the individual probability means not only that there is an increase in the probability of the majority decision, given that the required majority is obtained, but also that there is an increase in the probability of obtaining the required majority. The trouble with an unenlightened popular assembly is not so much that its decisions will be mistaken as that it will fail to make decisions: it will lack the energy and initiative needed for the radical reform of laws and institutions.

On some matters, it is more important to avoid a mistaken decision than to suffer the inconvenience of deferring decision to another time; on other matters, decision is imperative. Sometimes the burden of proof lies on one side of the question, and a mistaken decision is more or less grave according to which way the mistake is made. This holds for trial on a criminal charge, where a high probability is required for conviction (and, according to Condorcet, for any legislation which restricts the natural liberty of man.) This can be secured by requiring a sufficiently large majority, and if this majority is not obtained, the accused person is acquitted, even if he had some lower majority against him. But Condorcet does not share the admiration of some of his contemporaries, such as Beccaria, for the English jury system. In an English jury, unanimity was (and a special majority now is) required both for conviction and for acquittal, and the jurors were pressurized (and are still urged) to reach agreement if possible. Since the jury is composed of unqualified people, Condorcet holds that their individual probabilities are low, even if above $\frac{1}{2}$, and that therefore the probability of their naturally reaching agreement and agreement in favour of the truth is low also; no faith is to be placed in a forced agreement.

Condorcet assesses various other forms of judicial procedure found in the various countries of Europe: for example, elaborate systems of appeal from one tribunal to another. These are clearly intended to give greater certainty in the final decisions: but Condorcet's detailed analysis in terms of the calculus of probabilities seems to suggest that a reasonably sized majority in a numerous court of first instance gives a better chance of obtaining correct judgments than a system of appeals from one small court to another.[4]

In short, Condorcet was far from thinking that there was any magic either in majority decision, or any other procedure of collective judgment.

> Enlightened voters and a simple procedure, [he concludes] are the means to combining the most advantages. Complicated procedures will not make up for the lack of enlightenment in the voters, or will do so only imperfectly, or will even bring with them evils greater than those we wanted to avoid.

Critics have commented unfavourably on the unexciting

nature of this conclusion, after such a complicated analysis: but they would have commented even more unfavourably if Condorcet had come to the contrary conclusion that one *could* make up for the lack of enlightenment in individual judges by mathematical complications in the procedure.

Almost everywhere results will be found in agreement with what the simplest reason would have told us; but it is so easy to obscure reason with sophistry and vain subtleties, that I shall consider myself happy when I have done no more than support a single useful truth with the authority of a mathematical demonstration.

So far, Condorcet may seem to have given a tenable account of the grounds on which we will assess, and possibly accept, the authority of a procedure of collective decision. But the application of the calculus of probabilities to the question depends on an analogy with the case of testimony, in relation to which it was introduced. I accept the judgment of the court as true, or the act of the legislative body as wise, or the decision of the administrative committee as sound, because that judgment, or act, or decision, is all I have to go on. Either I have not looked at the evidence and arguments, or I do not consider myself qualified to assess them, so my judgment as to the probability of the collective decision is indeed based only on the probability I ascribe to the votes of the members of the body that decides. In the same way I might have to rely on combining the testimony of witnesses, when there is no other evidence, and I am not a witness myself.

But what authority does a collective decision have, over one who *did* himself participate in it? If I have already come to my own conclusions, and decided for myself, on the strength of the arguments and by the use of my own judgment, that a proposition has a certain degree of probability, how can I then decide, in the light of the votes both of myself and of others to whose judgment I ascribe a certain probability, that the proposition has a different degree of probability? If I know whether or not another voter agrees with me, then

surely the probability of truth I must ascribe to his judgment
in this instance, is simply the probability I ascribe to the
proposition itself? Condorcet offers an interesting solution to
this problem, both in the *Essay* of 1785 and in a paper, written
in 1792, *On the Nature of Political Powers in a Free Nation:*

> Reason, in accordance with nature, only places one limit
> on individual independence, only adds one social obliga-
> tion to the obligation of private morality: it is the necessity
> and duty of obeying, in respect of those actions which have
> to follow a common rule, not one's own reason, but the
> collective reason of the greater number: I say their reason
> and not their will, for the power of the majority over the
> minority ought not to be arbitrary.

It will be evident how in speaking of 'collective reason' Condorcet proposes a concept both analogous in form to Rousseau's
concept of a 'general will', and different in content. This is
how he puts it in the *Essay*:

> Indeed, every man has the right to conduct himself in
> accordance with his reason; but when he joins a society, he
> consents to subject to the common reason a portion of his
> actions, which ought to be regulated for everyone by the
> same principles; his own reason then prescribes such a
> submission to him, and it is still in accordance with his
> own reason that he acts, even in renouncing the use of it.
> Thus when he submits to a law contrary to his opinion,
> he must say to himself: *It is not now a question of myself alone,
> but of everyone; I ought not therefore to conduct myself according to
> what I believe to be reasonable, but according to what all, in dis-
> counting, like me, their own opinion, ought to regard as being in
> conformity with reason and truth.*

In the paper of 1792 he argues again that the right of the
majority cannot be based on its power, both because the
power, if it had it, would not give it the right, and because
in many cases it does not have the power:

> A majority is rarely strong enough to exclude the idea of

resistance. There is no necessity which can force, say, 100,000 men to obey the will of 150,000.

In this, I think, Condorcet is consciously contradicting Pascal, who observed that we follow the majority, not because they are right, but because they have force. Condorcet published an edition of Pascal's *Pensées*, and owes much to his thought. In Condorcet's own solution to the problem of authority we may, I think, find an echo, in this case affirmative, of Pascal. I may not need to remind you of Pascal's famous, or notorious, reason for believing in God. If I do believe in the God of Christianity, and my belief is true, I shall gain an eternity of life and happiness; if my belief is false, I gain and lose nothing. If I disbelieve in God, and my disbelief is correct, I gain and lose nothing. If my disbelief is mistaken, then I lose an eternity of life and happiness, which I should have gained if in those circumstances I had believed. However low the probability that belief in God is true, the gain it offers if it is true is so great, that any reasonable gambler would choose to believe in God. In this intellectual move, my reason is conquered by reason itself. Not only do I have to regard my belief as a matter of rational *choice*, I have to regard it objectively, and entertain, at the same time, perhaps, as I hold the belief, the possibility of its falsehood, and the consequences of this possibility. My own reason prescribes submission in such a case, and it is still in accordance with my own reason that I act, even in renouncing the use of it.

Condorcet's account of political society, though different in its conclusions, is essentially as anarchistic in its fundamental assumptions as William Godwin's:

In general, since, with a law which has not been voted unanimously, it is a matter of subjecting men to an opinion which is not their own, or to a decision which they believe to be contrary to their interest, a very high probability of the correctness of this decision is the only just and reasonable ground on which one could demand such a submission from them.

According to his theory, I *can* have a sufficient assurance of
the probable correctness of an opinion that I have personally
rejected, if I know that a large majority in an assembly of
enlightened persons is against me, and I *can* have an assurance
of the probable correctness of an opinion I support, sufficient
for compelling those who dissent from it, if, and perhaps
only if, a large majority of enlightened persons is with me.

Now there could be a quite understandable reason why I
should discount my own judgment to some extent, when I
become aware that another disagrees with me, for whose
judgment on the same matter I have some respect. It may be
that I *change* my assessment of the probability of the proposition,
because I am now basing it on a different total set of evidence,
evidence which now includes the fact of disagreement as well
as the grounds on which I originally judged. But can I go so
far as to rely entirely on the collective judgment, to which at
the same time I make a small contribution in the form of my
private judgment?

In that way a general argument of this kind for discounting
my own judgment does not go far enough. In another way
it goes too far: for Condorcet's argument does not apply to
all cases of disagreement, but only to those in which it is
necessary to act in accordance with a rule that applies equally
to me and to others, though he thinks that it is not only my
action but my reason too, that is subjected to a common rule
in such cases.

Now we do indeed think in this way. There seem to be two
ways in which I can have a right to act in a certain manner.
Either the facts of the case give me the right, or my belief
as to the facts gives me that right. If an accused man who is
in fact innocent is convicted after fair trial, by an unfortunate
but unavoidable mistake, then there is a sense in which his
judges have a right to punish him, as well as a sense in which
he has a right not to be punished. Now consider the standard
objection that would be made, to a proposal that I should
take private action against one who is not and will not be
convicted of a crime, but whom I have good private reason,

or so it seems to me, to believe guilty of it. It will be said that if I were to claim the right to act in those circumstances, then I should have to grant others the right to act similarly. 'Very well,' I may say, 'anyone who has equally good grounds, may act likewise.' But it will be retorted that what I will have to grant is not just that anyone who really has equally good grounds may act likewise, but that anyone who thinks he has, as confidently as I think that I have, may act as I do. And even if I am confident of my own judgment, I may not have equal confidence in theirs. Kant introduced into ethics the principle of universalization (which also, like Condorcet's concept of collective reason, owes much to Rousseau's concept of a general will). According to this, I may only act in accordance with a principle which I can consistently will that all moral agents should act on likewise. To ascertain the relevant principle, in an action that I propose, is to find my maxim of action. It need not be what I say it is, or even what I think it is, just as the *ratio decidendi* of a judicial decision need not be given by what the judges say while delivering it. Now in the case in question, it seems that I must universalize, not over all cases that are really like my case, but over all cases that *seem* to the agent involved to be like it. If I am not prepared to do this, then I cannot fairly consider myself entitled to act on my belief. It is not merely that I must refrain from acting: I must withdraw the claim to have the kind of justification for acting that would arise from the facts of the case being what I believe them to be. In short, I must regard my own belief with the same kind of neutral objectivity that I regard the analogous beliefs of others. This principle of universalizing over opinions rather than over facts, lies at the basis of every appeal to a collective decision procedure, or a public resolution of disputes.

It should now be clear how Condorcet's analysis offers to fulfil the hope expressed by Leibniz, that disputes might be calmly resolved by an appeal to calculation. Leibniz had in mind an inquiry which would eliminate disagreement on the issue in question: what Condorcet offers is the means of rational resolution in the cases of irremovable disagreement. Then we agree to derive our probabilities, not directly from the evidence and reasons available to us all, but from the very weight of our various individual judgments.

I have already hinted that the influence of Leibniz on Condorcet's work is to be found in the idea of analysing propositions atomistically. This was the idea that led Condorcet to his characteristic treatment of the problem of elections between numbers of candidates, and generally of voting on questions answerable in more than two ways, yes and no. It is in this respect, it seems to me, that Condorcet's theory contrasts most valuably with all modern treatments of the subject of collective choice.

Condorcet took it for granted that

> . . . any compound proposition is reducible to a system of simple propositions, and that all the opinions that can be formed by deliberating on this [compound] proposition are equal in number to the combinations that can be made of these [simple] propositions and their contradictories. Thus, for example, if the compound proposition being examined is formed of two simple propositions, there are four possible opinions; if it is formed on three simple propositions, there are eight possible opinions, sixteen for four simple propositions, and so on.

An answer to a question proposed for decision may be, not the sole alternative to its negation, but one of a set of contraries. If that answer is in effect the conjunction of two propositions p & q, then there are three other possible answers: p & $\sim q$, $\sim p$ & q, and $\sim p$ & $\sim q$. A simple vote between these views could fail to lead to the correct result, which for Condorcet means the most probable result.

> Let us suppose now that there are thirty-three voters; that the number of votes for the first opinion is 11, 10 for the second, 3 for the third, 9 for the fourth, and that consequently the decision is for the first. It is easy to see that this first opinion is composed of the two propositions p and q,

that the proposition p is adopted also by those who were of the second opinion, and so that this really has 21 votes in its favour, and 12 against it. The proposition q is adopted by all those who were of the first opinion it therefore has 14 votes for it and 19 against: for the same reason, the proposition $\sim p$ has 12 votes for it, and the proposition $\sim q$ has 19. It is therefore the two propositions p and $\sim q$ which ought to prevail, and the second opinion, not the first, which really has the majority.

Condorcet argues that a collective judgment on a complex question must be broken down in this way to collective judgments on simple questions, because, he says, individual judgment on a complex question is really analysable in the same way. He is led to this view both by the influence of Leibnitian philosophy and by the requirements of his probabilistic analysis. For the data on which we base the probability of a collective judgment are the probabilities of individual judgments: and when we say that an individual has a certain probability (on the average) of judging correctly, say $\frac{3}{4}$, that means that there is that probability of his judging correctly on each issue, and (on Condorcet's view of probability) that in the long run he will judge correctly three times out of four. The statement of this probability requires us to individuate the issues, to say what counts as one, two, three, and four occasions of making a judgment. The probability of the individual's judgment on complex issues is lower: for if he has a probability of $\frac{3}{4}$ of judging truly that p, and a probability of $\frac{3}{4}$ of judging truly that q, then he has only a probability of $(\frac{3}{4})^2$ or $\frac{9}{16}$, of judging truly that p & q.

This analysis assumes that the constituent propositions p and q are independent of each other; but it can be extended to the cases where complex propositions can only be analysed into propositions that are not independent. Thus, suppose a jury has to decide by majority vote, as in Scotland, between the three verdicts: guilty, innocent, and not proven. Condorcet describes such a case as follows:

Suppose that there is to be deliberation over the three following opinions:

It is proved that the accused is guilty.

It is proved that he is innocent.

Neither one nor the other is sufficiently proved.

Here we clearly see two systems of mutually contradictory propositions:

FIRST SYSTEM

(A) It is proved that the accused is guilty.

(N) It is not proved that the accused is guilty.

SECOND SYSTEM

(a) It is proved that the accused is innocent.

(n) It is not proved that the accused is innocent.

He then shows that the combination Aa, containing contraries, is absurd; that An gives the opinion 'It is proved that the accused is guilty', Na gives the opinion 'It is proved that the accused is innocent', and that Nn gives the opinion 'It is not proved either that the accused is innocent or that he is guilty'.

If we now suppose that the first opinion has 11 votes in its favour, the second 7, the third 6, we shall have 11 votes for the proposition A and 13 for the proposition N, 7 votes for the proposition a and 17 for the proposition n; it will therefore be the third opinion that ought to have the majority, although counting the votes in the ordinary way it appears to have a minority.

This example is not far from reality. In a Scottish Sheriff Court, in 1957,[5] the foreman of the jury reported a verdict of 'guilty' – it being a Scottish jury of fifteen, deciding by majority. Counsel for the accused requested to be told the voting figures. They turned out to be 6 votes for 'guilty', 5 for 'innocent', and 4 for 'not proven'. The Sheriff then directed the jury to bring in a verdict of 'innocent'. By Condorcet's argument, the verdict should have been 'not proven'. The absence of any clear rule of law or direction to the jury, even so recently, on the manner of forming a majority verdict, when there are three possible verdicts, and the foreman's declaration of 'guilty' in this case, which nearly went unchallenged, shows the contemporary value of Condorcet's work.

Condorcet's derivation of a collective view from the pattern of individual views depends, then, on a logical analysis of the views, extracting their common factors and tracing the logical relations between them. The relation of a given voter to other views than his own, is that of partial assertion or denial. This puts in an even clearer light, the contrast between Condorcet's approach to collective decision and that of recent times. On a modern analysis, the various options are objects, not of partial or total assertion and denial, but of preference, and they are thought of as essentially discrete and unconnected, related only externally by the order of preference. A voter who chooses one option (say the verdict 'guilty') is not thought of as thereby committed to a certain view of the verdicts 'innocent' and 'not proven', but rather as being at liberty to place the other options in an order of desirability as he pleases. Such a notion is clearly inappropriate in theory, and improper in practice, in the case of a criminal verdict.

But in relation to an election from among several candidates, the modern approach appears right. Candidates are primarily individual particulars, unlike propositions or possible states of affairs that have determinate relations of content. Condorcet, however, applies the same analysis to this case as well; and he is able to do so, by treating an *order of preference* as being itself a complex assertion analysable into simple ones. A voter who places three options in an order A, B, C, is thought of as asserting three propositions as to the relative merits of A, B, and C taken in pairs, namely that A is preferable to B, B to C, and A to C. It is conjunctions of such sets of three propositions, not the options A, B, and C, that constitute the complex alternative views. Of course these options may themselves consist in possible states of affairs logically related to each other. But the propositions describing the options are not the propositions voted on. A modern analysis treats the collective formulation of proposals as a species of election between options; Condorcet's analysis treats an election between options as a collective judgment of relative values.

But it is his attempt to atomize the logic of preference that leads him into paradox, or leads him to the discovery of paradox. For a ranking of items in linear order can never be analysed into the assertion or negation of independent simple propositions. This is immediately clear from the fact that the number of ways of ranking n items is $n!$, whereas the number of combinations of assertion and denial of m propositions is 2^m; and for no values[6] of n and m will $n!$ ever be equal to 2^m. So (putting it in terms of information theory) the amount of information contained in any pattern of assertion or denial by voting on simple questions will always either be too little information to determine a ranking of the items, or else contain redundant information and the consequent possibility of contradiction. This is a result analogous to Wittgenstein's disturbing realization that a set of contraries, such as simple colour qualities, or degrees of magnitude, had a kind of mutual incompatibility that could not be explained as analytic in terms of logical atomism.

In the simple two-proposition case there is no difficulty. Providing that one of the four mathematically possible combinations cannot be supported by any individual voter guarantees that the same combination will not result from the combination of the results of majority voting. Providing that no individual juryman will vote both for the proposition 'It is proved that the accused is guilty' and for the proposition 'It is proved that the accused is innocent', ensures that there will not be majorities for both these propositions. But if there are three simple propositions in the analysis, and certain combinations of the three or their negations are forbidden, then there is no guarantee that the majority votes, the consequent collective judgment, will obey the same restrictions as the individual voters. This is what happens if we try to analyse the ranking of three or more opinions. For any ranking of three options, A, B, and C, is a certain pattern of assertion or denial of the three propositions '*A* is above *B*', '*B* is above *C*', '*C* is above *A*', which are logically related, in that it is impossible either to assert all three or to deny all three.[7] But from the fact that individual voters are thus restricted, it does not follow that the majority voting will be. Thus there can be a majority for all three of these propositions: yet there is no rank ordering that corresponds to such a combination. These were the terms in which Condorcet perceived the paradox of cyclical majorities that now bears his name.

Yet even when the majorities are not cyclical, and are therefore not problematic from the modern point of view, there are difficulties which Condorcet's analysis will bring out. Condorcet himself was quite happy to accept that an actual majority for *A* over *B*, and a separate actual majority for *A* over *C*, together constituted a virtual majority for putting *A* first, above both *B* and *C*, despite the fact that *A* would not get an over-all majority against *B* and *C* together. But this is already to reckon with the fact that there can be a majority for each of two propositions *p* and *q*, at the same time as there is a majority for a proposition incompatible with what follows from the conjunction of the first two propositions. Here this third proposition is simply the negation of (*p* & *q*) itself. To show why this is not paradoxical, whereas the phenomenon of cyclical majorities is, would require not the abandonment of Condorcet's manner of analysis, but its elaboration by a clearer account of the logical relations between the propositions involved. That *A* is above *B*, and that *A* is above *C*, are the grounds for saying, and the facts that make it true, that *A* is first. But that *A* is above *B*, and *B* above *C*, are not the grounds for saying, or the facts that make it true, that *A* is above *C*, since this third proposition is on the same level, and is judged directly in the same way.

This is the point at which the logical aspect of Condorcet's theory becomes detachable from the theory of probability, in which it began. When a complex proposition is analysed into its simple constituents, then a collective judgment in its favour is taken as being constituted by separate majority votes for each of the constituent propositions, even though there is not an over-all majority for this complex proposition over its negation. This is the nature of its claim to be considered as the collective view. But it need not be the view that is made most probable by the probability of the individual votes. For suppose that there are three propositions '*A* is better than *B*', '*B* is better than *C*', '*C* is better than *A*', and that we are trying to find, not the entire collective ranking of *A*, *B*, and *C*, but the collective first preference. Putting *A* first is putting *A* above both *B* and *C*, that is, asserting '*A* is better than *B*' and '*A* is better than *C*'. It is independent of the third proposition '*B* is better than *C*', being equally compatible with '*C* is better than *B*'. Now suppose that there are majorities for '*A* is better than *B*', '*B* is better than *C*', and '*A* is better than *C*', and that these give probabilities for the three propositions, p_1, p_2, and p_3 respectively. Each probability is greater than its complementary: $p_1 > 1 - p_1$, $p_2 > 1 - p_2$, and $p_3 > 1 - p_3$. The probability of the complete ranking ABC ($p_1 \times p_2 \times p_3$) is greater than the probability of any other complete ranking. But the virtual majority candidate *A* need not be the one who is most probably the best. For the probability that *A* is best is $p_1 \times p_3$; the probability that *B* is best is $(1 - p_1) \times p_2$; and the probability that *C* is best is $(1 - p_2) \times (1 - p_3)$. Now if *B*'s majority over *C* exceeds *A*'s over *B* and *A*'s over *C* in sufficient ratios, it is possible for $(1 - p_1) \times p_2$ to be greater than $p_1 \times p_3$ and $(1 - p_2) \times (1 - p_3)$. Condorcet commented on this possibility, but argued on logical rather than mathematical grounds for counting *A* as elected none the less. He still rightly appealed to logic, and not to the simple weight of a majority preference.

NOTES AND BIBLIOGRAPHY

[1] See Sir Maurice Kendall, *Rank Correlation Methods* (Fourth Edition, London, 1970) Chapters I, II.
[2] H. L. A. Hart, *Punishment and Responsibility* (Oxford, 1968) p. 10.
[3] Since it is natural to take witnesses who separately have a less

than even chance of being right, as corroborating each other if they agree, thus raising – not lowering – the probability, this is made the basis for a criticism of some of the assumptions of the method of analysis Condorcet adopted. See L. J. Cohen, *The Probable and the Provable* (Oxford, 1977) Chapter 10.

[4] Condorcet was prepared to envisage courts having as many as sixty members, which was not out of keeping with French judicial practice in his day.

[5] Lord Advocate v. Nicholson, *Scots Law Times*, 1958, Sheriff Court reports, p. 17.

[6] Except for three degenerate or limiting cases: (1) when $n = 0$ & $m = 0$, $n! = 2^m = 1$; this is the case of no options and no simple propositions; (2) when $n = 1$ & $m = 0$, $n! = 2^m = 1$; this is the case of one option and no simple propositions; (3) when $n = 2$ & $m = 1$, $n! = 2^m = 2$; this is the only significant case, the case of two options and one simple proposition, that is, the case of a straight majority vote between two alternatives, or on an answer yes or no to a single question.

[7] For simplicity I assume with Condorcet that the options cannot be given an *equal* ranking, so that 'B is above A' is the contradictory, not the contrary, of 'A is above B'.

K. J. Arrow, *Social Choice and Individual Values* (London and New York, 1951).

K. Baker, *Condorcet: Selections* (Indianopolis, 1976).

D. Black, *Theory of Committees and Elections* (Cambridge, 1958).

C. Th. Guilbaud, 'Theories of the General Interest and the Logical Problem of Aggregation', in *Readings in Mathematical Social Science*, ed. Lazarsfeld and Henry (Chicago, 1966).

I. Hacking, *The Development of Probability* (Cambridge, 1975).

7

HUME AS MORALIST: A SOCIAL HISTORIAN'S PERSPECTIVE

Nicholas Phillipson

In this paper I want to discuss David Hume's views about morals, politics and citizenship and the role of philosophers and philosophizing in modern civil society – what I shall call his theory of civic morality.[1] This is a subject which has been neglected by philosophers, presumably because it is of limited philosophical interest. But it is of considerable interest to the historian who wants to understand Hume's development as a philosopher, to locate his thought within a specific, Scottish context and to arrive at some understanding of his surprisingly close and cordial relations with the literary and social world of enlightened Edinburgh. These are large claims and I cannot hope to substantiate them fully in a short paper. My purpose is first, to show that, historically speaking, Hume's preoccupation with civic morality was of central rather than peripheral interest to him as a philosopher and that it helps to explain his otherwise rather puzzling decision to give up philosophizing systematically in the manner of Hobbes and Locke, in favour of polite essay-writing in the manner of Addison and Steele. My second purpose is to suggest that Hume's interest in civic morality, his neo-Addisonian (or perhaps I should say, neo-Ciceronian) mode of philosophizing about it and the nature of his understanding of politics, citizenship and philosophizing in a modern age was, unlike his thought about religion, responsive to and consonant with some of the most important ideological preoccupations of his Scottish contemporaries. It was, I suspect, a shared interest which helped to contain some of the anxieties Hume's notorious religious scepticism caused his contemporaries. Without it, he could not possibly have emerged as one of the leaders of Edinburgh's intellectual life in the age of the Scottish Enlightenment.

Hume's *Treatise* was completed in 1740. It was his first and last exercise in constructing a comprehensive, systematic science of man. For much of the next decade he was to become immersed in essay-writing in the distinctive and fashionable manner of Addison and Steele's *Spectator*. The Addisonian essay was more than a literary genre. It was a vehicle for moralizing about human behaviour in a distinctive way and by Hume's day it had come to hold peculiar ideological associations for Scotsmen. In adopting it, therefore, Hume was allowing himself to be drawn into a distinctive ideological world. Addison and Steele had written, for an audience of men and women of rank, property and position in local and national life, who were preoccupied with questions of social role, personal conduct and private happiness in an increasingly complex, commercially orientated society.[2] How was one to achieve virtue and happiness in the turbulent world of courtiers, fops, pedants and speculators? Addison and Steele answered that it was to be found in the private world of family and close friends, not in the public world of affairs. It was only in a sociable but private world that one could hope to avoid the buffetings of fortune and acquire a sense of moral stability and a sense of ego. And without that, one could not hope to adapt oneself to a rapidly changing world with any ease and self-respect. But that private world was one which had, so to speak, to be constructed. Men and women had to learn to redirect their expectations of life from the public to the private world. They had to learn to detach themselves from society and to be spectators of it as well as actors in it. They even had to learn to cultivate the art, which Adam Smith was later to discuss with such uncanny skill, of seeing themselves as others

F

saw them. A private world, in which men felt at ease with each other and acquired a sense of virtue was one whose inhabitants had learned to defer to each other's tastes and opinions, to value consensus as well as truth in their discussion of ideas and things. In such a world conversation meant learning to discuss one's ideas and observations not simply in order to inform one's friends but to be sure that one's own understanding was as free as possible of affectation, idiosyncracy and personal prejudice. For Addisonian moralizing was based on the assumption that the form a man's actions took depended on the nature of his beliefs and that those beliefs were embodied in a distinctive frame of mind (it was a phrase Addison seems to have invented)[3] which could be regulated by means of self-criticism, detachment and a desire to cultivate private virtues of friendship and family affection. Only thus could one hope to acquire a sense of virtue.

Addison and Steele's essays were read throughout the Western world in the eighteenth-century – indeed they are one of the seminal influences on Western taste and manners – and it would have been extraordinary if they had been ignored in Edinburgh, where they were read, discussed and imitated throughout the century.[4] Contemporary historians invariably dated the revival of letters in Scotland from the date of their publication and in another paper I would be prepared to argue that they played an important part in encouraging the Scots to take an interest in manners, morals and society. What is curious and of relevance to this discussion is that although the Scots clearly had a voracious appetite for Addisonian moralizing, their interest was of a peculiar kind. For while Addison and Steele had only a passing interest in the public consequences of the improvement of manners, the Scots thought that was a matter of cardinal importance. The proceedings of the many clubs and societies which were devoted to the improvement of manners according to Addisonian principles, like the writings of Allan Ramsay, the first Scottish Addison, make it clear that they believed that the improvement of private morality was a matter of public importance to be undertaken by every patriotically-minded Scotsman anxious to revive the civic virtue of his country. Those who undertook the job, therefore, could be regarded as good patriots and virtuous citizens as well as decent men.[5]

As we shall see, this was a view with which Hume greatly sympathized and it is worth pausing, very briefly, to consider why the Scots should have attached so much civic importance to the improvement of manners.[6] In the seventeenth and eighteenth centuries it was customary for political moralists in the Western world to hold the classical view that a nation's liberties, independence and identity was founded on her constitution, enshrined in her laws and political institutions and preserved by a virtuous citizenry. It was on such foundations that a nation's grandeur and her wealth and excellence in the arts and sciences rested. But the Scots had long been accustomed to think differently. It was difficult for them to believe that the preservation of the liberties and independence of their country had had much to do with her underdeveloped laws and political institutions. It was much more plausible to believe, as every historian and chronicler had assumed, that she owed her independence and identity to the warlike manners of the gothic barons who had kept the English at bay, and had ensured the survival of a weak monarchy and undeveloped laws and political institutions. In other words, as far as Scotsmen were concerned, their liberties were founded on the manners of the people and it was the job of virtuous citizens to use their political resources to work for their preservation. Just what that meant had become clear in 1707 when, faced with the prospect of an acute economic and political crisis, and the choice of preserving their parliament or exchanging it for the opportunity of free trade with the English, the Scots parliament reluctantly decided that free trade was of more importance to preserving their country's manners than parliament. And it was in order to exploit the advantages the Union offered to stimulate the patriotism and virtue of a new generation that societies of aristocrats, professional men and literati sprang up in post-union Edinburgh to improve the nation's manners by encouraging trade and learning. By Hume's day, Edinburgh which had once been the seat of the old Scots Parliament had become a city of para-parliamentary clubs and societies of patriotically minded men devoted to the regeneration of the manners of a fallen nation and improving the virtue of its citizens. Hume's Edinburgh was, in its own remarkable way, a city dedicated to the pursuit of virtue and, in the process, Addisonian morality became one of the principal engines for bringing about the regeneration of the nation's manners. In turning to Addisonian essay-writing, in other words, Hume was, consciously or unconsciously, trimming his sails to meet the prevailing ideological winds of Enlightened Edinburgh.

Hume's decision to give up philosophizing in the grand manner of the *Treatise* has always made historians and philosophers uneasy. And although the vulgar view that he simply took to essay-writing for fame and money was effectively refuted by Ernest Mossner, his own alternative explanation, that Hume wanted a popular vehicle for bringing his philosophy forward is underdeveloped.[7] For a historian, however, Hume's decision to turn moralist is not altogether surprising. His interest in practical morality was long-standing. James Boswell reported that Hume had told him from his death-bed that he had been pious as a child. He had read *The Whole Duty of Man* and made 'an abstract from the catalogue of vices at the end of it, and examined himself by this, leaving out Murder and Theft and such vices as he had no chance of committing, having no inclination to commit them. This, he said, was strange work; for instance, to try, if, not withstanding his excelling his schoolfellows, he had no pride or vanity.'[8] His first known letter, written to Michael Ramsay in 1727 when he was sixteen, speaks of the pleasure Cicero and Virgil gave him, which was all the greater for the relief they gave him from the anxieties of metaphysical speculation. 'The Philosophers Wiseman, and the Poets husbandman agree in peace of mind, in a Liberty & Independancy on Fortune, & Contempt of Riches, Power & Glory' Hume wrote. 'Everything is placid & quiet in both; nothing perturbd or disorderd . . . My peace of Mind is not sufficiently confirmed by Philosophy to withstand the Blows of Fortune; This Greatness & Elevation of Soul is to be found only in Study & contemplation, this can alone teach us to look down upon humane Accidents.'[9] At an early age Hume had become engrossed in problems of personal conduct and practical morality and had turned to Cicero, whose writings formed the cornerstone of Western thinking about civic morality.[10] At the same time, his letter hints that he had already acquired what was to be a lasting interest in the nature of those moral beliefs which strike one as obviously attractive even though they do not appear to be founded on the principles of human nature.

Hume's long sojourn in a disturbing metaphysical wilderness, which seems to have begun in earnest around 1729, appears to have isolated him from the clubbable literary society to which he, almost more than any other eighteenth-century philosopher, attached so much importance. He withdrew to the country, hovered on the edge of a nervous breakdown, left Scotland for Bristol and later La Flèche, where he wrote the first two parts of the *Treatise*. The crucial first volume of that protean work was, as an early reviewer unkindly put it, marred by egotism.[11] It possessed many of the epic qualities Sheldon Wolin has noticed in Hobbes' *Leviathan*.[12] It was, as scholars have often noted, a quasi-autobiographical exploration of the mind, which raised as many questions as it answered, the *tour de force* of an extraordinary man who was in the process of resolving fundamental questions about the nature of philosophizing and his own role as a philosopher. It would have been reasonable for a contemporary to have asked what he was going to do next. Would he, like Thomas Reid, develop as a metaphysician and a student of perception? Would he develop, perhaps rather like Adam Smith, as a philosopher who was interested in the mechanics of the moral sense and the process of acquiring moral sentiments? Would his discussion of law and morality encourage him to take the

quasi-anthropological path he later sketched out in essays like
'Of National Characters' or 'The Natural History of Religion?.
He did none of these things. Instead, he decided to develop
the central principles of the *Treatise* as a practical moralist
anxious to reach an understanding of morality which was
founded on the principles of human nature and not on the
whims of a moralist. It was not an altogether surprising step.
After all, he had told Francis Hutcheson that the principles
of Cicero's *Offices* were never far from his mind while he was
writing the *Treatise*.[13]

But perhaps the most interesting evidence that Hume's
interests were moving, or perhaps returning to the paths of
practical morality is to be found in the remarkable last chapter
of the first book of the *Treatise*. Hume had been forced to the
conclusion that it was impossible to avoid holding beliefs about
events which had taken place in the external world. However,
those beliefs could only properly be described as lively sensations which ascribed certainty rather than probability to the
consequences of those events. What troubled him was that
although these conclusions seemed inescapable if one reasoned
from experience rather than final causes, they were completely
at odds with the understanding of ordinary men and the
teaching of all philosophy. It was a disturbing position for a
sociable man to be in and it seemed to have generated existential anxieties in Hume's mind, for he recalled himself asking
questions such as these: 'Where am I or what?' 'From what
causes do I derive my existence and to what condition shall I
return . . . I am confounded with all these questions and begin
to fancy myself in the most deplorable condition imaginable,
inviron'd with the deepest darkness and utterly depriv'd of
the use of every member or faculty.'[14]

Descartes had written of the existential anxieties his own
early scepticism had aroused in much the same way and said
he had resolved them by an act of mind. But Hume thought
that although scepticism was 'a malady, which can never be
radically cur'd' its debilitating intellectual and moral consequences could be brough under control by acquiring a

frame of mind and adopting a manner of living which was broadly similar to that which Addison had recommended.[15] The philosopher should remember that no matter to what sceptical conclusions he was driven by philosophy, Nature, in the form of the frame of mind men adopt in ordinary social life, would quickly expose their intellectual and moral limitations.

> I dine, I play a game of back-gammon, I converse, and am merry with my friends; and when after three or four hours amusement, I wou'd return to these speculations, they appear so cold, and strain'd and ridiculous, that I cannot find in my heart to enter into them any farther.[16]

The company of friends, a willingness to be guided by the natural beliefs which govern the behaviour of men in society, not the intellect; that was the real cure for excessive scepticism. What is more it was only in society that philosophers could learn to observe human behaviour systematically and philosophize about it properly. The company of friends was thus a cure for bad philosophy as well as bad morals. In spirit at least, Hume's position was a thoroughly Addisonian one.[17]

Hume turned to the business of Addisonian moralizing immediately after completing the *Treatise* in 1740. At first he and Lord Kames planned to produce a series of weekly essays exactly as Addison and Steele had done but the plan fell through.[18] Instead Hume collected the essays he had already written, added a few more and published them in two volumes of *Essays Moral and Political* published in 1741 and 1742. The preface to the first volume acknowledged debts to the *Spectator* and, interestingly, to the *Craftsman*, the first journal to attempt to bring political discussion into the world of polite morality. In this preface Hume promised to reflect with 'moderation' and 'impartiality' on political questions. These are key words in the Spectatorial vocabulary. The spectator could be expected to distance himself from the world, reflect on its follies and philosophize about them. And just as Addison had allowed a system of morality to evolve as the essays proceeded, so

Hume set out gradually to build up a system of civic morality which would appeal to the sentiments as well as to the intellect of the polite men and women at whom it was directed. In so doing he would broaden the intellectual range of the Addisonian essay by drawing the attention of polite readers to the problem of civic morality that had arisen in a modern age and had been overlooked by contemporary moralists.

Hume's first volume was largely devoted to a discussion of the follies of the contemporary political world; the second was largely devoted to the role of philosophers and philosophizing in a modern age.[19] Together they were designed to illustrate and develop the central thesis of Book III of the *Treatise* that liberty, commerce, refinement and progress in the arts and sciences only arose in countries with good laws and constitutions and were thus dependent upon them for their survival.[20] Thus all morality was, in an important sense, civic morality and all learning and philosophy could be shown to rest upon civic foundations. In the first volume, most of Hume's time was devoted to a sceptical discussion of some of the most fundamental beliefs which Englishmen held about the constitution and contemporary politics. Assumptions about the antiquity of the constitution, French despotism and English liberty, the nature of liberty and authority itself, the role of political parties in a modern state, and the virtues and vices of a free press were all discussed critically and philosophically. In the *Treatise* he had argued that all we can ever know from experience about the nature of authority in civil society stems from our own experience of family and social life and depends on a recognition of the curious fact that we have a natural disposition to respect established authority. Thus all that we can have any reason to expect from government is that it will prescribe the rules of justice on which an orderly social life depends and do its best to maintain them.[21] It was, he argued in the *Essays*, on such principles that we ought to discuss the merits of the English and French constitutions and evaluate the activities of political zealots who did not seem able to understand either the nature of our respect for established authority or the dangers which an excessive and abstract libertarian zeal posed for the preservation of an orderly social life. For it was Hume's primary principle of politics that 'Good laws may beget order and moderation in government, where the manners and customs have instilled little humanity or justice in the tempers of men.'[22] It was on the rules of justice, supported by the authority of a government and the natural loyalties of the people that liberty, commerce, progress in the arts and sciences and social ease depended. No man who had learned to value the private virtues that Addison had extolled ought to forget the civic foundations upon which his private happiness rested and it was his duty to reflect on the civic duty he owed to the society of which he was part. It was not a debt which could safely be overlooked.

But how could it be repaid? Hume's answer was the one a civic moralist might have been expected to give – political participation; but it was political participation of a peculiar kind and one that was by no means so discordant with the principles of Addisonian morality as one might suppose. For Hume, too, believed that contemporary party politics posed a threat to human happiness. The reason was that it was geared to the pursuit of political objectives founded in antiquated prejudices which had little or nothing to do with the problems of maintaining political stability and the rules of justice in a modern age. Modern party politicians were factious zealots who posed almost as much of a threat to an orderly social life as religious enthusiasts. Thus civic virtue consisted in standing back from party political warfare and learning how to hold one's instinctive political enthusiasms in check by thinking of one's political duty in relation to the sole end of maintaining the rules of justice. To put it another way Hume had turned the liberty of indifference into a civic virtue.

In purely ideological terms, Hume's conception of civic virtue is of some interest to a Scottish historian. Scotsmen had already learned to believe that their country's future liberties and independence depended on their ability to improve its manners. Yet they knew that was only possible within the framework of a British constitution which was the source of the laws, government and the economic hopes upon which any future national regeneration depended and as North Britons they were required to believe that a nation's liberties rested on political foundations. Thus virtuously minded Scotsmen found themselves obliged to think in terms of loyalty to two nations and were required to subscribe to two very different ideologies. In the past no Scots theoretician had managed to construct a satisfactory model which would define the relations between the two kingdoms and the two conceptions of civic duty. In the long and complex debate about the desirability of an act of Union, Scottish writers had tended to gloss the problem and had assumed that in practical terms there was no reason why one should not learn to be an equally virtuous citizen of both countries. Only Andrew Fletcher of Saltoun, a fiery and important political moralist, well known both in England and Scotland, had got as far as hinting at the outline of a model which would define the place of Scotland in a modern kingdom and the relations between the two types of civic duty. His model, which was underdeveloped and largely inspirational in character, cannot be properly discussed here.[23] In outline Fletcher saw Britain as a kingdom of regions or nations each of which was governed from local centres of power by a locally based and presumably landed élite.

So many different seats of government will highly encourage virtue. For all the same offices that belong to a great kingdom must be in each of them; with this difference, that the offices of such a kingdom being always burdened with more business than anyone can rightly execute, most things are abandoned to the rapacity of servants: and the extravagant profits of all great officers plunge them into all manner of luxury and debauch them from doing good: whereas the offices of the lesser governments extending only over a moderate number of people, will be duely executed, and many men have occasions to put into their hands of doing good to their fellow citizens. So many different seats of government will highly tend to the improvement of all arts and sciences; and afford great variety of entertainment to all foreigners and others of a curious and inquisitive genius as the cities of Ancient Greece did.[24]

Fletcher's model implied that a man's primary loyalty was to his nation or region and that his loyalty to the prince and the system of laws he embodied was somehow secondary. But so deeply did the irascible Fletcher dislike all princes and all systems of court government that he could not bring himself to think of Scotland as part of a larger kingdom which was governed by laws which had a positive role to play in the maintenance of Scottish liberties. By Hume's day, however, it was clear that politically minded Scotsmen had slipped quite easily and naturally into a pattern of political behaviour which implied ideas of primary and secondary loyalty. As I have already indicated, Edinburgh had become a city of clubs and societies which were para-parliamentary in character and dedicated to the enthusiastic pursuit of virtue by encouraging economic and cultural improvement in order to secure the all-important manners of the nation. In London, however, it was quite different. The forty-five Scots Members of Parliament and the sixteen Representative peers took almost no part in the party political warfare around which political life revolved, contenting themselves with offering passive support to whatever ministry was in power in exchange for pensions and places, only appearing on the active stage of Westminster politics when local or national interests were involved.[25] In fact, by Hume's day the Scottish political community at large was behaving as Fletcher and Hume had advocated. It had cultivated a congenial and sometimes lucrative passive indifference to the politics of Britain as a whole and had sought virtue and happiness by actively cultivating what one might call the more private, domestic, national virtues. In purely Scottish terms what Hume had done was to show that this sort of political behaviour could be regarded as a source of potential civic virtue. But it was a conception of civic virtue that was much easier to understand in Edinburgh than in London, where, understandably, it helped to earn Hume the unflattering and wholly misleading title of Tory.[26]

But Hume was no ideologue, and interesting as his discussion of politics is as evidence of the consonance of his thinking about public affairs with that of politically minded Scotsmen, that was simply a by-product of his central purpose as a moralist. He wanted to show how intelligent and responsibly-minded men could acquire the frame of mind which would allow them to make a positive virtue out of political indifference and allow them to define the relationship between the public and private world in which they moved. This theme was sketched out in the first volume of essays and developed at greater length in the second. 'Good will or ill fortune is very little at our disposal' Hume had written, in a thoroughly Addison vein, in the first essay of the first volume, 'Of the Delicacy of Taste and Passion'. Unless we appreciated the folly of pinning all our hopes and fears on external events over which we had little control, we would be unable to achieve any sort of moral control over our lives and our happiness. The key to acquiring a sense of moral autonomy lay in cultivation of the arts and sciences. This was something which everyone could pursue in private at will. It would help men to forget about the bustle of the public world and en-courage them to study human behaviour and reflect on the principles which governed its operations. If this was done seriously on the basis of observation and experience and not on the assumption that events ought to be explained in terms of final causes, it would teach men to value intellectual modesty and encourage them to moderate their enthusiasms and un-reasonable expectations of life. It would also produce 'an agreeable melancholy which, of all dispositions of the mind is the best suited to love and friendship'.[27] We would learn to be more selective in our choice of friends and we would come to love and respect those we had more highly.

Hume's idea of a private world in which ease, happiness and moral autonomy could be acquired is more complex than Addison's. He was to become increasingly impatient with agreeable Addisonian 'trifflings'[28] and with the notion of a social world which revolved around aimless and trivial conversation. The job of the philosopher was to serve as an ambassador from the learned to the conversable world in order to elevate its conversation and direct it to the sort of moral and political questions that were integral to the Science of Man and to the cultivation of virtue. At the same time he would learn from the conversable the sort of lessons which Hume said he had learned from ordinary men while writing the *Treatise* – how to curb unnecessary credulity or pyrrhonism with common sense and how to respect the natural beliefs of ordinary men.[29] This symbiotic relationship between the learned and conversable world would render philosophy useful to society and society of use to the philosopher. It was, moreover, a symbiosis which had only become possible in the modern age in the company of men of middling rank who were rich enough to be independent of the great; sufficiently leisured and literate to be able to relish the delights of studying human nature; sufficiently independent-minded to distrust the authority of received opinion; sufficiently practical to be able to reason from experience rather than final causes. Such men were unknown in gothic times when society was dominated by warlike barons, fanatical priests and a servile peasantry. As Harrington had observed, it was only with the passing of feudalism and the rise of monarchies, systems of laws, luxury and commerce that a middling class of men had come into their own.[30] Thus it was only in the modern age that it had at last become possible to envisage a true science of man and a system of morality which would rest on the principles of human nature and help to underpin the liberties and happiness of the citizens of modern civil society.

It was from the tightly knit, good humoured, sophisticated coteries of literati that met in the coffee-houses and taverns of an Addisonian world that Hume thought the new science and the new morality would emerge. Here they had

> A better chance for achieving a knowledge both of men
> and things than those of a more elevated station in life and
> everything appears in its natural colours before him; he
> has more leisure to form observations; and has, besides, the
> motive of ambition to push him on in his attainments,
> being certain that he can never rise to any distinction or
> eminence in the world, without his own industry.[31]

But it was to the importance of conversation in forging and
maintaining the friendship on which social life depended that
Hume continually returned. It was conversation, that 'mutual
deference or civility, which leads us to resign our own inclinations to those of our companion, and to curb and conceal
that presumption and arrogance so natural to the human
mind';[32] that art which was unknown to the ancients and was
as yet ill-cultivated by the moderns;[33] it was conversation
that made social life and the acquisition of moral principles
possible. It was through conversation that men were exposed
to the general principles of taste and morals upon which
their ordinary understanding of life depended. It was from
conversation with ordinary men that philosophers learned to
'consult experience', searching for it 'where it is alone to be
found, in Common Life'.[34] And it was through conversation
that philosophers could learn to temper their sceptical paradoxes with respect to those natural beliefs which guide men
through everyday life. It did not matter, said Hume, whether
one was an epicurean, a stoic or a sceptic by temperament;
whether one found it more agreeable to be governed by the
senses, by a love of hard work or by an instinctive distrust
of the moral and intellectual authority of others. Provided
one regarded the end of life as an ease, contentment and a
sense of ego; provided one realized that the senses, hard work
and scepticism must each play their part in forming one's
moral character, one might achieve wisdom and virtue.[35] It
was a lesson which could only be learned in the company of

friends and it was a lesson which would inform one's sense of moral and civic duty.

The tone of Hume's discussion was Ciceronian but it is Cicero underpinned by Humean scepticism and adapted to the social needs of a modern age. Cicero had written in a stoic spirit about civic virtue and the philosophical and political virtues of acquiring a lofty detachment from men, ideas and fortune. It was only thus that a statesman could distance himself from the pressures to which the great men who direct affairs are inevitably subjected. But Hume did not write for statesmen. His audience was composed of men of middling rank who had an active interest in public affairs but possessed neither the means nor the desire to be great statesmen. It would be foolish for such men to take the letter of Ciceronian stoicism too seriously. But equally, it would be foolish of them to ignore the spirit of his teaching. For Cicero's teaching could be used to create a new political class whose members had learned collectively to appreciate the values of stoic detachment. Paradoxical though it might seem, Ciceronian stoicism and Addisonian sociability were by no means incompatable. In the process, conversation, the supreme instrument by which friendships were created and maintained and philosophy improved, had become as important to the maintenance of virtue in Hume's world as eloquence was in that of Cicero.[36]

I have discussed Hume's moral preoccupations like this because I believe that they were of central importance to his philosophical development and that they arose quite naturally from that protean masterpiece the *Treatise*. It is also important to remember that it was only after he had completed his exploration of the problems of civic morality that he felt able to return to the central principles of the *Treatise*. The two *Enquiries* of 1748 and 1751 are remarkable and undervalued discussions of the principles of human nature and morals by a practical moralist anxious to instruct his readers in the principles of virtue. Every metaphysical or historical question which had been discussed in the *Treatise* was carefully stripped away or relegated to appendices if it was irrelevant to his moral teaching.[37] The conclusion to the second *Enquiry* contains Hume's final statement of his principles of civic morality. Moral behaviour is only possible in society and the foundation of all social life is the rules of justice. Our natural disposition is to submit to the authority of established rules and to acquire the beliefs and prejudices of those like ourselves. Our desire to acquire a sense of virtue will encourage us to look for an independence from the authority of received ideas by testing their credibility against the facts of experience. Our desire for ease, virtue and an active, useful life will prevent us from allowing our scepticism from degenerating into an absurd and enervating pyrrhonism.

> How little is requisite to supply the necessities of nature. And in view to pleasure, what comparison between the unbought satisfaction of conversation, society, study, even health and the common beauties of nature, but above all the peaceful reflection one's own conduct: what comparison, I say, between these and the feverish empty amusements of luxury and expense? These natural pleasures, indeed, are really without price; both because they are below all price in their attainment and above it in their enjoyment.[38]

It was a conception of civic virtue that could be learned and practised in the coffee-house and in the salon. For, as Hume remarked, 'why in the greater society or confederacy of mankind, should not the case be the same in particular clubs and companies'.[39]

Historically speaking, the consequences of Hume's emergence as a civic moralist were of some importance to the development of Scottish culture. He had adopted a mode of philosophizing that was in itself of great importance to the Scots and it allowed Edinburgh's social and literary élite to treat him with the respect that any society accords to a man whose work is deemed to be of public importance. It was as a civic moralist rather than as a religious sceptic that he quickly became a key figure in the organization of the city's cultural life. He was a founder member and an active patron of the Select Society, secretary of the Philosophical society and his patronage was eagerly sought by lesser societies. It was because they shared Hume's views about the role of philosophers and philosophizing in a modern age that moderate ministers and laymen fought successfully to rescue Hume and his kinsmen Lord Kames and John Home from the charges of infidelity which had been levelled against them by the orthodox wing of the General Assembly of the Scottish kirk. By the early 1760's he was generally looked on as one of the leaders of taste and learning in the city. His conversation was enjoyed by young and old alike and reported with care and he was looked on with approval even by those who were disturbed by his religious scepticism; for his literary reputation reflected credit on the city. By the end of his life his own literary reputation and that of Edinburgh were closely connected and when foreigners like Johnson or Gibbon, Franklin or Jefferson thought of Edinburgh, Hume's name was one of the first to spring to mind. The consonance of his views about civic morality with those of a distinctive social and literary élite was a necessary precondition of his social and intellectual pre-eminence in the city. It was for the same reason that those who enjoyed his company found it possible to neutralize the problems caused by his notorious infidelity by an agreement to differ which occasionally had to be spelled out in no uncertain terms. But scepticism was, for an increasing number of Scotsmen outside the charmed circles of the Edinburgh élite, a cuckoo which was already growing dangerously fast. For an Aberdonian moralist like James Beattie, Edinburgh had become part of a Castle of Scepticism which was sapping the self-confidence of young men destined for a life in the world of public affairs, destroying religion, morality and virtue.[40] It was because Humean scepticism had been legitimized by Edinburgh's élite that it acquired the capacity to arouse the hostility of moralists like Dugald Stewart and Adam Ferguson as well as James Beattie, who were, in their own ways as concerned with civic virtue as Hume had been. As such, it was to become one of the most potent forces shaping the intellectual development of Scotland in the age of the Enlightenment.[41]

NOTES

[1] I am grateful to David Fate Norton, Harry Bracken, Charles Robertson and Richard Teichgraeber for comments on an earlier draft of this paper.

[2] See, in particular, Donald F. Bond's introduction to his edition of the *Spectator* (Oxford, 1965) i, xiii-cix, and Peter Gay 'The Spectator as Actor: Addison in Perspective' *Encounter*, xxix, no. 6, December 1967, pp. 27-32.

[3] 'I am a Fellow of a very odd Frame of Mind' *Spectator* no. 167. 'Cast of Mind' is used in the same sense in *Spectator*, no. 225. See also *Spectator*, no. 634. Mrs. Hutchinson had used the expression 'Frame of Spirit' in a roughly analogous sense in 1665. OED *Frame*.

[4] See my 'Culture and Society in the 18th Century Province: the case of Edinburgh and the Scottish Enlightenment' in *The University in Society*, ed. L. Stone (Princeton, 1974), ii, pp. 407-48.

[5] *Ibid.*

[6] I shall develop this point at length in my forthcoming study of the Scottish Enlightenment *The Pursuit of Virtue*. See also J. G. A. Pocock, *Politics Language and Time* (New York, 1971), ch. 3.

[7] E. C. Mossner, 'Philosophy and Biography: the Case of David Hume', *Philosophical Review*, 59 (1950).

[8] *Boswell in Extremes 1776-1778*, ed. C. M. Weiss and F. A. Pottle (New York, 1970), p. 11.

[9] *The Letters of David Hume*, ed. J. Y. T. Greig (Oxford, 1952), I, p. 10.

[10] Peter Gay was the first scholar to point out the central importance of Cicero to the thought of the Enlightenment. See his *The Enlightenment: an Interpretation. The Rise of Modern Paganism* (London, 1966), esp. pp. 105-9.

[11] E. C. Mossner *The Life of David Hume* (Edinburgh, 1954), p. 121.

[12] Sheldon Wolin, *Hobbes and the Epic Tradition of Political Theory* (Los Angeles, 1970).

[13] 'Upon the whole, I desire to take my Catalogue of Virtues from Cicero's Offices, not from the Whole Duty of Man. I had

indeed, the former Book in my Eye in all my Reasonings.' *Letters of David Hume*, i, p. 34. See also *Letters*, i, p. 16.

14 *A Treatise of Human Nature*, ed. L. A. Selby Bigge (Oxford, 1967), p. 269.

15 *Treatise*, p. 218. See also J. Noxon, *Hume's Philosophical Development* (Oxford, 1973), pp. 8–16.

16 *Treatise*, p. 269.

17 That is not to say, of course that Addison regarded society as the prime cure for philosophical scepticism. That important role was reserved for religion. But society certainly was a cure for lesser ailments. See, for example *Spectator*, nos. 93 and 222. Hume, in his characteristically unnerving manner, simply saw no reason why greater and more profound ailments should not be cured in the same way as more trivial ones.

18 E. C. Mossner, *Life of David Hume*, pp. 138–9.

19 The order in which the essays were originally published is as follows. *Volume I.* 1. Of the Delicacy of Taste and Passion. 2. Of the Liberty of the Press. 3. Of Impudence and Modesty. 4. That Politicks may be Reduced to a Science. 5. Of the First Principles of Government. 6. Of Love and Marriage. 7. Of the Study of History. 8. Of the Independency of Parliament. 9. Whether the British Government Inclines more to Absolute Monarchy or to a Republick. 10. Of Parties in General. 11. Of the Parties of Great Britain. 12. Of Superstition and Enthusiasm. 13. Of Avarice. 14. Of the dignity of Human Nature. 15. Of Liberty and Despotism. *Volume II.* 1. Of Essay Writing. 2. Of Eloquence. 3. Of Moral Prejudices. 4. Of the Middle Station of Life. 5. Of the Rise and Progress of the Arts and Sciences. 6. The Epicurean. 7. The Stoic. 8. The Platonist. 9. The Sceptic. 10. Of Polygamy and Divorces. 11. Of Simplicity and Refinement. 12. A Character of Sir Robert Walpole.

Hume continually regrouped and reorganized his essays later in life, omitting some, adding others. T. E. Jessop, *A Bibliography of the Works of David Hume* . . . (London, 1938), pp. 15–18.

20. The importance Hume attached to his argument is emphasized by D. Forbes, *Hume's Philosophical Politics* (Cambridge, 1975), esp. Part I. My views on the ideological significance of Hume's position are slightly different from his.

21 This was a thoroughly Shaftesburian position to take. Anthony, Earl of Shaftesbury. *Characteristics of Men, Manners, Opinions, Times.* ed. J. M. Robertson (Library of Liberal Arts), i, p. 74. In this, as in so much else, Hume's implied critique of Addisonian morality takes the form of going back to the Shaftesburian sources in which it was founded.

160 *Nicholas Phillipson*

²² 'That Politics may be reduced to a Science'.
²³ Fletcher deserves better treatment from historians than he has so far received. But see J. G. A. Pocock, *Politics, Language and Time*, ch. 4 and *The Machiavellian Moment Florentine Political thought and the Atlantic Republican Tradition* (Princeton, 1975), pp. 426–31. See also my 'Culture and Society in the Eighteenth Century Province'.
²⁴ *The Political Works of Andrew Fletcher* (London, 1737), pp. 445–6.
²⁵ See, for example, J. Brooke and L. B. Namier, *The House of Commons 1754–1790* (London, 1964), i, pp. 169–70.
²⁶ The unfruitful debate about Hume's supposed toryism has recently been fully and critically discussed by D. Forbes, *Hume's Philosophical Politics*, ch. 5–6.
²⁷ 'Of the Delicacy of Taste and Passion'.
²⁸ *The Letters of David Hume*, ii, p. 257.
²⁹ 'Of Essay Writing'. Hume withdrew this essay in the second and subsequent editions of his essays.
³⁰ 'Of the Rise and Progress of the Arts and Sciences' and 'Of the Middle Station in Life'. This essay was also withdrawn after the first edition. Hume's general point was to be developed in the economic essays and in the History of England.
³¹ 'Of the Middle Station in Life'. Norah Smith has pointed out the striking similarities between Hume's general treatment of the subject and Addison's. 'Hume's Rejected Essays'. *Forum for Modern Language Studies*, 8 (1972), pp. 354–71.
³² 'Of the Rise and Progress of the Arts and Sciences'.
³³ *Ibid.*
³⁴ 'Of Essay Writing'.
³⁵ For an interesting though rather different discussion of these essays, see *David Hume: Writings on Economics* ed. E. Rotwein (Edinburgh, 1955), pp. xcv–xcix.
³⁶ See particularly 'Of the Rise and Progress of the Arts and Sciences' and 'Of Eloquence' for Hume's most conspicuous hints on this subject. As Sheldon Wolin points out, Cicero saw clearly the value of friendship as an instrument of political strategy as well as of private virtue. *Politics and Vision: Continuity and Innovation in Western Political Thought* (London, 1961), pp. 86–7.
³⁷ J. Noxon, *Hume's Philosophical Development*, pp. 18–19.
³⁸ *Humes Enquiry Concerning Human Understanding and An Enquiry Concerning the Principles of Morals* ed. L.A. Selby Bigge (Oxford 1902), pp. 283–4.
³⁹ *Ibid.* 281.
⁴⁰ See my 'James Beattie and the Defence of Common Sense' in *Festschrift für Rainer Gruenter*, ed. B. Fabian (Heidelberg, 1978) pp. 145–54.

[41] See my 'Towards a Definition of the Scottish Enlightenment' in *City and Society*, ed. D. Williams and P. Fritz (Toronto, 1973,) pp. 125–47.

8

DIDEROT: MAN AND SOCIETY

J. H. Brumfitt

Principal editor of the great *Encyclopedia*, novelist and prose writer of genius, contributor to the development of scientific thought and method, to the theory of the bourgeois drama and to the practice of art criticism, Diderot perhaps embodies the rich variety of the Enlightenment spirit more than any other man. His only real rival is surely Voltaire. Rousseau, whose influence was greater than Diderot's, would not thank us for classing him among the *philosophes*. The more profound philosophers – a Hume or a Kant – not only lack his range, but are less unquestionably 'Enlightenment men'.

Yet Diderot's profile in the subsequent history of thought differs strikingly from Voltaire's. 'I write in order to act', said the latter, and he made every effort to ensure that nearly all he wrote was disseminated as quickly and widely as possible. Diderot did not disagree with this sentiment, as is shown by the twenty years of toil he devoted to his greatest 'action' – the *Encyclopedia*. Great action it certainly was, yet today only a small number of scholars consult it. The works we now read – the novels and the dialogues – remained unknown to the majority of contemporaries. Some circulated among a small number of friends. Others, including the *Rêve de d'Alembert*, *Jacques le fataliste* and the *Supplément au voyage de Bougainville*, were published in Grimm's *Correspondence littéraire*. Yet 'published' is hardly the right word, for this manuscript journal appeared in only about a dozen copies and these did not circulate in France, but went mainly to the crowned Heads of other European States.[1] Moreover, *Le Neveu de Rameau*, now commonly regarded as Diderot's literary masterpiece, did not receive even this degree of publicity. Only a series of lucky coincidences led to its publication (initially in Goethe's German translation) early in the nineteenth century.[2] As for the later political writings – particularly those relating to Russia – it is only within the last few decades that many of them have been discovered.[3]

So when, in 1770, after the completion of the *Encyclopedia*, Grimm informed the King of Poland that Diderot was wasting his time producing oddments for periodicals and asserted that 'this man will die without ever having been known',[4] he was expressing an important truth, even though, considering that the principal periodical concerned was his own, he was hardly acting as a loyal friend.

In maintaining this degree of secrecy about works which we, certainly, would regard as 'enlightening', Diderot remained curiously untypical of the Enlightenment. Many explanations have been offered.[5] Diderot may have felt bound to keep his promise – made after his imprisonment which followed publication of the *Lettre sur les aveugles* in 1749 – to refrain from similar actions in the future. He may have regarded the safe publication – and possible republication – of the *Encyclopedia* as being of overriding importance. He was unwilling to publish dialogues in which friends appeared as characters, especially when they objected. He may have placed more weight than one suspects on the fact that he was read by the social élite who received the *Correspondance littéraire*.[6] He certainly proclaimed that he had more interest in the judgment of posterity than in that of contemporaries. Some works were addressed specifically to individuals – his friend d'Holbach, his mistress, Sophie Volland, or his daughter Angélique. Herbert Dieckmann has argued that he often wrote for those whom Stendhal was later to call 'the happy few'.[7] All these explanations have some validity, though perhaps none quite explains the fate of *Le Neveu de Rameau*.

In any case, the important fact remains that 'our' Diderot is one who remained unknown to the great majority of his contemporaries. And our Diderot is read by more than the 'happy few'. He attracts the attentions of students of literature and historians of ideas as much as do Voltaire and Rousseau. The major edition of his complete works, now in progress, is the second within little more than a decade – a significant indication of his growing popularity. Yet philosophers proper have often been less willing to attach the same importance to him. His name does not figure in Russell's *History of Western Philosophy*; in Berlin's *The Age of Enlightenment* he is mentioned (and 'mention' is the right word) only three times. His place in Sabine's *History of Political Theory* is larger, but still a modest one.

What follows is not an attempt to refute these authorities. On the contrary, one of its aims is to show that their silence is understandable. On many of the vital issues which have been central to the history of philosophy, Diderot has little new to say. Even when he is 'new', he rarely presents specific arguments in detailed, coherent form. His mastery lies in his ability to present a wide range of views on problems which demand an answer and to do so in a way which constantly stimulates the reader. He is not afraid to contradict himself and delights in presenting two or more sides of an argument with what appears to be equal force. He is more at home with 'chicken and egg' situations than with those which require deductive logic. This may explain why writers in the French Cartesian academic tradition – Daniel Mornet, for example[8] – have found his inconsistencies so irritating. It may equally explain why Marxists have often been attracted to him. Though he is certainly no historical materialist, his constant awareness of opposites prefigures the Marxist concept of the dialectical.[9]

Much of Diderot's earlier work falls mainly outside the scope of this study, which is concerned primarily with his social and political thought. 'I am writing about God', he

be refined in later years, they were never to be abandoned.

The *Lettre* was primarily a statement of a philosophical position. Yet it was also, in its advice on how to deal with the *malfaisant*, in a significant sense political. Diderot's growing interest in political questions – particularly questions of political theory – can also be seen in the *Encyclopedia* itself. At this time, he was closely associated with Rousseau, who had recently begun work on his projected *Institutions politiques*.[22] This may partly explain why Diderot reserved for himself a number of important political articles. As Jacques Proust has shown in his masterly *Diderot et l'Encyclopédie*,[23] Diderot's initial knowledge of the classics of political thought was slight. His first and perhaps most important contribution on the subject to the *Encyclopedia* was the article 'Autorité politique' which appeared in the first volume. Its outspokenness may have contributed more than its share to the Government's decision to withdraw the work's licence. It opened with a powerfully-phrased assertion that no man had the divine right of commanding others; it rejected the idea of the paternal origin of monarchy, and it insisted that the King belonged to the State and not the other way round.[24] Such views, conflicting as they did with the official doctrines of the French monarchy, were daring in a work which appeared with royal privilege. Yet viewed in the context of the writings of Hobbes, Locke and the exponents of natural law, they offered little that was new to the political theorist. Moreover, if the spirit of popular sovereignty clearly emanates from the opening paragraphs of 'Autorité politique', it is to no small extent dissipated in what follows. For though Diderot speaks of the possibility of the people taking power back into their own hands, his one concrete example of a situation in which this might happen is that of the total extinction of the French royal line.[25] Finally, in his discussion of the views of Henri IV, he comes close to accepting the idea of the right of the monarch (at any rate the good monarch) to override the expression of the popular will and even to asserting that the monarch may himself be the incarnation of that will.[26]

Diderot's views on pre-social man were also developed in the *Encyclopedia*, but were first expounded in the *Apologie de l'abbé de Prades* of 1752.[27] Rouseau's influence is again visible here in the concern shown with the question of the origin of society. Yet their views diverge. Unlike Rousseau, Diderot postulates the natural rationality and sociability of man. This sociability, he argues, is reinforced by the need for men to co-operate in the struggle against external nature. He is later to go further and to assert that it is from this need that civil society originates; if the need were removed, even today, organized society might cease to exist. This view would appear to preclude the Hobbesian one of the brutishness of natural man. However, Diderot (now coming closer again to Rousseau) suggests that the state of nature subsequently gave place to one of Hobbesian anarchy from which men rescued themselves by establishing civil society. As Proust has shown,[28] the *Encyclopedia* articles on 'Agriculture' and 'Besoin' help to explain this degeneration of natural man into warring hordes. Yet this stage of Diderot's account remains less cogently argued and less rooted in economic realities than that given by Rousseau in the *Discours sur l'inégalité*. Nor is one easily convinced by the suggestion in the article 'Grecs' that some men, like the Greek legislators, preserved their original rationality through the times of chaos and saw the way forward to the establishment of civil society;[29] though one may find it more acceptable than one does the legislator of Rousseau's *Contrat social*.[30]

Diderot's view of the social contract itself, expressed in the *Apologie de l'abbé de Prades*, also differs markedly from the one which, a few years later, Rousseau was to present in the *Discours sur l'inégalité*. For Rousseau, it was essentially a trick played by the strong on the weak and aimed at preserving the property of the former. For Diderot, it was a more equitable bargain, more like the contract of the *Contrat social*, though with none of the latter's rigour or moral implications. Certainly, it protected the strong against the violence of the weak, but it also defended the latter against oppression. Behind this conflict of views lay, of course, a fundamental opposition on the question of property – for Rousseau the source of evil; for Diderot, then as always, an inalienable and beneficial human right.[31] On this issue, it was Rousseau who, in the long run, was to prove the more inconsistent.[32]

Diderot's article 'Droit naturel'[33] again exhibits both affinities with and differences from Rousseau. Though neither can be said to have invented it, Diderot uses the term 'volonté générale' before Rousseau makes it famous in the *Contrat social*, and uses it in a somewhat similar way. The right to decide on what is just or unjust in civil society cannot simply be left to the individual; the only appropriate tribunal, Diderot argues, is the human race. 'The general will is always good; it has never deceived, it will never deceive.' This is more dogmatic than Rousseau, who followed a similar statement with a reminder that it did not necessarily follow that the deliberations of the people always had the same rectitude.[34] The two are more at odds on the question of how the general will is to be ascertained. Both would agree that it is the highest part of the individual's will, and Diderot also asserts that rational man can discover it within himself. However, Diderot's alternative way of discovering it lies in an appeal to a more general tribunal: 'the principals of written law of all civilised nations; the social actions of savage and barbarous peoples'. Rousseau is far more specific in his proposals, but above all, he could not accept a theory in which universal human rationality precedes, both temporally and morally, the establishment of specific societies. The chapter 'De la société générale du genre humain', which he wrote for the *Contrat social*,[35] was clearly aimed at refuting Diderot.

For twenty years the *Encyclopedia* was Diderot's principal occupation and, as far as political and social thought were concerned, the principal repository of his ideas. These did not change markedly, though the somewhat paternalistic and authoritarian attitude of the concluding pages of 'Autorité politique' was, if anything, intensified. The more radical, earlier part of that article had owed much to an English source,[36] but by 1765, influenced by d'Holbach's account of his visit to England, Diderot had become disillusioned with English practice.[37] The article 'Représentants', written in that year, whilst still arguing for popular representation, reveals this disillusionment.[38] Diderot's contact with the physiocrats and particularly his enthusiastic acceptance of the work of Mercier de La Rivière, with its concept of '*despotisme légal*', perhaps intensified this drift towards absolutism in his thought.[39] A letter he received from Allan Ramsay, attacking the liberal penal theories of Beccaria, may have had a similar effect.[40] He was certainly to quote it later to Catherine II, when arguing that reasons of state could be a justification for the harshest punishments.[41]

In general, too, the sixties constituted a difficult period in Diderot's life. The struggle to ensure the completion and publication of the *Encyclopedia* proved a long one.[42] The *Philosophes* in general, and Diderot in particular, were the object of a campaign of personal attacks, some of which (e.g. Palissot's play, *Les Philosophes*) had a measure of official backing. There were constant domestic troubles with his wife.[43] Yet if a somewhat harsher and more pessimistic tone sometimes crept into his writings, Diderot had by no means abandoned his sentimental enthusiasm for virtue. This can be seen from the admiration he expresses for Pamela and Clarissa in his *Eloge de Richardson* of 1760. His moralizing plays, *Le Fils naturel* and *Le Père de famille* sound a similar note, as does his aesthetic-ally much more satisfying novel, *La Religieuse*.

The problems which arose from this conflict of attitudes within him began to pose themselves more sharply. The determinist who was also a conscious moralist[44] could no longer be satisfied with the simple solution offered by the *Lettre à Landois*. In an undated fragment of a letter to Mme de Maux, he wrote of his fury at being stuck with '*une diable de philosophie*' which his mind could not but approve and his heart deny.[45] Too much has perhaps been made of this phrase taken out of its context – that of a love-letter – but the feeling was no doubt genuine. Diderot could not abdicate moral responsibility, but could he define it? The article 'Droit naturel' had envisaged two tribunals – the rational man's conscience and the laws of society; what if the two were in conflict? Again, in matters of sexual morality Diderot had advocated, and allowed himself, a good deal of freedom; but at what stage did this become irreconcilable with obligations to others? Materialist determinism seemed manifestly true, but how could one distinguish it from sterile fatalism, or from the crudely mechanical application of the pleasure-pain principle?

Diderot answered none of these questions clearly. Had he succeeded in doing so, his place in textbooks of philosophy would have been considerably greater than it is. Yet, mainly in the early seventies, he produced a series of works, mostly in dialogue form, which explore the issues involved and which, far more than the *Encyclopedia* itself, have assured him a readership among the posterity whose approval he coveted.

He had used the dialogue (albeit in an embryonic form) as early as the *Pensées philosophiques*.[46] It allowed him freedom to debate with himself on the many matters on which he was uncertain. It allowed him to do so in the context of real situations and precise examples. He had never been a predominantly abstract thinker, but now the concrete became increasingly dominant. 'All abstract science is no more than a combination of signs', argued his mouthpiece, the Dr. Bordeu of the *Rêve de d'Alembert*, 'the idea has been excluded by separating the sign from the physical object, and it is only by attaching the sign to the physical object that science becomes once again a science of ideas. Hence the need, so frequent in conversation and in writings, to take actual examples.'[47]

How Diderot applies this doctrine to moral science can be seen in the *Entretien d'un père avec ses enfants*. The coversation is based on reality, the characters are Diderot, his father, and members of the family circle, and there are enough details of setting, action and character to give intense life to the whole. The initial question – was Diderot's father right in giving effect to an outdated and unjust will rather than destroying it

– is reinforced by others in which the problems of individual conscience *versus* the law are highlighted. Two characters dominate the debate: 'Moi' (who is clearly Diderot himself, though it would be rash to assume that the character expresses the final views of his creator) and 'Mon père'. The former argues that the philosopher – and, indeed, the reasonable man – should obey the dictates of his conscience; the latter defends the supremacy of the law. The father has the final word, but it is by no means conclusive: 'I should not be too upset if there were one or two citizens in the town like you; but I would not live here if they all thought the same.'[48] Rather than resolving the debate, the ending provokes its continuation in the reader's mind.

The same is true of the *Supplément au voyage de Bougainville*, though here structure and argument are more complicated. Within the framework of a dialogue between 'A' and 'B', who discuss Bougainville's account of Tahiti, are incorporated a valedictory (or rather maledictory) address by an aged Tahitian to the departing French, and a long dialogue between the Tahitian, Orou and the ship's almoner, who has been persuaded to ignore his vows of chastity and follow the Tahitian custom of sleeping with the female members of his host's family. The old man's denunciation of colonialism (a theme on which Diderot has also much to say in his anonymous contributions to Raynal's *Histoire des deux Indes*) is a relatively straightforward defence of an idyllic primitive society un-corrupted by the sexual taboos (and diseases) of 'civilization'. The dialogue is less simple. The sub-title of the *Supplément* reads: 'On the disadvantages of attaching moral ideas to certain physical actions which do not call for them' and it is again the theme of sexual freedom (rather than the ideal of primitive communism which is also touched on) which rouses Orou (and Diderot) to heights of eloquence. Yet when Orou goes on to describe the structure of Tahitian society, primitive simplicity gives place to a social organization consciously geared to the aim of maximizing population, and if the young can enjoy a free sex-life, the woman who attempts to do so when she has passed child-bearing age ends up in exile or slavery. Diderot's utopia has its dark side,[49] revealing something of the ruthlessness we have already had occasion to note. Yet here the ruthlessness appears to be unconscious, for in the final dialogue, where 'A' and 'B' sum up, Tahitian society is clearly seen as idyllic compared with European.

Idyllic it may be, but 'A' and 'B' are at one in rejecting the idea of trying to live like Tahitians. 'We shall speak against absurd laws until they are reformed, and in the meantime we shall submit to them. The man who, on his own authority, breaks a bad law authorizes anyone else to break good ones.'[50] The emphasis here is different from that of the conclusion of the *Entretien d'un père avec ses enfants* and contrasts with the more radical spirit of the *Supplément* as a whole. Are we to accept it as Diderot's own view? We may be hesitant to do so, especially if we bear in mind the warning contained in a letter which he wrote, about the same time, to Hemsterhuis: 'You are yet another of the many examples of men in whom truth has been silenced by intolerance, which has forced them to dress their philosophy in Harlequin's clothes so that posterity, struck by their contradictions, of whose cause it will remain ignorant, will never be able to pronounce on their true sentiments.' Diderot continued: 'As for me, I have taken refuge in the most unfettered ironical tone I could find, in generalities, in laconicism and in obscurity.'[51]

Given these circumstances and Diderot's natural cast of mind, it is not surprising that clear sustained arguments between opposing viewpoints are rare in these dialogues. Nor, on the whole, are they usually what may be termed Socratic. The *Rêve de d'Alembert* is a partial exception here, but only in the *Entretien d'un philosophe avec la Maréchale* do we find a wise philosopher leading a less intellectually gifted character to greater knowledge both of her own nature and of 'moral' truth. This dialogue, with its lightness of touch and its superficially conciliatory attitude towards the Maréchale's Christian standpoint, shows Diderot at his argumentative best, for that standpoint is nevertheless relentlessly undermined. Yet here

G

too, the conclusion at which he arrives is equivocal: we should all behave as if God existed, and 'Moi' assures us that he will not fail to receive the last rites of the Church.[52]

If ambiguity is evident here, it is paramount in *Le Neveu de Rameau* which presents a dialogue between a 'Moi' who is clearly Diderot himself and a 'Lui' who is cynical, dissolute and totally immoral. Yet in the discussion which follows on the nature of genius and its relation to morality, and on the relation of this same morality to the factors which determine it, the personality of 'Lui' – Rameau's nephew – comes to balance that of 'Moi'. 'Lui' may be a rogue and a failed genius, but his character is presented with such vividness, insight, and, in a sense, sympathy, that critics have remained divided on the question of where, if anywhere, Diderot really stands in relation to his two creations.[53]

The problems presented by the discussion and exemplification of determinism in the novel, *Jacques le fataliste* (itself largely in dialogue form) are scarcely less involved. For, even more than Rameau's nephew, characters like Mme de La Pommeraye, whose ruthless revenge on the lover who deserted her makes her one of those 'moral monsters' who defy simple determinist explanation, turns this novel into what Lester Crocker has called *'une expérience morale'*.[54] 'You can hate or fear Mme de La Pommeraye', Diderot concludes, 'but you cannot despise her. Her vengeance is atrocious, but it is not sullied by any motive of interest.'

The monster had always obsessed Diderot.[55] Initially, it was the physiological monster such as those described in the *Rêve de d'Alembert*, whose nature was doubtless determined, but could not be predicted. Increasingly, it became the moral monster, like Mme de La Pommeraye, like Père Hudson in the same novel, or like the renegade from Avignon in *Le Neveu de Rameau*. 'One cannot refuse a sort of consideration to a great criminal', says 'Lui' in that same work.[56] To take a real-life example, Diderot could not refrain from expressing his admiration for the fortitude of Damiens, who had attempted to assassinate Louis XV and who, after listening impassively to the horrible details of the execution to which he had been condemned, remarked merely that '*la journée sera rude*'.[57]

Faced with these examples of the complexity of Diderot's moral and psychological thinking, we can hardly be surprised if the relatively simplistic determinism of the *Lettre à Landois* and the mechanistic sensationalism of Condillac and his disciples no longer satisfied him. But the occasion for the outburst which, for all its lack of literary form, constitutes, more than any other work, his philosophical testament, was the posthumous publication of Helvétius' *De l'Homme*. For Helvétius, as for Diderot, man was 'modifiable', and like Diderot, Helvétius sought to 'modify' him into a more virtuous being, living in a better society. For Helvétius, however, man was relatively simple. The product of his sensations and a few basic instincts, he could be transformed by education and wise government into the inhabitant of a brave new world. This view, Diderot now thought, conflicted both with human dignity and with the manifest facts of life.[58]

The *Réfutation d'Helvétius*, written between 1773 and 1775, did not amount to a repudiation of Diderot's own materialism, but led to significant modifications of it. The idea that sensitivity was inherent in all matter, propounded in the *Rêve de d'Alembert*,[59] now became 'a supposition' and no more.[60] If man was still 'modifiable', you could not, Diderot now argued, significantly modify his religious beliefs in a thousand years.[61] Above all, he focussed his attention on two questions. Helvétius had asserted that '*sentir c'est juger*'. Diderot insisted, more clearly than hitherto, that memory, judgment and human volition and action could only be explained in terms of a conscious mind which received, co-ordinated and transformed sensations. 'Yes, here are five witnesses', he said of the senses, 'but where is the judge, the *rapporteur*?' 'I am a man', he asserted, 'and I need causes appropriate to man'.[62] Helvétius had maintained that the average well-organized man was capable of everything. Diderot retorted that, if he had ever turned his hand to teaching, Helvétius would have soon realized that this was not the case; in particular, genius could not be manufactured by education. Turning to himself, Diderot asserted that there was one thing he had always passionately wished to be capable of doing: writing a proof of his profound belief that to be *'un homme de bien'* was the best way to ensure one's happiness. He had meditated on the question ceaselessly, but had never set pen to paper, for he knew that he could not succeed.[63]

The other main target of Diderot's scorn was Helvétius' simplistic pleasure-pain principle. Human motivation, Diderot argued, was infinitely more complex than Helvétius allowed. Men would sacrifice health and wealth in the pursuit of some outward symbol of renown, and a genius like Leibniz would attach far more importance to his work than to any form of material gratification. Helvétius himself, writing to enlighten his fellow-men, and risking and suffering persecution as a result, was an example disproving his own thesis.[64]

The *Réfutation*, like many works of this period, is characterized by a shift in Diderot's thought from the abstract and speculative to the more concrete and pragmatic. A similar development can be seen in his political ideas. It began with his espousal and defence of Galiani's views on the question of the export of grain, which criticized the rigid theoretical formulations of the physiocrats.[65] In the years that followed, stimulated not only by events in France, but also by growing hostility to Frederick of Prussia and by his contacts with Catherine II which resulted in his visit to Russia in 1773, his concern with political questions increased. Frederick was perhaps something of a political 'monster', but in dealing with political monsters, Diderot felt no need to suspend his moral judgment. In the *Pages contre un tyran*, written in 1770, he denounced the King in virulent terms for his intellectual arrogance in maintaining that truth was not made for all men, and still more for his defence of the warrior monarch – 'master butcher' – responsible for the loss of millions of lives.[66] In Russia, he did his best to prejudice Catherine against the Prussian King, and he later returned to the attack with his *Politique des souverains*.[67] Moreover, the idea of monarchy itself, which Diderot had earlier been inclined to accept, provided the monarch was an Henri IV, was now rejected in the name of liberty. In the *Réfutation d'Helvétius*, he asserted that even the wisest and most benevolent despot destroyed the spirit of freedom by eroding the people's powers of decision. A succession of three monarchs like Elizabeth of England would have put an end to that country's freedom.[68]

Maupeou's *coup* against the French *parlements* in 1771 seemed to Diderot to have the same effect. In his *Mémoires* for Catherine II[69] (to whom he could speak openly on French affairs) he denounced Maupeou, without ever actually naming him, as 'that perverse man'. Not that he admired the role the *parlements* had actually played. He denounced *them* as corrupt, selfish, bigoted and ineffective. Yet at least they had had some measure of independence. Diderot, who had always expressed his admiration for Montesquieu, was coming closer to him in political thought. The existence of some intermediary body between crown and people now seemed to him essential if monarchy were not to degenerate into despotism. If the *parlements* had not played this role very effectively, yet their mere existence had kept alive the idea of liberty among the people. Now even this image of freedom was gone.

Yet Diderot's view was not wholly pessimistic. Much of the programme of reform he suggested to Catherine applied as much to his native land as to Russia. Apart from insisting on the right to opposition and some degree of popular representation, he proposed a series of measures of economic reform and reduction in royal expenditure which Paul Vernière could describe as containing 'all the demands of the third estate'.[70] Among them we may note the plea for the recall of the States General, though this measure, Diderot suggested, was one which might be taken about the middle of the following century.

He could see more hope for Russia – a society still in the process of formation. The *Mémoires* he wrote for the instruction of Catherine are full of practical suggestions for establishing liberty by the creation of a permanent representative body which would safeguard the permanence of the laws and, in effect, transform the country into a constitutional monarchy. Though precisely who this body represented, and how, remained somewhat vague. He advocated the creation of a new middle class – possibly through the importation of skilled merchants and artisans from Switzerland, though he regretted the fact that the Russians, when they had occupied Berlin during the Seven Years' War, had not deported its industrious population to serve their own needs. His proposals for the introduction of compulsory primary education and the creation of scholarships for secondary education were supplemented by the very precise details of organization and curriculum contained in his *Plan d'une université*.[71] He called for a system of competitive examinations for all positions of importance in the State.

However, his enthusiasm for Catherine was short-lived. On his return from Russia he wrote his *Observations sur le Nakaz* – Catherine's original statement of her reformist intentions – and its comments were characterized by a note of disillusioned cynicism.[72] At other times, a similar note was sounded even more sharply. The ideal of patient reform, leading towards the establishment of a liberal, property-owning constitutional monarchy could give place to something more radical. Revolution, generally condemned,[73] was applauded in the case of the American colonists.[74] In his poem, *Les Eleuthéromanes*, which was probably not intended to be taken too seriously, but which *was* taken seriously when published during the Revolution,[75] he could echo Jean Meslier's words about the desirability of strangling kings in the bowels of priests.[76] He could also tell Wilkes that perhaps the only way to reinvigorate a nation was to do what Medea had done to restore her father's youth: cut him up and have him boiled.[77] And he was not far removed from sharing Helvétius' view that only a foreign invasion would revive France.[78]

If he did not entirely agree, it was because the French King was very old. In 1774, however, Louis XV died, to be succeeded by a monarch who recalled the *pamrleents* and placed *philosophes* like Turgot in high office. Diderot applauded Turgot's appointment and deplored his subsequent dismissal. Yet he did so in muted tones, partly no doubt because he could not approve of Turgot's physiocratic leanings, but also because he was growing old, losing some of his political enthusiasm, and occupying himself more with securing the future for his daughter and son-in-law.[79]

These factors may all help to explain his last work, the *Essai sur les règnes de Claude et de Néron*, which appeared in its final form in 1782. Essentially, the *Essai* was a defence of Seneca, whom Diderot admired as a writer and respected as a philosopher. Yet Diderot had been no stoic. Did he discern, in other fields, a kinship with Seneca? Certainly he had compromised himself (momentarily at least) with a monarch who had turned out to be a tyrant. Certainly he had not spoken out, in these last years, against the abuses he discerned in France. Yet he never draws a clear parallel in this work between his own position and that of Seneca in regard to Nero. His excursions into the contemporary are largely confined to attacks on La Mettrie and Rousseau. Otherwise, his biography of a man whose life was characterized by its political compromises exhibits a certain serenity of tone. And where it does touch on general 'political' issues, it reveals a more conservative Diderot. 'The people', whose claims Diderot had often advanced, are described as ignorant, credulous and stupid. It is the voice of the philosopher that is the voice of reason, and the people ignore it now as they did in Seneca's day.[80]

If these are Diderot's final words, they clearly do not sum up all his moral and political philosophy has to offer. Nor have subsequent attempts to reduce the complexity of his thought to a coherent system proved wholly satisfying. As an artist he continues to delight us; as a philosopher to excite us, to provoke us, and often to instruct us. With all his inconsistencies he probably remains the man of his generation who is most 'alive' today.

NOTES

[1] For details of recent research see *La Correspondance de Grimm et de Meister* (Colloque de Sarrebruck), ed. Bray, Schlobach and Varloot (Paris, 1976).

[2] For details see the edition by Jean Fabre (Geneva, 1950), pp. xiii–xiv.

[3] See the Introduction to the edition of the *Oeuvres politiques* by Paul Vernière (Paris, 1963), pp. ii–iv.

[4] See G. May's 'L'Angoisse de l'échec et la genèse du *Neveu de Rameau*' in *Diderot Studies* (Geneva, 1949), III, p. 287.

[5] Most of those which follow have been fully discussed by Herbert Dieckmann, *Cinq leçons sur Diderot* (Geneva–Paris, 1959), pp. 19 ff.

[6] This is suggested by Carol Sherman, *Diderot and the Art of Dialogue* (Geneva, 1976), pp. 41–2.

[7] *Op. cit.* pp. 24–5.

[8] See especially the Introduction to his *Diderot* (Paris, 1941).

[9] Engels makes this point in *Anti-Dühring* (ed. Dutt, London, 1934), p. 26. On the attitude of Russian Marxists see Arnold Miller, 'The Annexation of a Philosophe: Diderot in Soviet Criticism' in *Diderot Studies*, XV. Miller notes (p. 32) that Diderot was Marx's favourite prose writer.

[10] See the edition by R. Niklaus (Geneva–Paris, 1957), p. 3.

[11] For a full analysis see Aram Vartanian, 'From Deist to Atheist: Diderot's philosophical orientation, 1746–49', *Diderot Studies*, I.

[12] For examples see R. Niklaus, *A Literary History of France: The Eighteenth Century* (London, 1970), pp. 215–16.

[13] *Correspondance*, ed. Roth (Paris, 1955–70), V, p. 117.

[14] Though in the same year, in a letter to Voltaire (*Correspondance*, I, p. 78) he can still affirm his belief in God.

[15] See the Introduction to the latter work in Paul Vernière's edition of the *Oeuvres philosophiques* (Paris, 1956), pp. 249 ff.

[16] *Ed. cit.* p. 22.

[17] *Oeuvres philosophiques*, p. 119.

[18] *Ibid.* p. 92.

[19] *Correspondance*, I, pp. 209 ff.

[20] Anthony Collins's *A philosophical enquiry concerning Human Liberty* (1717) led many *philosophes*, including Diderot and Voltaire, towards determinism.

[21] For examples see Paul Vernière's edition of the *Oeuvres politiques* (Paris, 1963), pp. 395–6 and see below, pp. 170 and 173.

[22] The work was never completed, but the *Contrat social* embodies many of his findings.

[23] *Op. cit.* (Paris, 1967), pp. 341 ff. The following paragraphs are greatly indebted to Proust's work.

[24] *Oeuvres politiques*, pp. 9 ff.

[25] *Ibid.* p. 15.

[26] *Ibid.* pp. 16 ff.

[27] See *Oeuvres complètes*, ed. Assézat and Tourneux (Paris, 1875–7), I, pp. 431 ff.

[28] *Op. cit.* pp. 418–19.

[29] *Ibid.* pp. 421–2.

[30] *Contrat social*, Bk. II, ch. 7. Rousseau's 'legislator', as has often been remarked, is required to have almost superhuman qualities.

[31] See, for example, *Oeuvres politiques*, pp. 366, 403 and 484. See also Anthony Strugnell, *Diderot's Politics* (The Hague, 1973), p. 174.

[32] On the development of Rousseau's thought on property, see the edition of the *Contrat social* by C. Vaughan (Manchester, 1947), pp. 132–4.

[33] *Oeuvres politiques*, pp. 29 ff.

[34] *Contrat social*, Bk. II, ch. 3.

[35] It was not published, but survived in the Geneva MS and appears in many modern editions of the *Contrat social*, e.g. that by Ronald Grimsley (Oxford, 1972).

[36] This debt to the *Traité du pouvoir des rois de la Grande-Bretagne* was not acknowledged by Diderot, but was pointed out in a critical review in the *Mémoires de Trévoux*. See *Oeuvres politiques*, p. 5.

[37] Two letters from Diderot to Sophie Volland in 1763 describe d'Holbach's reactions. Diderot's meetings with Wilkes two years earlier may have already been leading him in the same direction.

[38] See *Oeuvres politiques*, p. 53. He is still expressing the same view in his *Mémoires pour Cathérine II* (*ibid.* p. 230).

[39] See Strugnell, *op. cit.*, pp. 93 ff. and *Oeuvres politiques*, pp. xviii–xix.

[40] *Correspondance*, V, pp. 245 ff.

[41] *Oeuvres politiques*, p. 395.

[42] For details see, for example, Pierre Grosclaude, *Un audacieux message: L'Encyclopédie* (Paris, 1952), or the relevant chapters in A. M. Wilson's masterly biography of Diderot (New York, 1972).

[43] See, for example, *Correspondance*, II, p. 124; III, p. 303, and IV, p. 288.

[44] Just how 'Victorian' his moralizing can be is seen from his upbringing of his daughter; see *Correspondance*, VII, p. 231.

[45] *Correspondance*, IX, p. 154. See also Wilson, *op. cit.*, pp. 576–7.

[40] For a perceptive study of his use of dialogue see Sherman, *op. cit.*

[47] *Oeuvres philosophiques*, p. 369. I am indebted to Rachel Eltis for drawing my attention to the relevance of this quotation.

[48] *Oeuvres philosophiques*, p. 443.

[49] Strugnell comments: 'The social values which flow from Diderot's materialist ethics are daunting in the extreme. Everywhere the individual is reduced to total subservience to the collectivity' (*op. cit.* p. 42). The problems raised by the *Supplément* are acutely analysed in the edition by Herbert Dieckmann (Geneva–Paris, 1955).

[50] *Supplément*, ed. Dieckmann, p. 64.

[51] *Correspondance*, XIII, p. 26.

[52] *Oeuvres philosophiques*, pp. 552–3.

[53] See Sherman, *op. cit.* p. 107 n., for a useful bibliography of conflicting interpretations of *Le Neveu*.

[54] L. G. Crocker, '*Jacques le fataliste*, an "Expérience morale" ', *Diderot Studies*, III, pp. 73–99.

[55] For a fuller discussion of this aspect of his thought see Emita Hill, 'Human Nature and the Moral *Monstre*', *Diderot Studies*, XVI, pp. 91–117.

[56] Ed. Fabre, p. 72.

[57] See Proust, *op. cit.* pp. 338 ff. and *Correspondance*, III, p. 98.

[58] On Helvétius (and on Diderot's reactions) see D. W. Smith, *Helvétius: A Study in Persecution* (Oxford, 1965).

[59] *Oeuvres philosophiques*, pp. 257 ff. See also *Correspondance*, V, p. 142.

[60] *Oeuvres complètes*, II, p. 302.

[61] *Ibid.* p. 289.

[62] *Ibid.* pp. 318 and 300. The significance and modernity of Diderot's view is brought out by I. W. Alexander, 'Philosophy of Organism and Philosophy of Consciousness in Diderot's Speculative Thought' in *Studies in Romance Philology and French Literature presented to John Orr* (Manchester, 1953).

[63] *Oeuvres complètes*, II, pp. 343–5.

[64] *Ibid.* pp. 308–14.

[65] *Oeuvres politiques*, pp. 61 ff.

[66] *Oeuvres politiques*, pp. 129 ff. Diderot's relationship to Frederick is examined by Adrienne Hytier, 'Le Philosophe et le despote: Histoire d'une inimité. Diderot et Frédéric II', *Diderot Studies*, VI, pp. 55–87.

[67] *Oeuvres politiques*, pp. 151 ff.

[68] *Oeuvres complètes*, II, p. 429. See also *Oeuvres politiques*, p. 272.

[69] *Oeuvres politiques*, pp. 237 ff.

[70] *Mémoires pour Cathérine II*, ed. Vernière (Paris, 1966), p. xviii.

[71] *Oeuvres complètes*, III, pp. 433 ff.

[72] *Oeuvres politiques*, pp. 331 ff.

[73] Vernière (*Oeuvres politiques*, p. xxxiii) notes that in 1772 Diderot

partly justifies the authoritarian *coup* of Gustav III of Sweden by referring to the danger of 'popular anarchy'.

[74] See *Aux Insurgents d'Amérique* (*Oeuvres politiques*, pp. 489 ff.

[75] See J. Th. de Booy and Alan J. Freer, '*Jacques le fataliste* et *La Religieuse* devant la critique révolutionnaire', *Studies on Voltaire and the Eighteenth Century*, XXXIII, pp. 41 ff.

[76] *Oeuvres complètes*, IV, pp. 15–16.

[77] See *Oeuvres politiques*, p. xxxii.

[78] *Ibid.* p. 288.

[79] *Ibid.* p. xxxvi.

[80] *Oeuvres complètes*, III. See especially pp. 111, 164 and 263.

9

JEAN-JACQUES ROUSSEAU, PHILOSOPHER OF NATURE

Ronald Grimsley

From the very outset of his literary and intellectual career Rousseau saw himself as an uncompromising critic of contemporary society. As he has vividly related in his personal writings, the famous moment of 'illumination' when he was on the way to visit his friend Diderot imprisoned in the Château de Vincennes not only gave him a vision of 'another universe' but transformed him into 'another man'. An overwhelming 'enthusiasm for truth, freedom and virtue' made him henceforth reject the corrupt values of the society he saw around him; 'to be free and virtuous and above fortune and opinion' seemed a greater and nobler attitude than servile acquiescence in the 'maxims of his age'.

In spite of its undoubted intensity, this sudden attack upon the society and culture of his time had been prepared by the earlier circumstances of his life. He himself admits that the success of the *Discourse on the Sciences and Arts* 'fermented in his heart the first leaven of heroism and virtue which his father, his fatherland and Plutarch had put there in his childhood' (I, 356).[1] Because he had been born a Genevan Protestant, had received little formal education and had felt himself to be a man of great sensitivity rather than a professional intellectual, his departure from Geneva at the age of sixteen made it likely that he would become an outsider in any foreign society. Admittedly, the *philosophes* were also fierce critics of traditional institutions and beliefs, but since their critical attitude was that of men brought up within the society they were attacking, their animadversions were less radical than Rousseau's. It is significant, for example, that Diderot and d'Alembert looked upon the argument of Rousseau's *Discourse on the Sciences and Arts* as a clever paradox rather than as a deeply felt personal conviction; they failed to see that Rousseau would not entertain an idea merely because he found it intellectually attractive; he had to feel that he was writing through a sense of vocation and with the serious intention of promulgating truths beneficial to humanity. This meant that he was impelled into a literary career almost in spite of himself.

The strongly critical emphasis of the first *Discourse* makes its message largely negative: Rousseau is more concerned with denouncing the evils of existing society than with producing an effective remedy. The positive aspect of the essay consists of an invocation of 'virtue' as the 'sublime science of simple souls'; the reader is also exhorted 'to withdraw into himself' and 'to listen to the voice of conscience in the silence of the passions'; by so doing he will soon realize that it is more important to 'do well' than to 'speak well'. This moral theme was reiterated in the controversy aroused by the publication of the *Discourse*, for Rousseau insisted that only 'the love of humanity and virtue' had prompted him to reply to his critics; he was animated by 'the simplicity and zeal of a friend of truth and humanity who puts all his glory in rendering homage to the one, and all his happiness in being useful to the other'. ' "Virtue, truth!" I shall constantly exclaim, "Virtue, truth!" If someone perceives those words alone, I have nothing more to say to him' (III, 33). This theme was to recur in all the early writings. The preface to the *Letter to d'Alembert on the Theatre*, for example, stressed that it was not a question of 'vain philosophical twaddle' but of 'a truth of importance to a whole people' (p. 8). 'Justice and truth', he insisted, 'those are man's first duties. Humanity, fatherland, those are his first affections' (p. 3). He stressed particularly how the direct-

ness and simplicity of such moral qualities and feelings contrasted with the 'subtlety' (almost always a pejorative term in
Rousseau) of existing attitudes. Simplicity also meant strength
and vigour in both body and soul – qualities again notably
absent from contemporary society.

If such moral values are natural in so far as they are 'engraved in the human heart', their precise connection with
'nature' in the broadest sense needs to be clarified. The moral
principles of the first essay are frequently illustrated by appeals
to the examples of the Ancients – the early Roman Republic
and Sparta, for instance – and to those small modern nations
(such as the Swiss) who have so far escaped irremediable
corruption, but Rousseau points out that for these nations
virtue was not always a difficult achievement; it was such an
intimate part of their way of life that peoples of old had no
difficulty in 'being' what they 'appeared' to be; their 'simplicity,
innocence and virtue' made them more natural than their
sophisticated successors. Modern man finds it difficult to
achieve virtue since he has to overcome the nefarious influence
of his environment and his own artificial character. When he
thinks of the remote past Rousseau evokes 'the image of the
simplicity of these early times'. 'It is a fine shore, adorned
solely by the hands of nature, towards which our eyes are
constantly turned and from which we feel ourselves moving
away with regret' (III, 220). A striking aspect of the life of
these 'innocent and virtuous men of old' was the way in which
they considered the gods as 'witnesses of their actions'. It was
not until they treated the gods as 'importunate spectators'
that they fell into vice and depravity. Already we see how
Rousseau's thoughts are directed towards the ideal of human
existence harmoniously and spontaneously related to a 'nature'
greater than itself.

Rousseau's initial description of the plight of modern man
inevitably involved him in an attempt to analyse its causes.
Whatever 'nature' may mean in its broadest and most immediate aspect, its absence from the modern world means
that the 'nature of man' has to be reconstituted through an

analysis of its gradual historical development, even though this can be done only imaginatively and hypothetically. Rousseau makes it clear that any consideration of man's historical origins must be subordinated to a discussion of his essential and 'original' nature; but because man's true nature has been corrupted and distorted by the historical process, Rousseau proposes to examine how this has come about. That is why he starts with 'nature' in its physical and physiological aspects. A proper understanding of primitive man's relationship with his physical environment will perhaps provide some insight into the reasons for his subsequent deterioration. Rousseau stresses, however, that at this primitive level man is not a truly human being in the full sense of that term, for he is a creature dominated by primordial instinctive urges such as self-preservation, and seeking little more than food, shelter and sex. He has no 'moral' needs since he lives isolated from his fellow-men; his lack of stable and permanent contact with others thus obviates the need for sustained reflection about his relationship with them. Moreover, the essential requirements of self-preservation can be adequately controlled by the natural pity which makes him spontaneously recoil from inflicting gratuitous suffering on others.

Rousseau's eulogy of the 'state of nature' is intended to contrast the unity and contentment of primitive man with the inner conflicts of modern man who has failed to cope with his simplest physical needs: he has been removed from the 'order of things' by his failure to understand such simple experiences as sexual appetite, sickness and death; instead of accepting them as part of the process of nature he has made them into objects of fear and anxiety; his attempts to protect himself from sickness by a vain recourse to medicine and from death by superstition, have merely aggravated his misfortunes. Primitive man, on the other hand, was content to 'give himself to the sole feeling of his present existence without any idea of the future, however near it might be' (III, 144), reflection upon it would have destroyed his peaceful way of life and made him into a 'depraved animal'.

Rousseau is not of course advocating a return to the state of nature or, in Voltaire's humorous phrase, urging men 'to walk again on all fours'. He knows that when once men have abandoned the state of nature, they can never return to it. 'Human nature does not go backwards and we never return to times of innocence and equality when we have once gone away from them' (I, 935). In any case, it would not be desirable to do so, since primitive man is an animal-like creature who has not developed his full human potentialities. From the very beginning, insists Rousseau, he was endowed with freedom and perfectibility, but these remained merely 'virtual' capacities because he had no need to use them: in the simple conditions of his primitive way of life he seemed to lead a static, almost timeless existence. Yet unforeseen changes in his physical environment eventually impelled him to move away from this state: he began to acquire a history and, with it, a goal and purpose hitherto lacking.

The true fulfilment of human nature comes only with the development of its highest possibilities. God did not intend man to remain restricted to the merely physical aspects of his being. Rousseau considers that the happiest period of man's existence was not to be found in the state of nature, but in the 'first revolution' which produced a simple communal life based on the 'establishment and distinction of families' and a 'kind of property'. Perhaps at this stage there had been some diminution in 'the pure emotion of nature, prior to all reflection' (III, 155) as well as in the 'force of natural pity' which marked the primitive state, but men had acquired other capacities such as the 'perception of certain relationships' and a 'kind of reflection' which enabled them to affirm their superiority over the animals. Although this new stage was also marked by the appearance of the 'first movement of pride' from which so many misfortunes were later to stem, the benefits undoubtedly outweighed the disadvantages since these first steps away from innocence and happiness had led to new forms of fulfilment; men were now 'placed by nature at an equal distance from the stupidity of brutes and the fatal enlightenment of civil man'.

'This period in the development of human faculties, keeping a just mean between the indolence of the primitive state and the irrepressible activity of our pride, must have been the happiest and most stable age' (III, 171). It was the 'true youth of the world', a veritable 'golden age'. Rousseau cannot forbear from referring to the idyllic moment when men sat 'by the fountains and experienced idyllic love'.

However happy it may have been, this mode of existence could not last, for men were developing their imagination, memory and reason and experiencing the effects of 'pride'. It is not necessary to retrace here Rousseau's account of the discovery of metallurgy and agriculture and the eventual distinction between 'mine and thine' as men vied with one another to acquire more and more of the earth's resources. Life became such a ferocious struggle for existence and the division between rich and poor, powerful and weak, so harmful to peace and security that people were ultimately persuaded to accept the formation of a political society as the only way of escaping from perpetual strife. Henceforth dominated by an 'evil propensity to harm one another', men put on a 'mask' which concealed their real selfishness, so that 'being and appearing became two different things' and from this distinction arose 'the imposing pomp, deceitful cunning and all the vices which follow in their train' (III, 174–5); in short, men gave up their freedom and independence for the enslavement imposed on them by modern society.

As the corruption of modern man becomes increasingly evident, so does the notion of his true nature gradually disappear, until, finally, 'nature' emerges only as an indication of what men might have been rather than of what they have actually become. At the universal level, nature has not changed, but modern man is incapable of heeding its lessons. Nature is revealed only to those who have eyes to see it. This means that from this point onwards in Rousseau's thought, nature, in the fullest sense, remains both a reality – for the most part a hidden reality – and a goal.

In spite of this difficulty, nature already emerges as an indispensable corrective to the distortions imposed by modern society and very often we can discern its meaning, as Rousseau himself says, by assuming it to be the very opposite of what we see before us. More positively, however, nature already appears as an effective background to any worthwhile human activity. This is clearly brought out in the *Letter to d'Alembert*. Whereas the modern theatre separates man from his own being and his fellow-men, true pleasures 'spring from his nature and originate in his labours, relationships and needs' (p. 20). Unlike the 'dark cavern' of the modern theatre – and its social counterpart, the *salons* or 'voluntary prisons' in which effeminate men immure themselves – the old Greek tragedy took place amid the beauty of the physical world. 'These great, superb entertainments, given beneath the sky, in the presence of a whole nation', were intended 'to raise up and stir the soul', for actors and spectators were 'animated by the same zeal' (p. 105).

When at the end of the *Letter* Rousseau depicts the entertainment most suited to his fellow-Genevans, he sees it as a spontaneously creative communal activity in which people are open to one another and the world of nature. Instead of these 'exclusive entertainments which sadly shut up a small number of spectators in a dark cave', 'happy peoples' celebrate their freedom with a true *air de fête*. 'It is in the open air, beneath the sky', he tells the Genevans, 'that you must gather and abandon yourselves to the sweet feeling of your happiness' (p. 168).

When he tries to give a more precise philosophical analysis of his fundamental conception of nature, Rousseau links it up with the principle of order – a theme to which he constantly returns in his didactic writings. Since cosmic order has been created by God, man is provided with a reliable guide in 'well-ordered nature'. The same consideration applies to the nature of man himself. Just as the physical universe expresses a spiritual principle which sustains it, so is man's body related to the animating principle of the soul. There is a 'conformity' between 'man's immortal nature and the constitution of this world and the physical order which he sees prevailing in it' (I, 1018). One of the objectives of human life ought to be the contemplation of this order, for true 'self-contentment' can be achieved by the individual only when he 'meditates on the order of the universe, not in order to explain it by futile systems, but in order to admire it unceasingly and adore the wise author who can be felt in it' (IV, 605). As the Savoyard priest also says: 'I acquiesce in the order established by him [God], certain of enjoying this order one day and finding my bliss in it: for what sweeter felicity is there than to feel oneself ordered in a system where all is good?' (IV, 603). Such a view clearly proves that Rousseau is no advocate of an irresponsible individualism. He affirms that whereas the wicked man tries to make the universal order conform to his own desires, 'the good man orders himself in relation to the whole' (IV, 602).

Yet the attainment of this supreme goal cannot be achieved without effort. If the universal order is already there, men do not easily perceive it. As we have seen, history reveals their failure to attain the type of existence for which God intended them. Reality, in the deepest sense, thus becomes a goal rather than an immediate fact. Nature is not simply there, but, as far as man is concerned, has to be recreated. If, therefore, the *Profession de Foi* occupies an important place in *Émile*, it represents a fairly advanced stage of human development. The intention of *Émile* is to explain the essential stages of man's development as they would take place if he were free from the corrupting influence of his present environment. As such, the work depicts an ideal, but an ideal elaborated in accordance with the 'original' features of human nature. More especially, it presupposes direct contact with the external world as found in the countryside and in an environment far removed from the evils of city-life. The main reason for this setting is Rousseau's overriding desire to free the growing child from the oppressive influence of the arbitrary human will, which he regards as a sign of physical and psychological oppression. Dependence, he is careful to point out, is not resented by the individual at any stage of his development as long as it stems from natural 'necessity' and not from the uncontrolled human will. From the very beginning of his life, the child must be allowed to develop in accordance with innate powers to which physical nature sets a definite but not irksome limit; in modern society these are frustrated and distorted by the environment and especially by the artificial constraints imposed upon him by adults. Rousseau sees, for example, tight swaddling-clothes as the first unmistakable indication of the enslavement to which the modern human being is destined for the rest of his life. Early education, therefore, must be 'negative', for it will consist mainly of removing possible obstacles instead of actively trying to stimulate activities which will develop of their own accord.

If the development of the human being is to take place under the guidance of 'nature', the educator will have to recognize that 'the first movements of nature are always right' and that 'there is no original perversity in the human heart' (IV, 322). Man's natural goodness is thus a reason for accepting 'negative education' since it is a question of keeping out bad influences rather than of being anxious about the cultivation of good ones; it is enough at this early stage to let the child be educated by 'the sole force of things'; for it is 'in human nature to endure patiently the necessity of things but not the ill-will of other people' (IV, 320). 'Let the child', says Rousseau, 'see necessity in things, not in the whim of men.' It is 'force' – not 'authority' – which must be the guiding principle of these early years.

If nature provides an overriding principle which gives man a secure and effective view of his situation in the world, it always remains a dynamic concept as far as his own being is concerned. In the course of his life the individual passes through different stages of development, each of which has its own distinctive features and its own 'perfection'. 'Nature', affirms Rousseau, 'wants children to be children before being men.' 'Childhood', he goes on, 'has its own ways of seeing, thinking and feeling, which are peculiar to it; nothing is more foolish than to want to replace them by our own' (IV, 319). This respect for the intrinsic features of childhood makes Rousseau enter an eloquent plea on behalf of the child whom he wishes to be a happy and free being, enjoying to the full the possibilities of his own particular nature. Too many educators, he maintains, have made the child miserable by their inordinate preoccupation with his future as a man.

Some human faculties mature slowly, for they do not consist of a simple homogeneous component. Reason, for example, is not a unique power possessing identical features at all phases of human life: it is 'a compound of all the rest and the one that develops late'. In the child it functions in connection with the senses – this is *la raison sensitive* – so that our 'first masters of philosophy are our feet, hands and eyes'; in our early years, 'our limbs, senses and organs are the instruments of our intelligence', it is only later on that we acquire the use of an 'intellectual reason' (IV, 369). The developing function of reason, however, does not bring it into conflict with 'nature', although it may at times have to play a subordinate role, for, in Rousseau's view, 'nature' is much more fundamental than reason. Contemporary thinkers are criticized for their failure to understand the proper function of reason, which is to harmonize with the other essential elements of the self. Powerless when it relies on its own strength and harmful when it lets itself become a mere instrument of passion and prejudice, it is none the less – like all genuine human attributes – good in itself. Moreover, as soon as it recognizes its proper place in the hierarchy of human attributes, it can be of great value in clarifying their true meaning. In other words, reason is an indispensable means of attaining true knowledge. As soon as man becomes aware of his true being and his position in nature, reason can help him to achieve greater understanding and fulfilment.

The link between reason and nature becomes evident in Rousseau's view of morality. The source of all morality, he insists, lies in one of man's deepest impulses – conscience. Now conscience is not a judgment but a feeling – a 'divine instinct' and an 'inner voice'; it is 'the voice of the soul, just as the passions are the voice of the body'. The 'subtleties' of reason may deceive us, but the simple voice of conscience never will, for it is 'man's true guide' and 'an infallible judge of good and evil', 'he who follows conscience obeys nature and need not be afraid of going astray'. Conscience is 'the sacred voice of nature, stronger than that of the gods' (IV, 598). The principle of conscience, therefore, can be explained independently of reason. Yet when all this has been said, reason still plays an important role in morality, for conscience 'cannot be effectively developed without it'; although it is 'an innate principle of justice and virtue in the depth of our soul', conscience cannot remain a blind impulse, for it is ultimately linked up with the 'order of nature'. Since this order sometimes requires the individual to act 'against the laws of men' (IV, 320), he may need to use his reason in order to apply his moral principles to particular situations.

Because morality is not restricted to the isolated individual, it involves relations – sometimes quite complicated – with other people. Apart from the co-operation of reason, morality requires the activity of the will. Whatever he may think and feel, the individual has to translate his thoughts and feelings into action by the use of his freedom. In the mature human being 'nature' will thus be a unifying principle, for a man can attain true happiness and fulfilment only when all his powers are functioning harmoniously; conscience, reason and will combine to produce a balanced and integrated view of human existence, for man has 'conscience to love the good, reason to know it and freedom to choose it' (IV, 605). This means that the 'order' which lies at the heart of the universal system will be reconstituted in the life of man himself. Since his ultimate goal will be the achievement of a 'self-contentment' based on his active participation in this universal system – so that even the next life will simply be a perfect extension of the good man's earthly existence – he will one day 'enjoy the contempla- tion of the Supreme Being and the eternal truths of which He is the source, when the beauty of order will strike all the powers of his soul' (IV, 591). This ultimate felicity will be possible, however, only to the man who has freed himself from the corrupting influence of his environment and attained a new kind of experience by 'withdrawing into himself' and rediscovering the meaning of his existence in the light of a new consciousness of 'nature'.

If an adequate understanding of 'nature' lay at the heart of Rousseau's philosophy, the main principles of his 'system' were not derived primarily from reflection or a critical reaction to other thinkers' views – although these obviously played an important part in the elaboration of his thought – but in a personal response to the basic intuitions of his own inner life. As he says in the *Dialogues*, 'whence could the portrayer and apologist of nature, today so disfigured and so calumnied, have drawn his model except from his own heart?' Yet as soon as he had discovered these principles intuitively, he had to reflect upon them with a view to making them comprehensible to others and this often meant clarifying them in relation to the ideas of other thinkers. There was never any question of falling into mere subjectivisim, for he was convinced that his ideas were based on 'principles engraved in the human heart' and the universal system of which it formed part. Speaking of his religious ideas in his very last – and unfinished – work, *Les Rêveries du Promeneur solitaire*, he refers to 'a whole body of doctrine so solid, so consistent and formed with so much meditation and care, so well adapted to his reason, his heart and his whole being and strengthened by the inner assent which he felt to be lacking in all the rest' (I, 1018). Moreover, such a philosophy contained 'eternal truths admitted by all times, all sages, recognized by every nation and engraved in the human heart in indelible character's (I, 1021).

If the concept of nature provides Rousseau's thought with a principle of unity and harmony at the religious and metaphysical level, it does not offer an obvious and easy solution to the problems of social and political life. Progress from the primitive state to the supreme felicity of true *contentement de soi-même* still requires a radical transformation of the individual who abandons a 'natural freedom' based on innate physical strength to a disciplined moral freedom derived from participation in civil life: this new kind of freedom thus requires a process of 'denaturation'. In an important passage in *Émile* Rousseau points out that the existence of both primitive and civil man involves dependence on 'necessity', the former on the necessity of physical nature, the latter on the necessity of the laws. Whereas the necessity governing the life of primitive man is provided by the individual's innate strength, the necessity of social life is created to a large extent by man himself. Faced with the responsibility of freely determining the conditions under which he will henceforth live, he finally chooses to submit to the rule of law. In this way he overcomes the disastrous consequences of an 'uncontrolled dependence on men' which engenders nothing but misery and vice by dividing mankind into masters and slaves. 'If there is some means of curing this evil in society, it is through substituting law for men and arming the general wills with a real strength which is superior to the influence of any particular will. If the laws of nations could have, like those of nature, an inflexibility which no human force could ever overcome, dependence on men would again become dependence on things: in the commonwealth all the advantages of the natural state would be combined with those of the civil state; to the freedom which keeps men exempt from vice would be added the morality which lifts them up to virtue' (IV, 311).

Yet such a view of civil life rests much less on spontaneous 'natural right' than on rational 'natural right', although the two are not absolutely distinct. It is no longer sufficient for the individual to give way to the promptings of natural impulse or his own spontaneous goodness, for he is deliberately choosing the way in which he will live with other people. Social life, therefore, is not a simple extension of natural life (for example, the family) and the ruler is no mere father-figure, but it is a carefully organized mode of existence in which all citizens participate on free and equal terms.

It is thus easy to see why the *Social Contract* should be Rousseau's last didactic work, for it is only through his participation in civil life that man attains true maturity: he is henceforth called upon to be a fully conscious individual, rationally and morally responsible for his membership of the community. 'Instinct' has given way to 'justice', 'appetite' to 'duty' and 'right', and 'from being the stupid limited animal he was in the state of nature' he has become 'an intelligent being and a man' (III, 364). Admittedly, the establishment of political and civil society is partially motivated by self-interest, in so far as all citizens are seeking security and protection, but it is also inspired by the desire for moral fulfilment. That is why, for Rousseau, politics and morality remain inseparable. In society alone can man acquire 'moral' as opposed to 'natural' freedom. Yet such a moral and political attitude requires constant effort if it is to resist not only the historical and physical pressures which ultimately destroy all societies but also those elements in human nature which constantly threaten to weaken the effectiveness of reason and will.

The apparently austere tone of the *Social Contract* is due partly to the moral demands made upon the individual by his membership of the political community; effective citizenship is impossible without a strong sense of personal responsibility and the achievement of genuine 'virtue'. Virtue, as Rousseau points out, implies strength and the ability to overcome natural feelings; 'virtue belongs to a being weak by nature but strong by will'. In society it is not enough for a man to follow the spontaneous impulse of natural goodness, for 'goodness breaks and perishes under the shock of the passions' (IV, 818); the 'simplicity of nature' alone cannot produce a fully developed human being, for 'the good man is good only for himself', whereas the virtuous man, being aware of his obligations to others, 'sacrifices inclination to duty and resists his heart in order to listen to his reason' (*ibid.*): 'he follows his reason and his conscience and does his duty'. This means that the individual can henceforth live 'in order', for virtue is 'love of order'. If, however, he is to adapt himself satisfactorily to the demands of the social and political order, a man may need the support of principles greater than those provided by his own moral strength. This explains Rousseau's tardy insertion of the chapter on 'Civil Religion' into the *Social Contract*: he felt that, to be effective, social morality needed a religious sanction. This was quite consistent with his general principles since the life of man, both as individual and citizen, was bound up with a 'nature' greater than himself.

The strongly moral aspect of Rousseau's philosophy of man has probably been obscured by the influence of his personal writings, in which he tended to portray himself as a simple 'man of nature' – a 'good and innocent man' persecuted by a wicked world; isolated from his fellows, he believed himself to be justified in following the promptings of his sensibility. Yet even in his very last work – *Les Rêveries* – he admitted that he might have been mistaken about his true virtue, for there was no virtue in 'following one's inclinations' but only in 'overcoming them when duty ordered it'. 'Born good and sensitive', he had never been able to do this (I, 1052–3). Moreover, the personal and imaginative writings had described aspects of the human personality which did not fit in easily with the controlled and ordered view of nature elaborated in the didactic works – for example, the yearning for the infinite and the awareness of an 'inexplicable void' in the presence of nature (described in the third of the letters to M. de Malesherbes) and Julie's longing for the absolute and her deep feeling of *ennui* (in *La Nouvelle Héloïse*). If these were the experiences of a sensitive man who believed himself to be cut off from society, they anticipated feelings and aspirations which were to become familiar to later Romantic generations. In his formal works, however, Rousseau strove to give nature a universal meaning based on the recognition of a reality greater than that of man himself.

NOTES

1 All references, indicated solely by volume and page-number, are to the *Oeuvres complètes de Jean-Jacques Rousseau*, edited by B. Gagnebin and M. Raymond, Bibliothèque de la Pléiade, Paris, Vols. I–IV, 1959–69 (to be completed in 5 volumes). As the *Lettre à d'Alembert sur les Spectacles* has not yet been included in this edition, all references will be to the critical edition by M. Fuchs (Lille and Geneva, 1948). Translations are my own.

10

BUTLER'S THEORY OF
MORAL JUDGMENT

Roger A. Shiner

It is something of a commonplace of Butlerian interpretation
that the main interest and achievements of Butler's moral
philosophy are in normative ethics, and not metaethics. He
wishes to bring moral enlightenment to citizens and not, to
philosophers, epistemological enlightenment. Nonetheless for
that he makes a number of remarks which, if we were collecting
for some bizarre purpose metacthical forms of words, we would
note down and include in our collection. Thus he makes some
progress towards the development of a moral epistemology, a
theory of moral judgment. My purpose here is to assess those
steps, and to see how far the structure which results can be
called a theory. I have the impression that much of the reluct-
ance among scholars to allow that Butler does have a theory
of moral judgment is caused by the metaethical blinkers that
they themselves wear; what is in fact the beginnings of an
unfashionable and unconventional theory is seen as un-
sophisticated confusion. But I shall not overdo praise of Butler.
I shall suggest that Aristotle does a somewhat better job of
developing this type of theory.

The bulk of moral epistemology in the history of philosophy
has been dominated by the model of the essential separation
of Reason and Sentiment as possible sources of moral judgment,
and by regarding Reason as having as its object matters of

fact and *a priori* truths, relations of ideas, if you like. As the last words indicate, Hume is one of the arch-exponents of this model, and, for ease of identification, I shall call it the 'Humean Model'. The psychological antecedents of moral judgment are assumed by the model to be *either* Reason *or* Sentiment, but not both. Either Reason is the slave of the passions (cf. Hume, *T*, II.iii.3)[1], or the passions are unruly horses to be subdued and controlled by the charioteer Reason (cf. Plato, *Phaedrus*, 246 a ff.). The task of moral philosophy is simply to decide which. In more modern clothes, the model has emerged in two forms – either as a reduction of moral statements to a straightforward species of factual or descriptive statement; or as the view that moral judgments are something like expressions of emotion, statements of personal feeling, prescriptions, commendations, and so on, which follow a discernment of the empirical facts. As Stevenson puts it, 'I approve of this; do so as well' (21); or, with vastly greater elegance, Hume: 'After every circumstance, every relation is known, the understanding has no further room to operate, nor any object on which it could employ itself. The approbation or blame which then ensues, cannot be the work of the judgment, but of the heart: and is not a speculative proposition or affirmation, but an active feeling or sentiment' (*IPM*, Appendix I, 240).

For the remainder of this lecture, one of the above parties will receive comparatively little attention, namely, the Rationalist or Cognitivist party. Both Butler and Aristotle are sceptical of the ability of Reason alone to produce moral agency, and they are at a commonsensical level quite right about this. That is, one who holds moral beliefs and exercises moral judgment is not one who merely utters propositions, states facts, and draws inferences. He is also one who has attitudes and emotions, feelings and concerns, sentiments and cares, all of which essentially result in actions. He is one who is *not indifferent* to the things about which he supposedly exercises moral judgment and holds moral beliefs. He is *moved and affected*, not merely cognizant.

I must however underline the following point. This commonsensical fact I take to be obscured or ignored by Cogniti-vism and Rationalism in moral epistemology. Nevertheless, in saying such theories err by ignoring the point about Sentiment, I wish to leave open for the moment *how* one is to include the point in an adequate theory of moral judgment. I am not at this stage to be taken as thinking that by rejecting, for example, Plato, Kant and Moore, I am opting for Hume.

There are several 'Humean' passages in Butler, which both suggest a systematic distinction between Reason and Sentiment, and emphasize the inability of Reason alone to produce virtue. Butler regards Conscience as a quite separate principle from self-love, benevolence and the particular affections. He often associates Conscience with Reason (cf. *P* 18, 24: *S* 6.12, 13.5). In the fifth Sermon, he says that 'Reason alone, whatever anyone may wish, is not in reality a sufficient motive of virtue in such a creature as man' (5.3), and that the affections are needed to supply the deficiencies of the higher principles. A little later (5.10), he says that 'reasonable and cool self-love' has enough problems moving mankind. 'It is therefore absurd to imagine that, without affection, the same reason [sc. that which tells us that 'the results of food and sleep are the necessary means of our preservation'] alone would be more effectual to engage us to perform the duties we owe to our fellow-creatures'. Our conviction of duty, he says, 'hath but a distant influence upon our temper and actions' (*S* 9.21), and, in an intriguing application of this thought for the sociology of law, claims that 'the cool consideration of reason . . . might indeed be sufficient to procure laws to be enacted', but it is 'resentment or indignation' that bring the offender to justice (*S* 8.14).

However, to rest content with these quotations would give a wholly misleading and one-sided picture of Butler's view of moral judgment. Despite the passages just mentioned, there are numerous others in Butler's 'official' explanations of Conscience which exclude the equation of Conscience with an enslaved Humean Reason. On many occasions, Conscience itself is said to do the approving or disapproving (*P* 19, 24; *S* 1.8, 2.2, 2.8, 2.9, 2.14; in the latter, Conscience is also said to influence us). Moreover, there seems no inclination on Butler's part to anticipate recent metaethical theory by investing ordinary language with special connotations. He does not harden notions as 'survey', 'distinguish', 'reflect', 'discern' into technical terms and codewords for the activities of a Humean Reason, restricted to relation of ideas and matters of fact. Nor does he regard such notions as 'approve', 'disapprove', 'influence' as equally technical, and as codewords for the activities of Humean Sentiments in relation to moral value. P 24 refers to a 'disapprobation of reflection'; S 1.8 describes how the human mind, employing its 'principle of reflection' by which it can 'distinguish between, approve and disapprove' its own actions, 'can take a view of what passes within itself'; and also how 'in this survey it approves of one, disapproves of another, and towards a third ... is quite indifferent'. In S 2.9, Conscience is said to 'survey, approve or disapprove'. DV 3 talks of a 'sense or discernment' of actions. In terms of their denotations and connotations in contemporary moral philosophy, these locutions are incomprehensible. A present-day philosopher will want to say to Butler, 'Conscience must *either* reflect *or* approve, *either* sense *or* discern; it cannot do both. It must either make factual/descriptive judgments, or evaluative/prescriptive judgments, but not both.'

Of course, in suggesting that Butler is, on the face of it, swimming against the tide of contemporary metaethical theory, I do not wish to overlook the fact that he was also seemingly going counter to the flow of thought of his own time. The seventeenth and eighteenth centuries saw the great debate between Rationalist and Sentimentalist theories of moral judgment. But we are attuned to the jargon and philosophical commonplaces of our own time. Since my concern here is as much with doing moral philosophy as with doing history of moral philosophy, I will continue to regard Butler as an antagonist of modern heroes. It has often been remarked that Butler, in Prof. Raphael's words, 'gives the [moral sense] controversy no more than a passing and rather contemptuous, notice' (219). The tendency, however, is to regard this as something of biographical or historical significance, but not of philosophical significance. Prof. Donald Mackinnon is almost alone among modern writers on Butler to suggest that there may be a deeper philosophical significance. He claims that 'the importance of Butler's work in ethics lies in the contribution which he makes to the problem of method' (201); he continues by remarking that Butler 'does insist that we bring together what prevailing forms of philosophical fashion have long encouraged us to separate, now in one way, now in another'. (*Ibid.*) The remainder of this lecture may be represented as a set of extended variations on this theme.

The difficulty in presenting Butler as an important radical innovator in metaethical theory has already been hinted at. Removing the spectacles from the eyes of metaethical theorists was not his main concern. But I think we may be able to put the things he docs say in some sort of context by comparing them with remarks made about moral judgment and moral virtue by Aristotle. He likewise sought to bring together what fashion encourages us to separate, and for him a theory of moral judgment *was* of major concern. Aristotle's moral philosophy, as unfolded in the *Nic. Ethics*, is complex and sophisticated. I can only sketch certain points here, but I hope the sketch will provide us with all we need. We shall concentrate on what is contained with greater or lesser degrees of explicitness in the definition of Moral Virtue in Bk. II. (1106 b 36 ff). Moral virtue is, says Aristotle, a disposition to choose according to the mean relative to us, defined as the man of practical wisdom would define it. There are six crucial elements in this definition – that moral virtue is a disposition; that it essentially involves choice; the celebrated doctrine of the mean; the idea that the mean is relative; the idea that, though relative, the mean is defined; and the equally celebrated doctrine of practical wisdom and the practically wise man. Although all parts are interconnected, of most importance are the notions of choice and practical wisdom.

Like others before and after him, Aristotle divides the human soul into parts, a rational part, an appetitive part, and a nutritive part (cf. e.g. *NE* I. 13). There are further more complex divisions, but these do not concern us. Human activities essentially consist in or are caused by the activities of the human soul. Human virtue consists in performing these activities well. Aristotle distinguishes between the Intellectual Virtues and the Moral Virtues (1103 a 4). The Intellectual Virtues are virtues of the rational part of the soul. The Moral Virtues, by contrast, are virtues of the appetitive part of the soul. So far, nothing sounds very revolutionary; in fact, it sounds depressingly 'Humean'. But the significant differences and innovations come when we start to examine in more detail the specific intellectual virtue of *phronesis*, practical wisdom, and Aristotle's concept of *proairesis*, moral choice.

Practical wisdom is to be distinguished, among other things, from speculative/scientific/theoretical wisdom. Practical wisdom is the virtue of the rational part of the soul as far as it concerns itself with *action*, and not merely thought (1140 b 20). The generalizations that can be made about practical matters, in Aristotle's view, are of a logically different kind than those that can be made about scientific/theoretical matters. The generalizations of science are universal truths; the generalizations of practice are simply 'true for the most part' (1094 b 12 ff). This is because practical matters are themselves different from scientific matters; we must, he says, expect no more precision in an enquiry than the nature of its subject-matter allows. Practical wisdom is the successful exercise of reason in the realm of practical matters. It involves awareness of these guarded generalizations. But because of the nature of those generalizations, it involves also, and possibly more importantly, the delicate task of the application of those generalizations to particular cases and circumstances. (1142 a 23 ff., 1143 a 25 ff.). Because moral truth is 'truth for the most part', one can never mechanically conclude that one's own case is covered by some given generalization. It could always, in principle, be an exception. Whether it is or not is also the province of practical wisdom to determine.

Despite this important modification, practical wisdom is

nonetheless, along with scientific or theoretical wisdom, still an intellectual virtue. Where does moral practice, moral agency, moral judgment come from? Aristotle's seemingly 'Humean' answer is that they come from the activity of the appetitive part of the soul. But, virtuous moral practice, agency and judgment occur just in case the activity of the appetitive part of the soul occurs in harmony with the deliverances of practical wisdom (1139 a 24). So, down, it seems, with Hume, now, and up with Plato. Appetites are fine and necessary, as long as they are not naughty and do exactly as Reason tells them. But, despite appearances, Aristotle is not pushing *this* line *either*. The crucial element is his concept of *moral choice*. Moral virtue is, as I quoted above, a disposition to *choose*. A man becomes virtuous by making choices, and by being influenced by the effects of those choices. Patterns of actions and choices produce dispositions. What, then, is moral choice? It clearly has to include both rational and desiderative or appetitive elements, but how does it include them? If Aristotle is to deserve the title of 'Rationalist', one would expect him to say moral choice is essentially rational and secondarily desiderative. If he is to be a proper 'Sentimentalist', one would expect him to say moral choice is essentially desiderative and secondarily rational. But he says *neither* of those things. Choice is, he says, *desiderative reason or rational desire, e orektikos nous e he proairesis dianoetike orexis* (1139 b 4). The moral choice, that activity of the human soul from which moral virtue springs, cannot be thought of as either primarily rational or primarily desiderative. It is primarily *both*. It matters not whether one thinks of it as reason qualified by desire or as desire qualified by reason; the distinction between reason and desire in moral choice is ultimately *artificial*. The morally virtuous man is not one in whom passions have subdued reason, or one in whom reason has subdued passions. He is one in whom reason and passions join forces in an undifferentiated whole to produce judgments and actions.

I think that, as a matter of fact, Aristotle is *dead right* about this. Part of the reason why metaethical theory has, in the

H

English-speaking world, ground to a halt in the last decade is
that such theorizing has gone about as far as it can go in terms
of variations on the 'Humean Model'. We are not going to
make any further progress until we give up the Great Divide
between Reason and Sentiment, and open ourselves to the
possibility of viewing moral judgment as essentially both. At
which point we can appropriately return to Butler. There is a
well-known and uncanny echo of Aristotle in Butler's discussion
of Conscience in the *DV*. Butler affirms in §1 the certain
existence of a 'moral approving and disapproving faculty', and
continues:

> It is manifest great part of common language, and of common
> behaviour over the world, is formed upon supposition of
> such a moral faculty; whether called conscience, moral
> reason, moral sense, or Divine reason; whether considered
> as a sentiment of the understanding, or as a perception of
> the heart; or, which seems the truth, as including both.

The expressions 'sentiment of the understanding' and 'perception of the heart', as Raphael remarks (230), 'to modern ears
. . . at first sound curious'. They sound curious, because
modern minds are committed to regarding them as incoherent.
Raphael's way of removing the strangeness does not succeed.
He argues that 'sentiment' could be used to mean 'rational
judgment' and 'perception' could be used to mean 'feeling'.
So, in his view, all Butler is saying is that conscience includes
both a rational judgment and an introspected feeling; the
paradoxical phrases disappear. But whether or not this is
historically plausible, it does not blunt the cutting-edge of
Butler's remark. If our faculty of moral judgment includes as
an essential part of itself *both* an element of reason *and* an element
of feeling, then Hume and Plato are left behind. The striking
metonymy may be removed, but not the striking thought; the
linguistic paradox, but not the philosophical paradox.

We can be certain that Aristotle's use of the conjoint expression is deliberate and designed to make metaethical points.
What entitles us to be certain is the fact that it is inextricably

embedded in a wider total theory, a view of knowledge, of the soul, and of the substance of moral virtue. Such a wider theory is at best skeletal in Butler. In particular, it is hard to decide the following quite central matter. Is, for Butler, the term 'conscience' the name for a whole faculty which includes both rational and affective elements, comparable to the Aristotelian *proairesis*? Or is 'conscience' the name simply for what would be for Aristotle the rational element in moral judgment, i.e. *phronesis*? My not very exciting solution to this problem is that there is a case to be made out for each view, and I find it difficult to see how they can both be reconciled. Thus there is a quite definite degree of interpretative charity in seizing on the above passage from *DV* 1, and attributing to Butler a comparably profound understanding of the issues to that exhibited by Aristotle. Rather, what we find in Butler is a barque afloat without a rudder, blown where the metaethical winds take it. Such an unstable theory is, I wish to underline, not without value. Through it, the complexities of the issue can be discerned. Butler is more sensitive than are, in the end, either Hume or Plato to the lie of the commonsensical land. In the last analysis that is the land of which philosophers are trying to give us a deeper understanding. Butler's remarks are, therefore, put in their proper perspective, illuminating.

First, let us see what evidence there is for conscience being analogous to practical wisdom, the Intellectual Virtue. The main evidence would be the passages referred to above (p. 201) in which we find a distinction between reason and affection, and conscience firmly on the side of reason and even equated with it. Butler takes pains when discussing benevolence in *Sermon* 12 to insist that benevolence is not blind. In reasonable creatures it is directed by their reason, 'for reason and reflection comes into our notion of a moral agent' (*S* 12.27). Being human, we have appetites and affections, one of which is benevolence. But the mere existence of this affection is not enough for virtue; it must be directed by reason. Again, in *S* 5.3, Butler says that a man will 'act suitably to our nature' only when 'those affections which God has impressed upon

his heart . . . are allowed scope to exercise themselves, but
under strict government and direction of reason'. These
passages suggest that reason is a separate faculty in moral
judgment, and that its role is like that of Plato's charioteer.
Although both reason and affection are necessary to produce
virtue, the two are not separate but equal; they are separate
and unequal.

On the other hand, the second group of passages quoted
above (pp. 201–2) suggest an analogy between conscience and
Aristotle's *proairesis* or choice. Conscience is said *both* to survey,
distinguish and reflect, *and* to approve or disapprove; conscience influences us; conscience is not indifferent (*DV* 8). I am
inclined to include the famous 'cool hour' passage (*S* 11.20)
in this category also. I accept Prof. White's account of the
passage (followed by Kleinig), that the 'justification' being
referred to is not objective, criterial justification, but something
like 'subjective rationality'. Before one can embark on a course
of action, one has to make sense of it within the particular
world-view and scheme of values one has. Two other passages
make the point clearer. In *S* 7.16 we find:

> As we are reasonable creatures, and have any regard to
> ourselves, we ought to lay these things plainly and honestly
> before our minds, and upon this, act as you think most fit;
> make that choice, and prefer that course of life, which you
> can justify to yourselves, and which sits most easy upon
> your mind.

The expression 'sit easy' is hardly an invitation to avaricious
selfishness. Analogously, in *S* 11.21, not only does virtue have
to make purely theoretical sense, but 'its very being in the
world [i.e., concrete virtuous action by a moral agent] depends
upon its appearing to have no contrariety to private interest
and self-love'. The 'appearing', as White points out (337),
is important. Butler is making a point about how it has to be
with the moral *agent*, about the springs of action. Moral
judgments are, in different jargon, intentional, and this
element of intentionality cannot be overlooked in moral

practice. Thus there is truth in Mrs. Foot's recent claims that reasons for action have an important relation to the individual agent. But it is an exaggeration to say that morality is therefore a system of hypothetical imperatives. The 'being of virtue in the world' is what is at stake, not the possibilities for the rational justification of moral claims.

The same duality of approach is evident in Butler's treatment of the authority of conscience, and in commentators' treatment of Butler's treatment. Broad (78) analyses the authority of conscience in terms of the thought that an action's being approved by conscience gives a conclusive reason for doing that action. This view is supported by, e.g. *P* 26, where the 'natural authority' of conscience is said to be 'an obligation most near and intimate'. It is implied by *A* II. viii.11, where the authority of conscience is spelt out as God's promise of reward and threat of punishment. It is implied by *P* 25, where the authority of conscience is something we enforce on ourselves. To say P is a conclusive reason for Q is to remark simply on an *a priori* relation between P and Q; it is to say nothing about whether some given person who knows P will infer Q, or, where P and Q are practical, whether a person who knows P and knows that P gives a conclusive reason for Q, will actually do Q.

Duncan-Jones, on the other hand, regards 'authority' as Butler's word for the 'mysterious bond which appears to hold between a moral disposition and the recognition of a moral truth' (186). Conscience's having *authority* is supposed to unite the rational and appetitive elements in human nature, so that from intellectual understanding proceeds virtuous action. *This* view is supported by *S* 1.8, where conscience is described as tending to restrain men from doing mischief to one another and leading them to do good, and *DV* 9 where conscience not only suggests but also *enforces* the moral rule of action interwoven in men's nature. The contrast between conscience's enforcing a rule, and our enforcing the dictates of conscience is clear.

The nearest Butler comes to reconciling these conflicting

views, and achieving a degree of stability is, I am inclined to think, in *S* 3.5. Here we find the following few lines:

> Conscience does not only offer itself to shew us the way we should walk in, but it likewise carries its own authority with it, that it is our natural guide; the guide assigned us by the Author of our nature: it therefore belongs to our condition of being, it is our duty to walk in that path, and follow this guide, without looking about to see whether we may not possibly forsake them with impunity.

Butler certainly has to erode here the autonomy of his natural-istic ethics to achieve stability; it may or may not be worth the price. He is making two basic assumptions. The first is of a human nature and a created world in which those who behave according to that nature will achieve happiness. The second is that life in accordance with that nature will simul-taneously satisfy the demands of virtue and of self-love. These assumptions, of course, represent enormous promissory notes, with dubious collateral. But, forgetting that for the moment, should one accept them, then the seeming triviality that human beings behave naturally takes on a different coloration. In that context it can be *both* a 'condition of our being' and a 'duty' to follow conscience. It will be possible both for us to enforce conscience and for conscience to enforce its rule in us; for conscience to have both a declarative and an action-guiding role.

   This is also the way to look at what, for Duncan-Jones, are a set of aberrations in Butler (189). If Butler was simply trying to recommend virtue on prudential grounds, then why does he distinguish conscience and self-love; why does he give con-science authority; why does he (cf. *S* 13.1, 13.5, *DV* 5, A intro 10, I.vi.11; 12, II.viii.11, etc.) recognize an eternal and immutable moral order? Assuming Butler to be not simply disingenuous, we have to see Butler as trying hard, with some but not total success, to preserve a number of different insights in the face of metaethical fashion. As Butler himself points out (e.g. *P* 21, 36, *S* 9.13, etc.) there simply is such a thing as benevolent and virtuous behaviour in general. 'In all common ordinary cases we see intuitively at first view what is our duty, what is the honest part' (*S* 7.14). At this ordinary level of common sense, 'obligation', 'duty', 'conscience' are terms which have a strong currency, to work contrasts with 'self-interest', 'option', 'desire', and so forth. Equally, the human animal being what it is, moral actions and choices stem from the individual's own perception of the world and his place in it. In general terms this vision is not idiosyncratic; it cannot be, otherwise there would not be human social life. But it is peculiar to the individual. Moreover, the feature of the individuality of moral perception is combined with the fact that virtue has to do with feeling, caring and so forth to place the individual's particular attitudes, affections and emotions in a position of some prominence for virtue. These points are, in my view, well brought out by the Aristotelian account of choice as 'desiderative reason or rational desire'. But they begin to be obscured by the linking of conscience with self-love, if that is to be taken in anything like a literal sense. Butler rightly argues against Hobbes that 'out of self-love' need not imply 'selfish' (cf. *Sermons* 1 and 5). But his own grip on this valuable distinction loosens, when he feels it necessary to supplement reason and affection with self-love in order to account for virtuous action. The need to involve the individual's affections if he is to act morally is not necessarily a need to involve the individual's *self-loving* affections. Butler, however, seems to have missed this. In *S* 9, for instance, on the forgiveness of injuries, he writes:

Since to be convinced that any temper of mind, and course of behaviour, is our duty, and the contrary vicious, hath but a distant influence upon our temper and actions; let me add some few reflections, which may have a more direct tendency to subdue those vices in the heart, to beget us in this right temper, and lead us to a right behaviour towards those who have offended us: which reflections however shall be such as will further shew the obligations we are under to it (§21)

These reflections turn out to be a straightforward appeal to self-interest, culminating in 'a forgiving spirit is therefore absolutely necessary, as ever we hope for pardon of our own sins'. The inconveniences of forgiveness on our part are a straightforward trade-off in the economics of self-interest for future considerations.

One could pursue the comparison with Aristotle further. The notion of virtuous behaviour as habitual is as important to Butler as to Aristotle (cf. *S* 3.8, *DV* 2, A I.v.4). Butler has a doctrine something like Aristotle's 'mean' (cf. *S* 1.14, 5.7, 6.9, 7.14, 12.5). As in Aristotle, so in Butler, this is saved from triviality by the insistence that the rule of nature does not present itself to man in a codified form for mechanical application – –*S* 10.10, 'a great part, perhaps the greatest part, of the intercourse among mankind cannot be reduced to fixed determinate rules'. Examples are as important to Butler's exposition of the substance of his moral views as they are to Aristotle's, and one should not be blind to the expository work that they do. As Mackinnon has rightly remarked, Butler is 'the enemy of the single formula' (181); 'his style is almost pointillistic' (186). But arguments from particular examples *are* arguments, and points well arranged form pictures. To stand back from a *Pointilliste* painting is to see its unity and profundity. So it is with both Butler and Aristotle on normative matters.

I wish to turn now to some other puzzles in the concept of conscience, puzzles which have been felt by moral philosophers, and which have caused hostility to a theory such as Butler's to which the concept is crucial. I hope to suggest that here too there are in Butler traces, perhaps not always wittingly, of the kind of solution that can be offered to these problems. These problems are three in number, the 'only one's own' problem, the 'not all cases' problem, and the 'redundancy' problem. These titles will become clearer in due course.

(1) The 'only one's own' problem is highlighted by a paper of Ryle's on conscience. He points out (156–7) that there is something wrong with a theory which regards conscience as a

general faculty of moral judgment. In fact, he says, the term 'conscience' is *not* used this way. 'We limit the verdicts of conscience to judgments about the rightness or wrongness of the acts only of the owner of that conscience.' This, it seems to me, is quite right, even in the special case where the action of one's own that is relevant is a proposed passing of moral judgment on another. Butler takes the opposite view. He states baldly in *S* 13.7:

> Now if a man approves of, or hath an affection to, any principle in and for itself, incidental things allowed for, it will be the same whether he views it in his own mind or in another; in himself or in his neighbour.

The reason why he takes this view emerges from a passage in *S* 1:

> There is a principle of reflection in men, by which they distinguish between, approve and disapprove their own actions. We are plainly constituted such sort of creatures as to reflect upon our own nature. The mind can take a view of what passes within itself, its propensions, aversions, passions, affections, as respecting such objects, and in such degrees. (§8)

Contrary to Roberts' footnote, the first sentence is, I think, not 'Rylean', but to be taken in conjunction with the second. 'Their own actions' does not mean 'the peculiar actions of each individual', but 'the kind of thing humans do'. The key is in the introspectionist terminology of the third sentence. The activity of conscience is represented as a cinema show on a private mental screen. Some of the pictures are of the owner himself doing things; some are of other people doing things. The pictures can be surveyed, distinguished, approved or disapproved all in precisely the same way. The fact that John Doe's private pictures are some of them of John Doe and some of them of Richard Roe is immaterial. The same psychological mechanism is employed in judging one's own activities and in judging another's; moreover, when it is employed in one's own case it is called 'conscience'. From here, together with his assumption of the uniformity of conscience and duty (cf. Duncan-Jones, ch. 3), Butler is very easily led to overlook Ryle's point, and regard conscience as a faculty of moral judgment generally. However, that said, what follows? Ryle takes the opposite course of removing any special role for conscience as a mental principle at all; I shall say more about that in discussing the 'redundancy' problem shortly. But has Butler been in any serious way misled by conflating the agency which tries to persuade us to do what we do not wish to do, or to reassess something we have already done, with the agency by which, generally, we make moral judgments and choices?

Given Butler's emphasis on the coincidence of duty and interest, I am inclined to think he is not misled. Without that coincidence, a certain undesirable type of argumentative slide would seem possible – 'We all have a general faculty of moral judgment called Conscience. Since Conscience tells us what is right and wrong, the next time your Conscience tells you to ignore self-interest and do your duty, you had better do it.' To one who contrasts duty and interest, and favours prudence as a guide to virtue, this move from a commonplace to an unpalatable conclusion would be just a conjuring trick. But if interest is, as in Butler's view it is, already built into the idea of conscience, the move is no trick, but quite explicable. Of course, unclarities do come in with Butler's pious hopes for the coincidence of duty and interest. That is a well-worn topic, to which I decline to add further superfluities.

(2) The 'not all cases' problem is somewhat different, although it is again related to a distinction between a general faculty of moral judgment and a faculty which is, in Ryle's happy phrase, 'an internal competitor' (159) in moral struggles. The problem is this. If conscience is a general faculty of moral judgment, why is it that we only sense its operation in certain cases, e.g. so-called struggles of conscience?

There is a cheap way and a useful way of dealing with this question. The cheap way is to say, 'Conscience is not a general faculty of moral judgment at all. It works only in struggles of conscience; otherwise it is inactive.' But this does not help us much in understanding conscience, and, in particular, it won't do much for Butler, who *does* think that conscience is a general faculty of moral judgment. Can Butler's conscience be saved from this apparent paradox? I think that it can, and that Butler himself has done so. As noted above, he does emphasize, especially at length in the first part of the *Analogy*, that in the virtuous man virtuous behaviour becomes *habitual*. Broad remarks, 'I do not think that Butler means to say that every trivial detail of our lives must be solemnly debated before the tribunal of conscience.' (79) I am myself absolutely certain that Butler doesn't mean that: he says so himself in *S* 7.14 – 'there are many operations of the mind, many things pass within, which we never reflect upon again'. But Broad's image of the regulator ('the main function of conscience is regulative' (*ibid*)) does not seem to me quite right. God has certainly installed conscience in man, as Butler sees it, as part of the divine Utilitarian beneficence. But the regulator image suggests something like a thermostat. The thermostat functions to facilitate the proper working of, say, a central heating system under certain conditions. But the system has its proper functioning given to it independently of, or at best along with, the thermostat. The function, however, of conscience in man, for Butler, is as much and as importantly *educative*. Conscience is a guide; it leads us; it directs us. A regulator just regulates; it does not improve the quality of the system that it regulates, but rather merely maintains whatever quality was originally built in.

This educative aspect of the operation of conscience is of course, in Butler, firmly linked to the theological background of his ethical theory. But it can be 'demythologized'. Indeed, only as a 'demythologization' of this role of conscience can I make sense of something Taylor claims. He says that Butler seems to have meant by 'conscience' 'the body of moral convictions which is common to the "best" men of a society', and not 'something peculiar and private to the individual man'

216 R. A. Shiner

(316). This remark, taken literally, strikes me as just plain false, and I have quoted enough to show that. But if one thinks of the way in which the general climate of moral opinion in a society does, and, I think, necessarily must, affect moral education, then certainly one dimension of Butler's conscience is indeed illuminated.

(3) We are left with the most powerful objection to Butler's concept of conscience, which has been put forward in a recent analysis of Butler's ethics by Nicholas Sturgeon. This objection is simply that, given the role played by the concept of human nature in Butler, the concept of conscience as the supreme and authoritative principle of the mind is totally redundant.

Sturgeon's argument is set out with great care and length. Since I do not wish to dispute the soundness of the argument, but rather question how significant an objection it is, I shall here give merely the essence of it. His argument turns on showing Butler to be committed to what Sturgeon calls the Full Naturalistic Thesis, that conscience never favours or opposes any action, except on grounds which include its naturalness (328). He shows that Butler is therefore committed to various consequences of the FNT, including the following (his numbering):

(6) A man's conscience will favour a current action of his only if the action is favoured by the highest of the superior principles in his nature, other than conscience, which either favour or oppose it; and his conscience will oppose a current action of his, similarly, only if the action is opposed by the highest of the superior principles in his nature, other than conscience, which either favour or oppose it. (346)

(7) It makes no difference whatever to the naturalness or un-naturalness of any action whether or qot conscience is superior to any other principle of action (347)

Sturgeon concludes that therefore Butler, 'to achieve the stated central objective of his moral philosophy, must abandon his doctrine of the supremacy of conscience' (356).

If I may pick up on a distinction drawn earlier (p. 209)

between the two ways of taking the notion of 'authority' in Butler ('authority' being the same as 'supremacy'; cf. e.g. *S* 2.13–4), it seems to me that Sturgeon's argument concerns the authority of conscience *only* in the 'reason-giving' sense. That is, Butler may be under the impression that the rule 'if conscience approves of some action A, it is morally obligatory to do A' plays a significant role in his programme of normative justification. Such an impression, Sturgeon undoubtedly demonstrates would be a mistake. The virtuousness of actions is a matter of their being natural, not a matter of their being approved by conscience. Moreover, in the *Analogy* (cf. e.g. I.vi.12, II.viii.11) Butler expresses a belief in moral value as being not relative to man's perception of it, and as independent of all will. I do not wish to say that Sturgeon is attacking a straw man, for certainly from time to time Butler sounds like one who is under said misapprehension. But much of the time conscience does not seem to be playing such a purely justificatory role at all. I do not believe Butler's shade will rotate in his grave with the same degree of embarrassment that Sturgeon's *Schadenfreude* implies. Certainly conscience functions for Butler in what John Hunter has called an 'argument-stopping' role (320) – if conscience approves there is no further deliberative question to be asked. But I do not think that Butler would deny that the approval of conscience is the symptom of moral virtuousness, and not the criterion.

However, even if I am right about this, we are not out of the wood as regards the redundancy of conscience. The second way of taking the authority of conscience placed conscience in an action-guiding role. But it can surely be argued that this is dangerous anthropomorphizing. Ryle in fact, in the paper already mentioned (163 ff), argues that:

Conscience is one species, among others, of scrupulousness; and scrupulousness is the operative acceptance of a rule or principle which consists in the disposition to behave, in all modes of behaviour, including saying to oneself and others, teaching, chiding, etc. in accordance with the rule.

Thus Ryle offers us an adverbial reduction of conscience: to say a man acted as his conscience told him, or was bothered by his conscience, or had a clear conscience, is just to describe how he did something that he did. There are no consciences implied by such locutions any more than 'he did it for the sake of the regiment' implies there are such things as 'sakes'. If this line of argument is correct, then we seem to have eliminated consciences altogether. We are left with the nature of man as a logical ground for virtue, and the behaviour of man as a series of brute events to be characterized adverbially. There seems no object, to paraphrase, on which a theory of moral judgment can employ itself, nor further room in which such a theory can operate.

In order to try to create such room, we have to try to peel away Ryle's philosophical theory from the common-sense facts of which it is a philosophical description. As often in philosophy, this is not easy to do, as philosophical theory has pre-empted some of the commonsensical words for its own purposes. But we must try. In one ordinary life context, Dr. Kildare may ask Mrs. Mopp whether the pain in her back is as bad today as it was yesterday. In answering ,'No, it ain't', Mrs. Mopp does not beg any questions against Ryle or Skinner about what it is to be in pain. People will go on having pains in this ordinary sense, whether a Rylean or a Cartesian account of pains is popular among philosophers. Conversely, in another ordinary life context, a headmaster may say to a parent that her daughter has a considerable capacity for learning languages. This in turn does not beg any questions against Descartes or Butler about what it is to have a capacity or a faculty. People will go on having capacities and faculties in this ordinary sense, whether a Rylean or a Cartesian account of capacities and faculties is popular among philosophers. It is therefore possible for it to be perfectly true that a conscience is a capacity for behaving in a certain way, without 'George has a conscience' being translatable without remainder into 'George's body behaves thus and so in circumstances C'. Indeed there is one passage in the *DV* where Butler uses precisely the form of words one would use to make this point about conscience. He is presenting evidence for the existence of conscience, and writes that the certainty of its existence 'appears from our exercising it unavoidably, *in* the approbation and disapprobation even of feigned characters' (*DV* 1). I emphasize the 'in' purposely. Contrast it with the form of words in *S* 1.8, where the talk is of a principle *by* which men approve. The 'in' form of words, while still retaining a distinction between us and our behaviour, suggests a material identity of conscience and the appropriate behaviour, an identity which is implicitly denied by the 'by' form of words.

This needs some unpacking. It may be that Ryle's adverbial elimination of conscience is prejudicial, and does not follow from merely linking conscience at a commonsense level with certain patterns of behaviour. But one needs to show in more detail why it is that a concept of conscience as an independent part of the mind can make some contribution to our understanding of moral judgment. I shall canvass three possibilities, the second and third of which, in my view, show the most promise.

(a) The role for conscience I am inclined to be wary of is one remarked upon by Mackinnon. He talks of Butler's insistence that 'taking stock of our nature as we find it, refusing to be distracted from acknowledgement of its actualities, is, where human beings are concerned, necessarily pregnant with moral import' (188). 'Psychological self-scrutiny is not morally neutral . . . psychological self-scrutiny is morally significant' (*ibid*). I beg leave to state that the ice is here thinner than, if I understand him aright, Mackinnon takes it to be. If I were to hear Aristotle talking in such terms about the moral significance of the actualities of human nature, I would worry less. I know that Aristotle has a quite 'this-worldly' view of human nature. But in Butler's case I am more apprehensive. Although from time to time he officially declares it is of no interest to him (e.g. *S* 2.8), nonetheless he is clearly concerned with men as imperfect creatures (cf. *S* 5.3). This becomes more pronounced in the *Analogy*, culminating in the view of Christ as Mediator in II.v. Certainly there is no *angst*-ridden grand eschatology here; but there is straightforwardly the claim that the role of Christ on earth was to give men insight into the real nature of moral virtue, insight which they would so signally be unable to gain if they merely surveyed their fellow-creatures. Thus, in this sort of context, psychological self-scrutiny, whether of man in general or of oneself in particular, is likely to lead to obsession with failings, with inadequacy, with guilt. Such obsessions in my view are not productive of virtue, but are a form of egoistic self-absorption. 'Look what I have failed to do for my fellow-men' is an effective way of turning to oneself and away from one's fellow men and away from action to meet their needs; it is quite as effective a way of doing that as is 'Look what my fellow-men can do for me'. I am not wishing to push this too far, for a little conscience is certainly a good thing. But conscience over-burdened with religious guilt, I am equally sure, is not. So I approach somewhat gingerly the recommendation of a concept of conscience on the grounds that it facilitates 'psychological self-scrutiny', and hastens the arrival of the putative benefits that such scrutiny allegedly brings.

(b) The second possibility involves comparing Butler again with Aristotle. The latter, as is well known, distinguishes between merely performing a just, e.g., act, and being just, that is, performing just acts as the just man performs them (cf. e.g. 114 a 14 ff.). The just man is one who has the disposition to choose according to the mean in the realm of justice. That is, his practical wisdom and his desires have developed by habituation to the point where his doing of something just is not a fluke, but the manifestation of a settled character. This seems to me an enormously important distinction, for human capacities of all kinds. There is some evidence that Butler was aware of it too. In *P* 25 he contrasts the person who does good on a casual, noncommittal basis with the person who brings their 'whole conduct before this superior faculty [sc. conscience]' and makes it 'the business of [his] life'. The concept of conscience is certainly one perfectly valid way of drawing to our attention *this* important feature of moral virtue. (c) The third possible role for conscience in a theory of moral judgment requires us again to contrast the Butlerian approach with the Rylean. In the cases where the notion of conscience has a grip, the events we feel comfortable interpreting in terms of conscience occur at datable points of time. A person's conscience bothers him or her on specific occasions; he or she has a clear conviction that no blame attaches to them for some specific action. The fact that on certain occasions of moral choice an important antecedent to the action is the consulting of and/or listening to conscience can easily suggest to philosophers indulging the craving for generality that *all* cases of moral judgment and choice are like this. Conscience then comes to be represented as a general 'faculty of approbation and disapprobation'; it is the source of *all* moral judgments and choices, even though we are, paradoxically, only aware of its operation in certain cases.

In contrast, there may be taken as the paradigm those cases where there is no obvious operation of a faculty called conscience, where the behaviour, the action, occurs immediately, and the choice does not seem separable from the chosen behaviour. Taking their cue from these cases, other philosophers indulge the craving for generality by saying that it must be in the conscience cases too that there is no independent mental activity called 'consulting one's conscience'. There is only another pattern of behaviour, which is another kind of choice, and which is singled out by the application of a different epithet to it.

Both of these accounts are suffering from the defect of partiality. Both are taking certain characteristics of certain cases of moral judgment, and thinking that these must be characteristics of all cases, that they are the essence of moral judgment. But why should there not be different cases with different characteristics, but all connected to form the family of cases of moral judgment? Moral behaviour is rule-governed behaviour, not regularity-governed behaviour. Following a rule, as Wittgenstein has shown in the *Philosophical Investigations* (cf. e.g. §232) is not a matter of obeying an inner voice. Suppose one is doing a sum and writes 156 as the product of 12 × 13. What makes that an act of calculation is not that one obeyed an inner voice which said '156', although that *may* have happened in *that* case. It is rather that one acted in accordance with a long-established practice of recognizing 156 to be the product of 12 × 13, *and* that one shows oneself capable on other occasions of performing that and other acts of calculation. So it is too if declaring every single one of one's tips to the taxman is to be an act of moral agency. But the obverse of the distinction between rule-governed and regularity-governed behaviour is that one doesn't fully understand moral behaviour unless one takes into account what Hart has called (55 ff) the 'internal aspect' of rules, including moral rules. It is not just that humans often, as a matter of fact, refrain from actions which they perceive to cause injury to others. It is rather that such refraining is moral behaviour, when it is, because the agent takes the injurious consequences of the action as a *reason* for refraining from it.

Of the two ways of representing conscience, the Butlerian way pays attention to the feature of the 'internal aspect', a feature which appears most prominently when moral deliberation is self-conscious and agonizing. But it mistakes the 'occurrence' in these cases of the internal aspect to be a feature of all cases. The Rylean way sees correctly that the rule-governed characteristic of moral behaviour frequently does not manifest itself in any occurrent internal feeling at all, and therefore mistakenly concludes that the internal aspect is never any part of human moral behaviour. We need to be able to see how conscience can perfectly well be the name for a mental activity that occurs in certain cases of moral judgment and choice, *without* that prejudicing either the Rylean emphasis on behaviour in moral agency or the Butlerian emphasis on internal feelings.

By way of summing up, let me say again that I have been as much concerned to do moral philosophy as to do history of philosophy, with enlightenment as well as The

Enlightenment. The moral philosophy has had two themes. (i) There is a need to represent moral judgment as a mental activity in which Reason and Sentiment are inextricably entwined. (ii) There is a need to represent conscience as neither an omnipresent inner voice nor as a figment of philosophical imagination. The history of philosophy has come in by way of seeing how well Butler's remarks about conscience succeed in bringing matters out aright. On the first issue, there are undoubtedly passages in Butler which do not make sense unless one assumes an unwillingness of some kind on his part to espouse a traditional dichotomy between Reason and Sentiment. But, unlike, for example, Aristotle, in Butler's case these are not accompanied by either a terminological consistency or an extent of metaethical theorizing which can make us entirely confident about attributing to him profound metaethical iconoclasm. In particular, his tendency to think that *self-love* has to be the spring of action, rather than affection or sentiment in a broader sense, produces an imbalance in relation to the emphasis on conscience, duty, obligation and the like, an imbalance which only faith can resolve. On the second issue, there is again a revealing instability between conscience as the arbiter of one's own duty in a narrow sense, and conscience as a general faculty or moral judgment. Butler tries to bring these together in his notion of the authority of conscience; but that simply transfers the instability to that notion. We can avoid this only by some more piecemeal account, a fraction of which has just been presented.

Despite these complaints, I wish to end on a positive note by saying that the root reason of this problematic instability is Butler's acute sense of the legitimacy of the claims of both Reason and Sentiment, both Duty and Interest, both internal voice and external behaviour, for inclusion in an adequate moral theory. In this respect, he is to be commended over most moral philosophers who have plumped for one or the other set of claims exclusively.

NOTES AND BIBLIOGRAPHY

[1] This is the standard interpretation of Hume. David Falk has recently argued (*Phil. Studies*, **27** (1975), 1–18 and *Cdn. Jnl. of Phil.* **6** (1976), that Hume's view is more like the view held by Aristotle, as expounded here.

All references in the text are to works listed in the bibliography below.

Aristotle, *Nicomachean Ethics*, ed. I. Bywater (Oxford U.P., 1890). In-text references use the following abbreviation: *NE*.
Broad, C.D., *Five Types of Ethical Theory* (Routledge & Kegan Paul, Oxford, 1967).
Butler, J., *Fifteen Sermons and A Dissertation on Virtue*, ed. T. A. Roberts (SPCK, London, 1970). In-text references use the following abbreviations: *P.* (*Preface*). *S* and *DV*.
Butler, J., *The Analogy of Religion* (Ungar, New York, 1961).
Duncan-Jones, A., *Butler's Moral Philosophy* (Penguin, Harmondsworth, 1952).
Foot, P., 'Morality as a System of Hypothetical Imperatives', *Phil. Rev.*, **81** (1972).
Foot, P., 'Reasons for Action and Desires', *ASSV*, **46** (1972).
Hart, H. L. A., *The Concept of Law* (Oxford U.P., 1961).
Hume, D., *Treatise on Human Nature*, ed. L. A. Selby-Bigge (Oxford U.P., 1896). In-text references use the following abbreviation: *T*.
Hume, D., *Inquiry into the Principles of Morals*, eds. L. A. Selby-Bigge and P. H. Nidditch (Oxford U.P., 1975).
Hunter, J. F. M., 'Conscience', *Mind*, **72** (1963), pp. 309–34.
Kleinig, J., 'Butler in a Cool Hour', *Jnl. of History of Phil.*, **7** (1969), pp. 399–411.
Mackinnon, D. M., *A Study in Ethical Theory* (A. & C. Black, London, 1957).
Raphael, D. D., 'Bishop Butler's View of Conscience', *Philosophy*, **24** (1949), pp. 219–38.
Ryle, G., 'Conscience and Moral Convictions', reprinted in *Philosophy and Analysis*, ed. M. Macdonald (Blackwell, Oxford, 1954), pp. 56–65.
Stevenson, C. L., *Ethics and Language* (Yale U.P., New Haven, 1944).
Sturgeon, N. L., 'Nature and Conscience in Butler's Ethics', *Phil. Rev.*, **85** (1976), pp. 315–56.
Taylor, A. E., 'Some Features of Butler's Ethics', reprinted in his *Philosophical Studies* (Macmillan, London, 1934), pp. 291–328.

White, A. R., 'Conscience and Self Love in Butler's Sermons', *Philosophy*, **27** (1952), pp. 329–44.
Wittgenstein, L., *Philosophical Investigations*, 2nd edition (Blackwells, Oxford, 1958).

11

KANT AND
THE SINCERE FANATIC

Bernard Harrison

I

'I see well enough what poor Kant would be at' said James Mill on first looking into the *Kritik der reinen Vernunft*. No one would wish to say that the reception of Kant in England has remained at this level: abundance of sound scholarship, innumerable Kant seminars and the swell of interest in transcendental argument which has developed since the Second World War all exist to prove the contrary. But in spite of all that, Mill's response still touches a chord in English breasts. We are prone to think Kant a conjurer. If we are to accept, or even to work seriously with, any version of Kantianism it must be a demythologized, logically aseptic version. Strawson's Kant, for instance, is a Kant freed from the 'strained analogy' between the study of the conditions of sense, or intelligibility, and the study of the human cognitive system. And in moral philosophy too, the English Kantianism chiefly represented by the work of Professor R. M. Hare has scrupulously avoided those parts of Kant's ethics which have a suspiciously speculative flavour: the notion of an unqualified good, for example, or that of treating moral agents as Ends-in-Themselves; and more generally the whole notion, which permeates Kant's moral philosophy, that morality can only ultimately be understood in terms of a set of ideal relationships that entirely transcend all considerations of common-sense mutual accommodation or rational self-interest: transcend all such considerations so radically, in fact, as to point mutely towards the possibility of a life after death.

I am half in, and half out of sympathy with this English caution. In one way it seems to me entirely proper. Nobody could seriously suppose, for example, that Kant's account of the understanding, or of synthetic *a priori* judgment, could stand unmodified against the assaults of later epistemology and philosophy of logic. But cautious reading passes easily over into mis-reading, particularly when the urge to caution springs from underlying philosophical commitments which may be themselves neither particularly defensible nor very clearly formulable.

The urge to demythologize the work of a major philosopher is less likely to mislead us if it is carried on against the background of an effort to restore and reconstruct, as far as possible, his original intentions in a form in which they can withstand contemporary criticism. Such studies are of historical interest, but they are not without contemporary application as well. By making the effort to reconstruct the thought of a great writer against the drift of contemporary reinterpretation we can stave off for a moment what C. S. Lewis called 'the provincialism of the present'. In the gap between what our contemporary concerns urge us to make of a major writer, and what his work can be got, with a little effort, to say in defence of his original intentions, we may glimpse something which, normally, we are no more able to perceive than we are able to see the backs of our own heads: namely the peculiar cast of our own minds and of the cultural milieu which formed them.

Such an enterprise is what I have in mind. I want to try to rescue some neglected parts of Kant's moral philosophy from the oblivion of the customary respect paid to a historical monument. It will be necessary to begin at some apparent distance from Kant; with a problem, in fact, over which Kant never troubled his head at all: the problem of 'fanaticism' as it appears in Professor Hare's book *Freedom and Reason.*

II

The position Hare takes up in *The Language of Morals* (*LM*), and in an expanded and slightly modified form in *Freedom and Reason* (*FR*), is so well known as to need only a brief résumé.[2] We can, if we wish treat judgments of the form, 'I ought to do X' as in certain cases entailing the command 'Let me do X'. When they carry this entailment they are value-judgments; when they do not they are merely statements of sociological or psychological fact ('Common standards of behaviour require one to do X', or 'I have a feeling that I ought to do X'). Hare's claim that ought-statements, when they express value-judgments, entail imperatives, is offered as 'a matter of definition' (*LM*, p. 168). The definition has the disadvantage of raising well-known, but perhaps ultimately soluble, problems about 'weakness of will'. But perhaps it has advantages as well: as Hare puts it (*LM*, p. 169), 'I am merely suggesting a terminology which, if applied to the study of moral language will, I am satisfied, prove illuminating.'

The first fruit of the definition is that it frees us from the Humean belief that reason has nothing intrinsically to do with evaluation. Sentences in the imperative mood can stand in logical relationships to one another, just as ordinary descriptive sentences can. Thus, a universal imperative sentence, taken together with an indicative minor premiss, entails a singular imperative conclusion, as in the example (*LM*, p. 27)

Take all the boxes to the station.
This is one of the boxes.
∴ Take this to the station.

If we allow that ought-statements, when they express value-judgments, entail commands, then ought-statements, too, stand in similar logical relationships to one another, as in the example (*FR*, pp. (90–91)

(1) Anyone who is owed money should put his debtor into prison if he does not pay.

(2) I am unable to pay C, who is my creditor.

∴ (3) Let C put me into prison.

Although it is a universal imperative, however, (1) might not be being advanced as a moral judgment. It might be being advanced simply as a maxim of prudence: as an injunction to be heeded, for example, by any rising young merchant in 1680, say, who has come to the City with a view to getting up his crumb (Pepys' lovely phrase). But, on the other hand, it might be being advanced as a moral principle. The claim might be, for example, that we show moral frivolity when we do not go the full distance the law allows in exacting payment from debtors, although of course it is also in our own interest to use the law to its fullest extent: that leniency in such cases encourages others to run up debts they cannot repay, or something of the sort. What *in general* differentiates the speaker who utters (1) with a moral intention from the speaker who utters it with a merely prudential one?

Hare's answer is that a universal imperative advanced as a moral judgment is not restricted in its application to any particular person or group of persons, or to particular times or places. A moral judgment is by its nature a universal imperative addressed to all persons everywhere and at all times. It contains no proper names; no references to particulars of any type, in other words. Universal imperatives contrast with singular imperatives like 'No Smoking', glossed by Hare (*LM*, p. 177) as 'No one is ever to smoke in this compartment'. Hare argues that if we remove all references to particular compartments or particular railway companies we get something like 'No one is ever to smoke in any railway compartment anywhere', and that this, although it would certainly be a very odd moral principle, is hard to make any sense of, because of its universality except as a moral principle of some sort.

Thus a moral judgment, since by its nature it applies to anyone without restrictions of time or place, constrains anyone who makes it to act in accordance with it himself if he should find himself in the situation to which it applies. Hare calls this feature of moral judgments their *Universalizability*.

It is important to notice, because it is essential to Hare's position, and a point which he himself repeatedly emphasizes, that the Principle of Universalizability is itself not a moral principle, but a principle of *logic* (*FR*, p. 30 f.). The principle simply says that someone who asserts a principle of the form 'Anyone in circumstances *xy* ought, morally, to do *a*', but then refuses to do *a* when he himself happens to be in circumstances *xy*, is not, or cannot, logically, be held to be really using the word 'ought' with *moral* force: that such a person is abusing language in exactly the way in which somebody who said, for example, 'I call "red" anything which is exactly the same colour as *y*, but although *x* is the same colour as *y* I wouldn't want to call *x* "red",' would be abusing language.

This account of the logical status of the principle of universalizability is Hare's principal defence against the accusation of naturalism. It enables him, as he sees it,[3] to claim that his theory gives a substantive and correct account of the nature of morality without committing its proponents to the acceptance of any substantive moral principle. In what is to follow, part of what I shall try to show is that the bulwark which Hare here throws up against the imputation of naturalism is very much stronger than it need be to counter the – I believe largely imaginary – threat which occasioned its building. Certainly, Hare's insistence that the principle of universalizability is a principle of logic, or a meaning-rule, commits him to what seem to me at least, very odd views about the category of persons whom he calls 'fanatics'.

A 'fanatic', in Hare's terminology, is someone who holds, on what he says are moral grounds, principles which can only be applied at the cost of inflicting very great suffering upon other people. Hare's example is that of a Nazi who believes that all Jews ought to be killed, and who believes it, presumably, on pseudo-moral grounds having to do with saving the soul of Germany, ensuring a racially pure culture, restoring the Aryan virtues recorded in Tacitus' *Germania*, and other stuff of the like kind.

Hare's exemplary Nazi, however, is not deaf to the demands of moral rationality as Hare's theory represents it. He believes, like Hare, that a man has no (logical) right to affirm a moral principle unless he is prepared to accept every particular prescription which may follow logically from it in any conceivable set of relevant circumstances. Hence, he believes that, if some quirk of the Registry Office were to reveal his mother's maiden name to have been not, as he had always supposed, Stolz, but Mendelssohn, he ought, morally, to submit himself to the proper authorities for shipment to one of the places appointed for the Final Solution to the Jewish Question. And he is an honest and upright man: we need not seriously doubt that when he learns the truth about his ancestry he will give himself up to the authorities. He is in short, Hare says, a fanatic, or as I shall say, a 'sincere fanatic'.

The problem now (it is a problem for Hare, but also I think for all of us, in that I think most of us would like Hare's project, or something like it, to succeed) is that if Hare's account of the nature of moral reasoning is correct we cannot say that the sincere fanatic is in any absolute sense guided by wrong or bad principles, that he is in any sense morally confused, or that he has no right to the abominable principles which he espouses. He fully understands the nature of moral reasoning and responsibility. He has thought long (and, we may even suppose, to give the screw its final turn, in anguish) before making his moral choice. It is just that the choice he has made is one which we happen to detest. *We* can do nothing really, in other words, but froth.

Hare deals with this problem in a way which I, and I fancy many other philosophers, find unsatisfying. He says (*FR*, pp. 171, 220 for example) that the psychology of the sincere fanatic is such an extraordinary one that it can for all practical purposes be neglected, since even if such minds are not psychologically impossible or inconceivable, they must nevertheless be very rare indeed.[4]

It would be pleasant if this were so, but I don't see that it is so, or why it should be so. In the face of the vast harm which political fanaticism has done in the world this century, it is not merely dangerous but to a certain extent morally frivolous to underestimate its psychological resources. Academic discussions, even in philosophy, should not sit quite so lightly to the facts, especially when the facts concerned are so unsurprising. The sincere fanatic is, after all, merely a man who is prepared to proclaim what he takes to be moral truths *whatever the cost to himself*. Self-sacrifice of this sort is not all that uncommon; in pessimistic moods it can seem very much commoner than ordinary decency, kindness or common-sense. Martyrs are made every day for causes whose claims will scarcely bear a moment's examination. We need not, in fact, suppose a very bizarre psychology for the sincere fanatic. We need not even suppose him to be a man very much given to hatred, at least in the emotional, operatic sense of the word. He might just, for example, be a very cold, dry, self-absorbed and overly theoretical man who has made a life for himself out of abstract nationalism and racialist politics: a life which offers him certain benefits in terms of power and a sense of personal significance, and allows him to see himself in a more heroic and self-flattering light than would otherwise be possible; as well as making up, through a spurious political connection, for the isolation from other people into which the natural operation of his character would otherwise lead him.

It does not seem to me believable, now, that a man like this (and there are plenty of other possible ways in which we could provide Hare's lay figure with a plausible naturalistic psychology) would suddenly draw back and experience a moral illumination of the sort repeatedly envisaged by Hare (for example in Chapter 11 of *FR*), simply as a result of belatedly discovering himself, on the basis of documents, to be Jewish. On the contrary, I think, such a man might at first suffer a crisis of horror and despair, but then, if he were sufficiently strong-willed, and sufficiently lacking in imagination and humanity, he might well rise above his initial abjection, and come to see in his willing submission to the Final Solution the path to moral regeneration: the only course, in fact, which could give back meaning and moral significance to his life. He would tell himself, no doubt, that he remained spiritually Aryan, despite his tainted blood, and that it was his duty, having discovered that taint, to purge it from the body of the Aryan *volk* by his own death, just as a leper might voluntarily exile himself from the society of men.

In real moral terms, of course, his assumed duty and his self-sacrifice have no weight at all. What he thinks of as moral reasoning is a mere farrago of self delusion. But we, as moral theorists, can hardly rest content with that thought. Our business as moral theorists is to show *why* his moralizings about his situation fall short of genuine morality. Without some theoretical means of grasping the exact nature of his mis-guidedness we can do nothing but watch impotently, beset by a sense that we are, morally speaking, in cloud-cuckoo-land, but quite unable to say why, or how, as his former Party comrades, some of them openly weeping quite real tears, give him a guard of honour to the gas-chamber, and at the subsequent Party funeral deliver eloquent eulogies upon his moral fervour and unflinching steeliness of Will. Given what we know in abundance about the atmosphere of the Third Reich, I should not be at all surprised if a few such cases actually occurred.

Hare's view about the sincere fanatic has two components. On the one hand Hare holds (implausibly, as I have tried to show) that there is something psychologically strained or bizarre about such a position. But on the other hand he holds that if anyone did really choose to adopt such a position he would be *morally* unassailable. He would have satisfied the formal requirements of moral rationality, and we should have to admit him as a man with genuine moral principles however flatly contradictory to our own.

This second component of Hare's position on fanaticism seems to me to be quite as misguided as the first. To see why, we must look a little more closely at the role of the concept of universalizability in Hare's account of moral reasoning.

The criterion of universalizability functions, in Hare's system, as we have seen, as a criterion simply for whether or not a universal imperative can be held to be being advanced, or held, as a moral principle. It is not necessarily a criterion of rightness. A person may hold a particular principle, and be prepared to accept all its consequences, only because he or she has not reflected sufficiently to see that there is some more complicated, though equally universal principle which he might hold, and which he would certainly think morally superior to his present principles if he were to become conscious of the possibility of holding it. And that principle might lead him to act differently in certain circumstances from the way in which his present principles would lead him to act. Both principles would, we may suppose, be moral principles by the criterion of universalizability, but the *right action* in those circumstances would be the action dictated by the second, more complex principle, and not that dictated by the principle the person in question adheres to now. The criterion of universalizability, therefore, only entitles us to say that the person who satisfies it is *thinking morally*, not that he subscribes to a correct, or ultimately adequate, set of moral principles.

But even so, the criterion of universalizability, if we take it both as a necessary *and a sufficient* condition for someone to be said to be thinking morally, seems to me to give far too much to the fanatic. Hare's position seems to me, indeed, to be flatly contrary to common-sense: that is, to the ordinary moral intuition which everyone without a philosophical theory to defend would bring to bear upon the situation. What ordinary moral common-sense tells us, it seems to me, is that a man who hates Jews so much that he wishes to see all Jews dead is simply a man given over to hatred. We need not suppose his hatred to be the product of moral ratiocination, or his anti-semitic principles to be moral principles: indeed, it would be absurd, a mere abuse of language to do so. What Hare tells us, now, is that if such a man is really prepared to accept that he should be killed if he should turn out to be a Jew, the whole situation mysteriously changes. His hatred of Jews is transformed into a matter of moral principle which could, in theory at any rate, issue from a serious process of moral reasoning. Instead of regarding the Jew-hater as a man with a tedious and morally detestable mania, we have to regard him as a man who holds *moral* views on the Jewish Question, however much his morality differs from ours.

From the point of view of ordinary moral intuition this seems altogether wrong. Mere willingness to submit oneself, under certain circumstances, to anti-semitic persecution surely cannot of itself turn hatred of Jews into a *moral* principle of any kind. However willing a man may be to commit himself to the flames if he should himself by some improbable accretion of evidence turn out to be Jewish, his hatred of Jews remains, it seems to me, just commonplace hatred and nothing more. It is not ennobled by his 'heroism', or 'sincerity' (by the consistency with which, in the ultimate corner, he accepts the consequences of his principles). On the contrary, the fact that his 'sincerity' forces him to submit in his turn to the naked power of hatred vitiates it. Real heroism will not submit to the arbitrary and unjust exercise of power. Real sincerity does not cling to the last logical consequences of a crumbling moral point of view: it makes the difficult motion of comprehending its own consciousness as it appears to, and affects, others, and therefore rejecting it. In short, the parade of moral seriousness and self-abnegation with which the Nazi in Hare's example seeks still to give meaning to his life and his beliefs by offering himself up for sacrifice, must seem to a dispassionate eye no more than the last access of an adolescent spiritual pride which becomes the more odious and the more corrupt the more it seeks still to express itself through pedantic adherence to the forms and rhetoric of the moral life: a form of life whose inner, living reality it has long since betrayed and abandoned.

That, it seems to me, is what common-sense tells us about the condition of the Harean fanatic. To the extent, therefore, that the goal of Hare's theory is to reveal the rational basis of ordinary moral intuition, Hare's theory must be judged a failure. Willingness to universalize an imperative judgment may still (for all we have said to the contrary) be a necessary condition of that imperative judgment's recording a moral commitment, but it cannot be a sufficient condition.

III

Can Kant's moral theory do any better? I think it can, provided we adopt an interpretation of the structure and functioning of the illustrations in Kant's *Groundwork of the Metaphysic of Morals* (hereinafter *GMM*) which is, I shall argue, true to Kant's intentions, but which differs from the interpretation most favoured by Kant's English critics.

Kant's illustrations are formulated in terms of the second of Kant's four versions of the Categorical Imperative, which Paton identifies as the Formula of the Law of Nature:[5] 'Act as if the maxim of your action were to become through your will a universal law of nature'. The four illustrations which Kant offers exhibit a common pattern of argument which can be roughly outlined as follows. First, in contemplating a given course of action, we formulate a general rule, or *maxim*, of which the particular act we have in view can be seen as an application, or special case. Examples of such maxims are 'From self-love I make it my principle to shorten my life if its continuance threatens more evil than it promises pleasure',[6] or 'Whenever I believe myself short of money, I will borrow money and promise to pay it back, though I know that this will never be done'.[7] Next, we consider this maxim not just as a maxim which *we* are going to act upon in certain circumstances, but as one which every rational being is *always* going to act upon in relevantly similar circumstances; that is, as a principle which is going to govern the behaviour of rational beings with the force of a law of nature.

When we do this, Kant says, we find that an immoral maxim 'cannot possibly hold as a universal law of nature', for one or other of two reasons: either because the maxim in question cannot be conceived as a universal law of nature without contradiction, or else because it cannot be willed as a universal law of nature, because such a will 'would contradict itself'.[8] The chief exegetical difficulties arise over the question of what exactly Kant means when he says that a given maxim cannot be *conceived* as a universal law of nature, or that a will which wills an immoral maxim as a universal law of nature *contradicts itself*. English critics, from John Stuart Mill onwards, have argued that no consistent interpretation of these phrases can be extracted from Kant's discussion; and that in fact the term *contradictory* in Kant can often, with the best will in the world, only be taken as meaning something like *inconsistent with the functioning of specific social institutions*, or *inconsistent with the welfare of the agent*: in other words, that Kant's general position reduces in the end to enlightened self-interest, or to utilitarianism, or to some form of social functionalism.[9]

There is, I believe, a comparatively simple way of reinstating Kant's intentions against these objections; one which gives a clear and consistent interpretation of Kant's text in the *Groundwork*. It requires us first to reconsider what Kant means by a *maxim*. It is easy to take a Kantian maxim as being simply any kind of general injunction or prescription: on this interpretation, 'Never tread on the lines in the pavement', or 'Look before you leap', would be maxims in the required sense.

In fact, I think, a Kantian maxim consists of two mutually dependent elements: a goal, or end, together with a plan for achieving that end. By contrast, a general injunction like 'Never tread on the lines in the pavement' leaves it open what goal might be attained by following the injunction, and therefore also leaves it open how following the injunction is supposed to contribute to the attainment of any goal. Kant's formulation of maxims in his examples displays this double structure of goal and plan clearly enough (*'From self love* I make it my principle to shorten my life if its continuance promises more pain than pleasure; *Whenever I believe myself short of money*, I will borrow . . .,' etc.); as does his general contention that all action, including virtuous action, is relative to some end or goal.

If we understand the notion of a maxim in this way, then

I

it is evident that in adopting a maxim we adopt a goal. Further-more, if I, as a Universal Legislator, can bring it about that everyone – every rational being – acts upon a certain maxim as a law of nature – as a psychological necessity, that is – then in doing that I bring it about that every rational being acts *as if* he desired to attain the goal written into the maxim. Of course, since *ex hypothesi* the adoption of the maxim by each rational being will have come about as a result of my activity as a Universal Legislator with power to determine natural law, there is an obvious sense in which no rational being (except myself) will have chosen the maxim. But I, as Universal Legislator, *have* chosen it, and that means that I have chosen, as a goal, whatever general result may flow from every rational being acting upon that maxim as a psychological necessity (a law of nature).

I thus have, potentially, two goals: the goal which I have in view when I adopt a maxim simply as a private person, and the goal which I find myself adopting (because it is the *result* of every rational being's acting in accordance with the maxim in question) when, in my capacity as Universal Legis-lator, I will that maxim to become a universal law of nature. The two goals may conflict, in the sense that the pursuit of the second may frustrate the first. When they conflict, the will is, in Kant's sense, *in contradiction with itself.* If the contradiction is so radical that pursuit of the goals set for me by my decreeing a given maxim as a universal law of nature would frustrate the pursuit of goals essential to human life, then the maxim in question cannot be conceived *as a universal law of nature* or *subsist as a system of nature.*

No doubt this still sounds suspiciously sonorous and vague. But I think we can make it a good deal less so by recasting one or two of Kant's illustrations according to the pattern which it suggests. Let us begin with the first, and as it happens, almost the most unpromising illustration: Kant's proof of the im-morality of suicide.[10] A man 'feels sick of life as the result of a series of misfortunes', says Kant, and is inclined to take his life. But he is still sufficiently in control to ask himself whether the maxim, 'From self-love I make it my principle to shorten my life if its continuance threatens more evil than it promises pleasure', can really become a universal law of nature. And he 'sees at once' that it cannot, because 'a system of nature by whose law the very same feeling whose function (*Bestimmung*) is to stimulate life should actually destroy life would contradict itself and consequently could not subsist as a system of nature'.

At first sight this looks open to exactly the sort of objection we canvassed above, and in addition it appears to constitute a flagrant instance of the Naturalistic Fallacy. The result of suicide is that the human species is diminished by one member. And it looks superficially as if what Kant is saying is that this result is inconsistent with the biological 'purpose' of furthering the increase of the species which we can ascribe to the 'feeling' of self-love on the basis of a commonplace teleology redolent of Paley or Bernardin de Saint-Pierre.[11] But of course, such an 'argument' would scarcely help Kant's case: indeed, from the point of view of Kant's overall programme it would be a *non sequitur* on more than one level. Even if we can take seriously the idea that our instincts have 'functions', why should this have any *moral* significance, except by virtue of some decision of ours to invest 'the system of nature' with moral significance: to take, in other words, Pope's 'Whatever is, is right' as our maxim, and so to abandon moral reflection altogether in favour of a comfortable acquiescence in the requirements of the natural order of things? And what is the real force of the claim that a 'system of nature' in which self-love might prompt suicide 'would contradict itself and consequently could not subsist as a system of nature'? Self-love manifestly does lead people to commit suicide: hence, just such a system of nature as Kant affirms to be self-contradictory and so incapable of subsistence actually does subsist. Not only, it appears, does Kant endeavour to draw moral lessons from the factual requirements for a possible system of nature, he is wrong, and quite blatantly and trivially wrong, about what those requirements actually are.

When we find a great philosopher out as dramatically as this the odds are somewhat more in favour of our having misunderstood him than in favour of our having really found him out. Great thinkers occasionally leave chinks in their armour, but seldom gaping holes. Let us see what can be done to rescue Kant.

The maxim of suicide, Kant tells us, is, 'Shorten your life if its continuance threatens more evil than it promises pleasure'. The terms 'threatens' and 'promises' suggest that hope is not out of place. In other words, the kind of suicide that Kant is discussing is not that of, say, a terminal cancer patient for whom we can predict with absolute certainty a very short and very painful span of life. Kant is discussing the kind of suicide which a man commits when he balances up the forces running counter to his interests against the forces operating on his side, and decides to throw in the towel. 'Evil' and 'pleasure' are presumably to be judged, in following the maxim, from the point of view of the would-be suicide's immediate personal interests and concerns at the point of suicide. To adopt Kant's maxim of suicide, therefore, is to leave out of account all considerations of hope, fortitude, concern for others, trust in the powers of the self to make something positive out of the wreckage of a former life, and so on.

I now ask whether this maxim can 'become a universal law of nature'. What I am asking is whether it could become a natural law that every rational being necessarily commits suicide – is psychologically unable not to commit suicide – when considerations of utility, construed in a narrow and egoistic way, lead it to suppose that the future threatens more evil than it promises pleasure. It seems to me, now, that Kant is on rather strong ground when he says that such a state of affairs 'could not subsist as a system of nature'. The continuance of life very often threatens more pain than pleasure, and it is often just at those very points that people need to stand firm and exercise the virtues of hope and fortitude if the prospects for humanity are not to become bleaker still. If suicide were the invariable response of human beings to the overthrow of their hopes: to bereavement, or financial crisis, or failure, or betrayal of love, or exile, or tyranny, for example, the human race would by now no longer exist.

In willing that the maxim of suicide 'should become through my will a universal law of nature', therefore, I cannot avoid adopting as my goal universal death: the end or absence of rational life. And this goal is certainly inconsistent with the modest private goal of optimizing my own personal utility for the sake of which I adopted the maxim of suicide in the first place. For that initial maxim is logically equivalent to 'Live as long as you can if the continuance of life promises more pleasure than it threatens evil'. And that is not a maxim I could hope to remain in a position to follow if the maxim of suicide were to become a universal law.

It should now be clear how Kant can evade the objections I raised a few paragraphs ago; or rather, why those objections fail to hit their mark. The 'contradiction' which Kant has in mind is not a conflict between the result of my committing suicide and the 'function' for which nature has ordained that men should be motivated by self-love: it is a conflict between the end, or goal, for the sake of which I initially adopt the maxim of suicide, and the end, or goal, which I necessarily find myself pursuing when I will that maxim as a universal law of nature. Similarly, when Kant says that 'a system of nature by whose law the very same feeling whose function is to stimulate the furtherance of life should actually destroy life would contradict itself and consequently could not subsist as a system of nature', he does not mean, what would in any case be manifestly false, that it is impossible for men to commit suicide out of selfish fear of what the future will probably bring.

He means that a system of nature in which every rational creature invariably allowed the choice between death and continued life to turn, from moment to moment, upon the best estimate of the future balance of personal utility, would be one in which self-love *could* not operate to 'stimulate the furtherance of life' – would be one, in fact, in which, after a very short time, there could be no further question of 'the furtherance of life'.

Kant, indeed, makes this last point quite explicit in his comments on the illustrations. Kant says in effect (*GMM*, pp. 91–2) that what we really want is that other people should continue to endure hard and difficult circumstances where necessary to maintain the ordinary everyday world in which it makes sense for us to worry about optimizing our personal utilities – that 'the opposite of our maxim should remain a law universally'; but that *we* should be free (just this once) to adopt the maxim of prudent suicide. If we ever considered these two desires together from the same point of view we should see the contradiction implicit in their conjunction: 'the contradiction that a certain principle should be objectively necessary as a universal law and yet subjectively should not hold universally but should admit of exceptions'. But in practice we are prevented from seeing the contradictoriness of what we will by the fact that we habitually consider the very same action from two different points of view which we manage to keep separate in our minds; the point of view of reason and the point of view of inclination. Because of this it is possible for a 'system of nature' to subsist in which people commit suicide out of self-love. But that does not mean that it would be possible for a system of nature to subsist in which the principle of prudent suicide was enshrined as a natural and invariable practice for every rational creature, or that the will of a person who commits suicide out of self-love while supposing himself also to be upholding a moral principle (a 'right to commit suicide') is not self-contradictory in the sense – a perfectly good one, I think – which Kant intends.

All four of Kant's illustrations can, I think, easily be assimilated to the pattern of a contradiction between the goal for the sake of which an agent initially proposes to adopt a given maxim, and the goal which he finds himself pursuing the moment he envisages turning that maxim, by a mere act of will, into a universal law of nature. Thus, in the second example, the goal of self-enrichment, which leads an agent to adopt the maxim of obtaining money on a promise of repayment which will never be kept, is at odds with the goal of subverting the institution of promising, which such an agent finds himself pursuing, the moment he wills that it should become a universal law of nature that any rational being who needs anything will make any wild promise at all, without the slightest intention of keeping it, in the hope of getting what he needs. Similarly, in the third illustration, the goal of enjoying a comfortable and idle life which leads the agent to adopt the maxim of neglecting his talents is at odds with the goal which he finds himself pursuing when he wills that neglect of talents 'should be implanted in us as . . . a law by a natural instinct'. For in willing *that*, what he is willing is that he should be incapable of developing his talents, and thus incapable of acquiring skills which might on occasion be essential to secure for him the very comforts and pleasures for the sake of which he proposed in the first place to adopt the maxim of neglecting his talents in favour of enjoying the pleasures and comforts which happen at the moment to be available to him.

That will have to do, for the moment, by way of an exegetical sketch of how Kant's illustrations in the *Groundwork* ought to be read. The interpretation is, I think, inherently plausible, and I shall try to show in a moment how it fits into the larger fabric of Kant's theory in the *Groundwork*. For the present, then, I shall leave the reader to fill in the fine detail of the interpretation for himself, and return to Hare's problem about the moral credentials of sincere fanaticism.

We have first to decide on the nature of the maxim upon which the sincere fanatic proposes to act. 'Kill Jews whenever possible' will hardly do as a maxim, if I am right about the character of Kantian maxims, because it makes no reference to the goal, or end, which killing Jews is supposed to further. What the fanatic wants presumably, is that the German nation, German culture, etc. should be freed from destructive and parasitic foreign influences (we can argue with him on the factual question of whether Jewish influences *are* destructive, of course, but it isn't the heart of the matter and for present purposes we can let it pass). His maxim must therefore be something like, 'Whenever I consider the activities of another nation or race to be inimical to the development of my own nation or race, I will exterminate that nation or race to the last child'.

It seems clear, now, that adopting this maxim simply as a rule to govern his own conduct might prove, in the phrase Kant uses in developing the second illustration, 'quite compatible with (his) entire future welfare'. In other words, he might very well get away with it.

What, then, makes it a wicked maxim? It seems clear that, for Kant, the test has nothing whatsoever to do with the question of what the sincere fanatic would do *if he discovered himself to be Jewish*. Kant's criterion does not depend upon *Gedankenexperimente* or counterfactual suppositions of any kind. What it turns upon is the question whether the fanatic's maxim could *become through his will a universal law of nature*: whether, in other words the goals which he would find himself pursuing in making the principle of preemptive genocide a psychological necessity for all rational beings are consistent with the goals which led him to adopt the maxim simply as a rule for the guidance of his own actions.[7]

It seems clear now, that if every human being, every national leader, and so on, were committed by psychological necessity to the principle of preemptive genocide, no nation, including the fanatic's own nation, could develop its national culture freely in the way the fanatic originally intended (intended that is, when he adopted the maxim of preemptive genocide merely as a rule for the guidance of his own actions). The result of making the maxim of preemptive genocide a universal law would be a Hobbesian war of all against all fought with paranoiac ferocity. Nor can the fanatic evade this conclusion by alleging that his maxim applies only to communities living within the body of larger communities. If the Jews can be regarded as a cancerous growth within the body of Greater Germany, why cannot the Germans, the French or anyone at all for that matter, be regarded as a cancerous growth within the body of Europe, or the World Community? The principle of preemptive genocide, in short, 'cannot subsist as a system of nature'. In willing that it become by his will a universal law of nature the fanatic commits himself to goals which conflict with the goals for which he originally adopted the maxim for the guidance of his own actions. Every nation must sooner or later suffer a decisive reverse of arms; certainly every European nation has several times suffered a military reverse so catastrophic as to make possible genocide, had the victors wished to inflict it upon the defeated. And what the Nazi is willing, in converting his maxim into a natural law, is, among other things, that genocide should be the natural and inevitable consequence of any sufficiently complete and definitive military victory, and thus, of any such victory over German arms.

From Kant's account of the nature of moral reasoning, then, it does not follow that the Sincere Fanatic possesses an 'alternative morality' of his own; a morality whose status *as* a morality, worthy to stand beside, or rather in opposition to, our own, is secured by the Fanatic's willingness to accept every consequence of his own principles. What follows is simply the conclusion which ordinary moral common-sense prompted us to draw in the first place, but which we were unable, then, to see how we could be entitled to draw: namely, that the Sincere Fanatic is merely cold-hearted and vicious, and self-deluded about the nature of his viciousness.

IV

Now for some brief comments on this conclusion. First of all, both Kant and Hare find the essence of morality to consist in the avoidance of something which might be called 'practical (or moral) self-contradiction'. The kinds of contradiction which they have in mind are, however, if I am correct, quite different from one another. For Hare, moral inconsistency is primarily *logical* inconsistency; inconsistency between *sentences* in the imperative mood. For Kant, if I have interpreted him correctly, it is primarily incompatibility between *ends*: specifically, between the ends which I will as a private person and the ends which I find myself willing when I consider the maxims which I am led to adopt in the pursuit of my private ends in the light of Acts of a Universal Legislator with power to decree that whatever he wills shall become, merely by that fact, a universal natural law.

According to Kant's theory, therefore, the Sincere Fanatic cannot endow his genocidal principles with the status of *moral* principles merely by being willing to accept their application to his own case, even if that willingness is perfectly genuine and even if it is capable of withstanding Hare's crucial test involving the discovery by the Nazi of his own unsuspected Jewish antecedents. In general, a man's willingness to abide the application to his own case of immoral principles does not make those principles any the less immoral – it is simply irrelevant to the moral issue. If the purposes for which he proposes to adopt a maxim for the guidance of his own actions are inconsistent with the goals which he would find himself pursuing if he were to transform that maxim into the decree of a Universal Legislator, then the maxim is immoral, and it makes no difference at all that he would be willing to accept the application of the maxim to his own case by, for example, his present political friends. All that *that* shows is that he is serious enough about being a Nazi to accept the attendant risks: it does not show that he is *morally* serious.

It might be argued that Hare could get around this objection by simply reformulating his requirement. What the Sincere Fanatic has to accept in order to prove his moral seriousness is not the application of a policy of genocide to *him*, personally, but to the German nation. But that simply makes my point – or Kant's – more sharply. The Sincere Fanatic might well be willing to *risk* the application of genocide to the German people, just as he is willing to *risk* his own life upon the probability that he is not himself of Jewish descent. But that, according to Kant, is not what is at stake over the issue of whether his principles are moral principles. What *is* at stake

is whether the *ends* which he would have to will in willing
the maxim of genocide as a natural law are consistent with the
ends for which he was led to adopt the maxim of genocide
in the first place: – and they clearly are not. He can avoid
perceiving the inconsistency, as Kant says (*GMM*, pp. 91–2),
only by shifting the point of view from which he considers the
question, taking the ordinary moral view that genocide is
immoral when it is a question of his own nation suffering
genocide but 'making an *exception* to it for himself (or even just
for this once) to the advantage of his inclination'.

Again it might be objected that I have made the fanatic's
maxim too egoistic. Why should he not believe that the world
will be a better place *for everyone*, and not just for his nation,
if all Jews are exterminated?

Kant's answer would be, I think, that in that case his maxim
could be construed as something like: 'When any theory of
mine leads me to suppose that a great future good may be
obtained through the sacrifice of others' present interest I will,
in order to achieve that good, do whatever my theory seems
to demand'. Once again the maxim construed as a natural
law – as a psychological necessity for all rational beings,
defines a world of destructive conflict in which the Fanatic's
original intentions – those which tempted him to adopt the
maxim as a rule for the guidance of his own conduct – could
not possibly be realized.

Of course, to give the Fanatic's maxim this form I have had
to assume that the Fanatic does not possess certain knowledge
about the results of exterminating the Jews: that he only
possesses a *theory*. But then, what would it be to be *certain*
about a matter like that? In practice, the Fanatic will merely
be sure enough to *feel* certain; certain enough at any rate to
refuse to take seriously the fact that many people disagree with
him. But if he makes *that* refusal, what becomes of his claim
to philanthropy? He wants, he says, to improve the lot of his
fellow-men. But if he discounts their claim to criticize his
attachment to his theories, he is scarcely thinking of them as
fellow-men: he is thinking of them as pawns in the working out

of his theories, which therefore take on the status of fantasies *even if they happen to be correct.*

Hare, as we saw earlier, puts forward the Universalizability Criterion as a 'logical thesis' and regards it as merely an extension to prescriptive language of a condition of intelligibility with which we are quite familiar in the case of descriptive discourse: that one cannot apply a description to one thing and then refuse its application to another thing exactly similar in all relevant respects. Kant's criterion, of whether a maxim can be enacted as a Law of Nature, does not, if I am correct, turn upon *logical* consistency between sentences at all; not even consistency between sentences in the imperative mood. It turns upon the coherence, or compatibility of ends, or goals. We cannot, therefore, it seems to me, take Hare's theory as constituting a modern, logically and philosophically more rigorous way of saying something which Kant was trying to say, but was prevented from saying clearly by the constraints of an antiquated methodological outlook within which no clear distinction could be drawn between naturalistic and non-naturalistic moral theories, or in general between empirical and conceptual enquiries. Whatever the merits of Hare's views on their own account, they seem to me simply and wholly different from Kant's. Indeed, the notion of universalizability which forms the central pivot of Hare's thought seems to me to play no part whatsoever in Kant's.

We can put the same point in another way. Neither Kant's ethics nor Hare's is, in the end, purely formal. Both of them found moral distinctions, ultimately, not upon formal incompatibility but upon empirical incompatibility. But the kind of empirical incompatibility which is at issue differs in each case. For Kant the ultimate question concerns the empirical compatibility of the ends which rational agents find themselves adopting when they consider themselves as occupying each of two distinct roles; the role of private person and the role of Universal Legislator. For Hare the ultimate question concerns the empirical compatibility or incompatibility between the particular prescriptive consequences of the universal prescriptive principles which an agent wishes to proclaim as his own, *and the agent's own fundamental desires*. Thus the Harean moral agent can, as it were, trade off his interests against his 'moral' right to hold the principles he holds; and thus, by making a sufficiently radical renunciation of his interests he can, as it were, purchase the right to hold any principle whatsoever as a moral principle.

This technique of trading off interest against principle is not open to the Kantian moral agent. He, as a private person, has whatever goals and interests he happens to have. The question for him is whether those goals are or are not empirically compatible with the goals he acquires when he transforms his plans for achieving his private goals (his maxims, that is) into Universal Laws of Nature. For both Kant and Hare, in other words, morality stands in a definite relationship to the psychology of the individual moral agent. But for Hare the relationship is such as to allow the individual moral agent, within limits, to *make moral* whatever principles he pleases; whereas for Kant the relationship is not such as to allow the moral agent any freedom to choose the content of morality by making individual acts of renunciation of interest: indeed, it precisely rules out that possibility. Morality for Kant is social, or as Hegel would say, universal.

(On the other hand, I am not at all sure that Kant is right to suppose that there is only one possible morality. Kant's mistake here may parallel his mistake about geometry. But to take up that question would require a much longer article.)

We shall see the extent of the gulf between Kant and our own moral rationalists even more clearly if we now turn to examine the relationship between the structure of Kant's illustrations and two other parts of his doctrine: the concept of an *unconditioned good* and that of a *Kingdom of Ends*.

The concept of a Kingdom of Ends is that of a community of rational beings who treat each other always as ends in themselves and never as means to other ends (*GMM*, p. 101). The notion of treating people as ends in themselves is explained in terms of the notion of a universal harmony of ends, and that notion in turn in terms of the very notion of incompatibility of ends which, we have argued, stands at the heart of Kant's treatment of moral choice in terms of the Formula of Natural Law. The test of attempting to will a maxim as a Natural Law locates precisely that configuration of goals with respect to which all human wills can be in systematic harmony with one another. Kant says:

> I understand by a 'Kingdom' a systematic union of rational beings under common laws. Now since laws determine ends as regards their universal validity, we shall be able – if we abstract from the personal differences between rational beings, and also from all the content of their private ends – to conceive a whole of all ends in systematic conjunction . . . ; that is we shall be able to conceive of a Kingdom of Ends which is possible in accordance with the above principles.

Another way of putting Kant's argument is this: in adopting the standpoint of one who can make Natural Law simply by the decree of his will, I adopt as my own the goals which every being subject to the Natural Law in question will seek as a consequence of being subject to it. I thus take up a universal viewpoint – a viewpoint which includes not only that of every other human being, but also that of myself at other times or stages of my life (which is why Kant finds it easy to derive principles of personal, as well as social morality from the Categorical Imperative) while simultaneously retaining the viewpoint of my present desires and interests. Conflict between the ends which I find myself pursuing from the two viewpoints thus necessarily reveals that my present private ends cannot be included in a 'systematic conjunction' of ends. Elsewhere, in the *Critique of Practical Reason* (section 4), Kant makes the point that no such harmony of ends can be constructed upon the basis of any concrete, 'phenomenal' end, such as the maximization of general happiness, or the improvement of the race. From such principles we can derive only a parodic harmony of ends, 'like the pledge which is said to have been given by Francis I to the Emperor Charles

V, "What my brother wants (Milan), that I want too" '.[12]

This, I think, is the clue to Kant's contention that the only unconditioned good is a Good Will. To say that something is a good is to say that it is attractive as a possible end. A good is 'conditional' if it is possible for it on occasion to conflict with (hamper the achievement of) some other end which may be good in itself. But if the *will* is good; that is, if it wills only ends whose maxims can without contradiction be simultaneously willed as Natural Laws, then clearly it can never will any end which is inconsistent with any end which is not *itself* inconsistent with some part of a systematic harmony of ends. From that it follows trivially that a Good Will is an unconditioned good, and the only one.

V

We now come finally to the heart of the matter. So far I have argued that a moral rationalism like Hare's, founded upon a purely 'logical' or 'definitional' conception of moral reasoning, leads to paradoxical conclusions concerning the logical status of certain alleged 'moral principles' maintained by Sincere Fanatics, and that Kant's version of moral rationalism, in many ways a more full-blooded one than Hare's, allows us to avoid such conclusions. But many of my readers may have begun to feel, as the familiar slogans and arguments of Kantian moral theory have paraded past once more over the last page or two, that Kant's victory over the Sincere Fanatic may, after all, be a hollow one. For if the Categorical Imperative is not supposed to be a 'logical thesis', or a 'matter of definition', then, surely, Kant's general position must reduce to one of the many forms of ethical naturalism. The Formula of the Kingdom of Ends strongly reinforces this suggestion. Kant appears to be saying that an end is good if, and only if, it can form part of a systematic harmony of ends. But this, it might be argued, is itself a moral judgment. Surely it is at least conceivable that some end might be good, morally speaking, and that we might have a moral obligation to pursue it, even though it would not cohere with all other good ends in a systematic harmony. In elevating the pursuit of such a harmony into the fundamental principle of morals, Kant, it might seem, is proceeding no differently from other writers who assign other principles, such as the maximization of the general happiness or the improvement of the race, to a similar status: that is, he is merely revealing the nature of his own most fundamental moral convictions. But if that is so, then the short way with Sincere Fanatics which I derived from Kantian principles must presumably cease to have much force or interest. For it is of very little interest that the Sincere Fanatic appears as vicious and self-deluded by the light of Kant's theory of the foundations of morals if that theory is not, in the end, a theory of the foundations of anything, but merely a statement of a set of rather general moral convictions which the Sincere Fanatic happens not to share. In that case we are back where we began.

Moore certainly took this view of Kant's theory. Moore regards Kant's theory as an example of 'Metaphysical' ethics, by which he means that it identifies goodness with some super-sensible reality; with something which, it is held 'does exist, but does not exist in Nature'.[13] Such an identification is made by Kant, Moore says, 'when he tells us that his "Kingdom of Ends" is the ideal'.[14] Pursuing this line of interpretation Moore argues that 'Kant identifies what ought to be with the law according to which a Free or Pure Will *must* act, with the only kind of action which is possible for it'[15] and proceeds to convict Kant of naturalism by the usual Moorean arguments. If the definition of what ought to be in terms of the way a Free Will must act is accepted, says Moore,[16] we have also to accept the absurd consequence that, the question 'Is the law by which a Free Will acts a good one?' is meaningless. And in accepting that we make the very existence of moral distinctions dependent upon the truth of certain propositions about the nature of Reality. Unless Reality is such as to contain a Free Will of the sort allegedly postulated by Kant, in other words, 'no assertion that "This is good" can possibly be true: it can indeed have no meaning'.[17]

This is, I suppose, less absurd than Mill's sublime assimilation of Kant to the company of Utilitarians-unbeknown-to-themselves which also includes Christ and Epicurus. But it still seems to me a strikingly perverse piece of misreading.

The phrase 'A Pure Will' does not function for Kant as the name of a 'super-sensible reality'. Nor is it a primitive notion for Kant: it is a defined notion, and the definition is neither obscure nor particularly 'metaphysical'. It goes, as I have tried to show, like this. We constantly find ourselves adopting plans of action (*maxims*) in order to achieve one or another private end. Often we find that if we were to will that every rational agent in like circumstances should, as a law of its nature, adopt the maxim in question, we should, in willing that, be committing ourselves to the pursuit of ends whose realization would conflict with the realization of the ends for the sake of which we are tempted to adopt the maxim in question in the first place. A rational agent possesses a Pure Will, now, if, and only if, whenever it finds itself in such a predicament it abandons the maxim in question together with the course of action which that maxim prescribes.

Kant is not, in other words, defining rightness, or moral obligatoriness, in terms of any statement or set of statements, metaphysical or otherwise about 'the nature of Reality'. He is offering us a *procedure*, a pattern of reflective activity, which will enable us to distinguish right from wrong. Kant, in effect, introduces the terms 'right' and 'wrong' as mere arbitrary labels to mark the two resultant heaps into which this procedure sorts the array of possible maxims. But, of course, he is also claiming that the terms 'right' and 'wrong' introduced in this way behave logically in discourse exactly as our ordinary everyday terms 'right' and 'wrong' behave; and that no other competing moral theory (Utilitarianism, for example) yields as complete and satisfying a match with ordinary usage. What I have been doing in this paper is, in effect, to defend this claim of Kant's by showing that his theory yields an intuitively satisfying account of sincere fanaticism, whereas Hare's theory yields a radically counter-intuitive account.

If we accept the procedure which Kant proposes as fixing the sense of the terms 'right' and 'wrong', then we cannot say that the assertions 'x is right' or 'x is wrong' are equivalent in meaning to any statement about 'the nature or reality' or about 'what is the case' or about 'facts', unless of course, we are prepared to accept a verbal formula which merely outlines Kant's procedure as constituting such a statement. Certainly, the 'facts' about a given course of action which bring it about that the maxim governing that course of action passes or fails Kant's test for the morality of maxims will vary indefinitely from specific case to specific case. What makes the maxim of prudential suicide fail is that to will the maxim as a universal natural law is to will universal death (the maxim 'cannot subsist as a system of nature'). What makes the maxim of neglecting my talents fail is that willing it as a natural law is equivalent to willing that I should be incompetent to pursue any of my ends; and so on. None of this rich concrete detail (although in a sense it is what *accounts* for the rightness or wrongness of particular maxims) is in any way essential to the *concepts* of rightness or wrongness. It represents the matter of morality and not the form: the form, which *is* essential, has to do merely with the notions of willing a maxim either privately or as the enactment of a Universal Legislator, the concepts of an end, of conflict of ends, and so on.

Kant is not, then, deriving an 'ought' from an 'is'. Nor is he, I think, deriving an 'ought' from an 'ought'. His method is not, that is, to begin with the *moral* thesis that we ought to seek to create a Kingdom of Ends, or a systematic harmony of ends, and then to derive a series of subordinate obligations by working out what is required of us if we are systematically to seek that end. He begins with the commonsense distinction between a qualified good (a good which may in certain circumstances turn into an evil) and an unqualified good; and he argues that only a Good Will, a will which never runs into the kind of contradiction which I have devoted most of this paper to elucidating, can be an unqualified good: a good which can never under any circumstances turn into an evil. Now, the

concept of a *good* from which Kant begins is no more a specifically *moral* notion than the Greek concept of *Kalokagathia* which
it very much resembles. Wit, wealth, health and power are all
things which Kant cites as 'goods' in the sense of 'good' which
he intends (*GMM*, p. 61). Kant shows, in fact, one way in
which what we would be inclined to regard as a non-moral
distinction between good and evil can develop into a distinction
between moral good and moral evil. But so far as I can see
there is no point in the transition at which the argument rests
upon any moral judgment on Kant's part.

In short, Kant really does offer a *formal* characterization of
the nature of morality: that is, a characterization which does
not itself contain, or rest upon, any substantial moral judgment. But at the same time, the characterization of morality
which he offers is not a 'formal' characterization in the sense,
originating with Frege, Wittgenstein and the Vienna Circle,
in which logic is generally regarded nowadays as a 'formal'
study: that is, a study concerned with sets of stipulative rules
for the manipulation of symbols. Truths of logic, it is customary
to say, are true irrespective of how things are in the world,
precisely because they merely record certain conventions of
symbol-manipulation ('All the sentences of logic', says Wittgenstein in the *Tractatus*, 'say the same thing: namely, nothing'!).
It is to logic in this sense, presumably, that Hare wishes to
assimilate the Principle of Universalizability when he says
that it is a *logical* thesis.

For Kant, the concepts of right and wrong are certainly
defined by a *procedure*; but it is not purely a procedure of
symbol-manipulation. To say what the procedure is we have
to bring in all sorts of empirical concepts: the concepts of an
agent, an end, a maxim, and so on. But the fact that these
concepts are empirical ones does not mean that statements
about rightness and wrongness can be analysed in terms of
any set of non-moral statements of fact. The situation is not
unlike that which obtains in the measurement of time. In
order to measure time I have to stipulate criteria for determining the rate of passage of time which necessitate the mention

of physical objects of one or another kind: graduated candles, clepsydras, clockwork mechanisms, and so on. But that does not mean that statements about time can be analysed in terms of statements about graduated candles or clepsydras, or, in general, about any of the physical or chemical properties of material objects. This analogy has another point of relevance to Kant's procedure. In treating a graduated candle as a measure of time I have to treat it as an approximation to something 'ideal', something which, as Moore says of the Kingdom of Ends, 'does not exist in Nature', namely, a candle which burns at a perfectly regular and constant rate. There is nothing absurd or metaphysical about defining scientific concepts in terms of such idealizations, and so it is hard to see what can be wrong with Kant's defining moral concepts in terms of a similar idealization, that of a perfect and systematic harmony of ends. Certainly it is not the case that Kant's moral terms lose their meaning if a Kingdom of Ends does not exist, any more than the terms of classical mechanics lose their meaning if such idealizations as frictionless surfaces fail to exist.

VI

I want now to move briefly back to the topic with which we began: the discomfort and difficulty which English-speaking philosophers feel, by and large, in reading Kant's moral philosophy, and the reasons for it.

Part of the reason, I believe, is that analytic philosophy is still deeply influenced by logical positivism.[18] The most characteristic thesis of positivism is the doctrine that a meaningful declarative sentence must express some statement of empirical fact, unless it is analytic, or expresses a logical or mathematical proposition of some sort. Moral judgments, which do not fall very obviously into either of these categories are, positivists have been prepared to say, perhaps not altogether meaningless, but if they are not, it is only because moral judgments neither say anything about the world nor express any formal proposition, but merely express 'feelings' or 'emotional attitudes'. The nature of Hare's achievement can only be understood, I think, if one sees his work as a response to the positivist-inspired emotive theories of the 1930s and 1940s. Hare has managed, as it were, to find a logical niche, in the shadow of positivism, for sentences expressing moral judgments, without going to the lengths of reducing them to expressions of feeling. Hare's move, as we have seen, is to treat the Principle of Universalizability as a principle of logic. Moral discourse can thus be assimilated to one of the two major categories of meaningful discourse which a positivist outlook allows. It becomes a branch of logic, having to do not, indeed, with questions of empirical fact, but with questions of the consistency or inconsistency of sentences in the prescriptive mood. Moreover, Hare's theory itself becomes a purely analytic study of the logic of moral discourse. We are relieved, in short, both of the need to postulate special categories of moral 'facts' and of the danger of dismissing morality as a matter of irrational emotional response.

Kant's theory, on the other hand, is not a way of accommodating moral discourse to the procrustean bed of the familiar positivist dichotomy between the empirical and the formal. Rather, it implicitly denies the validity of any such dichotomy. If Kant is correct, moral discourse is neither a branch of empirical discourse nor a branch of logic (i.e., the logic of prescriptions). The procedure of willing a maxim as a universal law of nature which serves Kant as his fundamental criterion of rightness does not yield statements of empirical fact as the outcome of its application (Hume was right to say that the wrongness of an act is not to be found in even the most exhaustive empirical description of the act and the circumstances under which it was performed), but neither does it yield propositions about the logical consequences of assenting to certain prescriptions, or about the logical consistency of sets of prescriptions. Equally, it does not yield expressions of feeling, or sentiment.

Nor, for that matter, do the sentences which describe Kant's theory fall into any of the categories offered by conventional positivist classifications of the kinds of meaningful sentence. They are not statements of empirical fact, but neither are they 'analytic' propositions, or for that matter propositions of logic. Their function is to explain the workings of a *criterion*, in a sense of that term which I believe, though I have no space to argue the point, to be not all that far from Wittgenstein's sense.

Analytic philosophers see that Kant's theory is fundamentally at odds with the positivist proprieties, and they find that deeply suspicious. One can see such suspicions working in the mind of even as perceptive and sympathetic a commentator as H. J. Paton. Paton, for example, finds Kant's conception of a will in contradiction with itself 'difficult to make sufficiently precise', and opts for an interpretation which has the effect of bringing Kant's position very close to Hare's:

> There is clearly a contradiction in willing that a maxim should be a universal law and willing at the same time that we should make arbitrary exceptions to it in our own favour.[19]

This, Paton says, 'is sound enough practically', if we know what the law is – know, that is, what law ought to govern our actions universally – but gives us no means of discovering what that law is, nor even any assurance that it is possible to discover what the law is.

The movement of Paton's thought here is clear, and fascinating. Like Moore, he suspects that Kant's concept of a Pure, or Free, or non-contradictory Will has just to be swallowed whole as a piece of metaphysics if we are to make any sense of it at all. He therefore sets out to extract what sense he can from Kant, short of a wholesale acceptance of Kant's presumed metaphysic of the Pure Will, and emerges from Kant's discussion at *GMM* pp. 91–92 with an account of moral contradiction as the *logical* contradiction involved in accepting a universal prescription while refusing to accept a particular prescription which follows from it. But Paton also sees clearly that consistency in *this* sense, while a logical virtue, is morally neutral. Any principle at all can, in other words, be held with this sort of consistency. We have here in embryo, in other words, the paradox of the Sincere Fanatic.

Paton's procedure here accurately represents, it seems to me, the way in which most of us read Kant's ethics at present. We take it for granted that a moral theory which is not couched in 'purely logical' terms must of necessity either derive 'ought'-statements from 'is'-statements through the agency of some more or less crude and naive form of naturalism, or else derive them from unacknowledged 'ought'-statements on some more fundamental level: must come in the end, that is, to preaching. Wishing to save Kant from both of these fates worse than death, we try to do the best we can for him, and emerge from his text with an interpretation in terms of *logical* universalizability which emasculates his thought, and is in any case entirely foreign to it. As a result Kant's ethics is, I suspect, largely inaccessible to us as a living piece of philosophy.

I hope, therefore, that I may have partly, at least, succeeded in showing that Kant's moral theory is simpler, less obscure, and stronger, than it is generally credited with being; and that his relegation to the status largely of a historical figure is a real impoverishment to moral philosophy.

NOTES

1 During the academic year 1976–7, when this essay was written, I was a Leverhulme Research Fellow, and, for part of the time, a Visiting Fellow of the Humanities Research Centre at the Australian National University in Canberra. I wish to express my gratitude for the support of both institutes, and to the University of Sussex for granting me leave of absence during this period. In addition to forming part of the present Royal Institute lecture series, the paper was read to audiences at the universities of Bradford, Sheffield and Western Australia; the present version has, I hope, profited from the discussion at those meetings, and from detailed comments by Julius Kovesi, Benjamin Gibbs, David Angluin and Patrick Hutchings.

2 R. M. Hare, *The Language of Morals* (Oxford U.P., 1952); *Free-*

dom and Reason (Oxford U.P., 1963). All page references in what follows are to these editions. I am indebted to Julius Kovesi for pointing out certain inaccuracies and some clumsiness in this section in an earlier draft of this paper.

[3] Hare, *Freedom and Reason*, p. 31 – 'The logical thesis (of universalizability) has, as we shall see, great potency in moral arguments; but for that very reason it is most important to make clear that it is no more than a logical thesis – for otherwise the objection will be made that a moral principle has been smuggled in disguised as a logical doctrine. . . .'

[4] 'Now it may be that there are people so fanatical as to be prepared for all these things in order to avoid miscegenation. But they are surely very few.' (*FR*, p. 220.)

[5] H. J. Paton, *The Moral Law, or Kant's Groundwork of the Metaphysics of Morals*, Hutchinson (3rd edition, 1956), p. 89 f. All further references to Kant will be to this edition of the *Groundwork* (*GMM*).

[6] *Ibid.* p. 89.

[7] *Ibid.* p. 90.

[8] *Ibid.* p. 91.

[9] See, for example, John Stuart Mill, *Utilitarianism*, Everyman's Library edition, 1910, p. 49: 'To give any meaning to Kant's principle, the sense put upon it must be, that we ought to shape our conduct by a rule which all rational beings might adopt *with benefit to their collective interest*' [Mill's italics].

[10] *GMM*, p. 89. The morality of suicide was a major crux of moral debate in the eighteenth century. Most of the *philosophes* denounced the laws on suicide, and defended suicide with, or without, reservation. Rousseau devoted two letters of the *Nouvelle Heloise* (part iii letters 21–2) to rehearsing the arguments for and against. A number of celebrated cases occurred of actual suicides who left reasoned defences of their actions, some along the lines of Kant's unfortunate's maxim. See, for example, Lecky's *History of European Morals*, ch. 4.

[11] This is the intention ascribed to Kant by H. J. Paton in his discussion of the example in *The Categorical Imperative*, Hutchinson, 1947, p. 154.

[12] Kant, *Critique of Practical Reason*, IV, tr. Lewis White Beck, Library of Liberal Arts edition, 1958, pp. 27–8.

[13] G. E. Moore, *Principia Ethica*, Cambridge, 1903, p. 113.

[14] *Ibid.*

[15] *Ibid.* p. 126.

[16] *Ibid.* p. 127.

[17] *Ibid.*

[18] The only book on ethics written since the war which is wholly free from the influence of positivism is, so far as I am aware, Julius

Kovesi's *Moral Notions*, Routledge & Kegan Paul, 1967. I have adapted some of Kovesi's ideas in Section V of the present paper, though I do not know whether he would agree with the use I have made of them.

[19] H. J. Paton, *The Categorical Imperative*, Hutchinson, 1947, p. 139.

INDEX

Addison, Joseph, xvii, 31, 140 ff., 147 ff.
d'Alembert, Jean, vii f., ix, x, xii ff., xv ff., xvii, 57, 58 f., 62, 69, 72 ff., 75, 185
analytic philosophy, 256 ff.
Arrow, Kenneth, 113
associationism, 48
authority (political), 148, 167

Battersby, Christine, ix f.
Beattie, James, 49, 52
belief, 36 ff., 84 f.
Berkeley, George, 67 ff., 72
Bernouilli, James, 121
Borda, 113 ff.
Brown, Stuart, x, 38
Brumfitt, J. H., xii, xv
Bunyan, John, 31 ff., 49 f., 52
Butler, Joseph, vii, viii, xvi, 47, Ch. 10 passim

chance, 63
characteristica universalis, 5
choice, collective, 112 ff., moral, 205, 207 f.
Christ, 219 f.
Cicero, 143 f., 155
civic morality, Ch. 7 passim
coherence theory of truth, 68
'collective reason', 128
common sense, 52 f.
comparative politics, xiv, 103 ff.
Condillac, Etienne, x, 57, 61 ff., 66
Condorcet, Marie Jean, vii, xi, Ch. 6 passim

conscience, 193 f., 197, 201 ff., 206, 209, 212 ff., 216, 219 ff.
Copernicus, 70 f., 84, 89
cosmic harmony, 87
cyclical majorities, paradox of, 137

Daunou, P. Cl. F., 120
Descartes, René, xv, 7, 16, 22, 23, 29, 58 f., 89, 91, 146
determinism, 166, 171
Diderot, Denis, vii, xii, Ch. 8 passim, 185
dualism, 4, 13–21

ease, 84; Hume's epistemology of, Ch. 2 passim
education, 191 ff.
election, 116
empiricism, xvi, 58; of Locke and Newton, Ch. 1 passim
Encyclopédie, vii, viii, ix, xii, 162, 163, 167 f.
Ends, Kingdom of, 242, 249 f., 254
Enlightenment, vii f., x, xii–xviii, 25, 57, 77, 93, 116, 162; Moderate, 1, 93; Scottish, xiv, xvii f., 94, 97, 140, 144
enthusiasm, 81
epistemology, Hume's, 31 ff.; Locke and Newton on, 6–9
experimental method, ix, xvi, 85

fanatic (sincere), viii, Ch. 11 passim
Ferguson, Adam, 95 f.
Fletcher, Andrew, 150 f.
Forbes, Duncan, xiv, 48
force, Newtonian, 18 f.

God, existence of, 4, 62, 75; idea of, 73, 165; intervention of, 19; nature of, 64
gravitation, 18 ff., 59
Grimsley, Ronald, xvi

Hare, Richard, viii, 226, 228 ff., 245 ff. 257
Harrison, Bernard, viii, xvi
Hart, L. A., 119
Helvétius, 175 f.
Hume, David, vii, viii, ix, x, xiv f., xvi, xvii f., Ch. 2 passim, 57, 59 f., 62 ff., 69 ff., 75, 77, 79 f., Ch. 5 passim, Ch. 7 passim, 200
Hutcheson, Francis, 44 ff., 83, 85, 97
hypothesis, x, xv, 5, 8, 13, 21 ff., 29, 61, 73

idealisations, 256
idealism, 70, 72
imagination, xvii, 84 f., 89 f.
indifference (political), 152
inductivism, 4, 23,
innate ideas, xv, 6 ff.

judiciousness, xvi
jury system, 126 ff., 133 ff.
justice, 78 f., 97, 149

Kant, Immanuel, vii, viii, xvi, 72 f., 131, Ch. 11 passim
Kemp Smith, Norman, 43

Leechman, William, 45
Leibniz, Gottfried, xvii, 66 f., 111, 131 f.
liberty, 102 f.
Locke, John, vii, ix f., Ch. 1 passim, 45
logic, 255
logic of justification, 3

Mach, Ernst, 70
Machiavelli, Niccolò, 104 f.
Mackinnon, Donald, 219
Magee, William, 79
Malebranche, Nicholas, 55, 69, 99 ff.

Mandeville, Bernard, 46 f., 90
materialism, 175
memory, 14
metaphysics, xvi, 16, 39, 50 f., 72, 146, 252
Millar, John, 95 f.
miracles, 63
monarchy (civilized), 104 ff.
Montesquieu, Charles, 106 f.
moral judgment, Butler's theory, x, Ch. 10 passim,
moral philosophy, 85, 91
More, Henry, 27

naturalism, 239, 251, 259, Hume's, 33, 48; Rousseau's, 186 ff., 189 ff., 196 ff.
natural law, xiv, 97, 238, 247, 250
natural man, xi f.
natural morality, xiii f., xvi
nature, state of, 187 f.
Newton, Isaac, vii, ix, xi, Ch. 1 passim, 34 f., 47, 58 ff., 66
Newtonianism, 67, 94, 97; Hume's, 33 ff., 43 ff., 48; Smith's 88

order, cosmic, Ch. 3 passim, 190 ff.
ought-statements, 228 ff.

parsimony, principle of, 38, 66–75
Pascal, Blaise, 110, 129
Paton, H. J., 258 f.
probability, theory of, 110 ff.
Passmore, John, 34, 48
perception, Locke and Newton on, 9–13
Phillipson, Nicholas, xvii f.
philosophe, vii, viii, xvii, 162, 170, 185, 260
philosopher (role of), 153, 157
philosophy, vii–xii, 81, 87, 100 f.
physics, deductive, 23, 29
Popper, Karl, 74 f.
positivism, 256 f.
practical wisdom, 204 f.
principle of natural order, 38, Ch. 3 passim
propositions, compound, 132 ff.
punishment, 119

Raphael, David, xi, 206
rationalism (moral), 200 ff.
realism, 4, 69, 72; scientific, 57
Reason, xv f., 46, 193, 199 f.
religion, Hume on, 50 ff.; natural, 77, 93; revealed, xii f., 77 f., 80
Rogers, G. A. J., ix f., xv
Rousseau, Jean-Jacques, vii, xvi f., 128, 131, 162, 168 f., Ch. 9 passim
Ryle, Gilbert, 212 ff.

scepticism, x, 23; enlightened, x, Ch. 3 passim; Hume's, 32, 38 40, 48, 62, 69, 146 f., 157
science, natural, 80 f., 91; social, 82 f.
self-love, 211 ff., 223, 241
Seneca, 179
Sentiment, 199 f.
Shaftesbury, Anthony, 45 f., 165
Shelley, P. B., xvii
simplicity, 71, 74, 84
Smith, Adam, vii, x f., 34, Ch. 4 passim, 94 f., 100 f.

Spectator, 141, 147
spirits, 20 f.
Sturgeon, Nicholas, 216 f.
substance, 4, 13–21
suicide, 238 ff., 242 ff., 260
sympathy, 88
system, xvi, 58, 61

unity of knowledge, x
universalizability, 229 ff., 232, Ch. 11 passim
universalization, principle of, 131

virtue, 185 ff., 197
Voltaire, vii, xii, xiii, 57, 61 ff., 162
voting, theory of, Ch. 6 passim

welfare judgments, 112 ff.
White, A. R., 208
White, Ian, xi
witnesses, reliability of, 120 ff.